LEGALLY ARMED

CARRY GUN LAW GUIDE

COVERING ALL 50 STATES AND D.C.

LEGALLY ARMED

CARRY GUN LAW GUIDE

4TH EDITION

1974 Chandalar Drive • Suite D • Pelham, AL 35124

ISBN: 0794845169
Printed in China

The writers, editors, and publishers of this book assume no legal responsibility concerning the content of this book. This book was compiled with accuracy in mind, but does not and cannot act as a substitute for professional legal advice. Given the changing and somewhat ambiguous nature of gun laws, the writers, editors, and publisher of this book suggest contacting a lawyer, member of law enforcement, or district attorney before carrying a firearm in public or discharging a weapon in self-defense. We are not lawyers and therefore relinquish all responsibility concerning this book's content.

1 Introduction

2 Chapter 1: Concealed Carry Permit

7 Chapter 2: Restrictions on Permit Holders

13 Chapter 3: Firearms and Self-Defense

18 Chapter 4: Traveling with a Firearm

22 Chapter 5: Using *Legally Armed*

26 Map and Legend

28 Alabama

31 Alaska

33 Arizona

36 Arkansas

40 California

43 Colorado

45 Connecticut

47 Delaware

49 Florida

52 Georgia

56 Hawaii

59 Idaho

61 Illinois

65 Indiana

67 Iowa

69 Kansas

72 Kentucky

74 Louisiana

77 Maine

79 Maryland

84 Massachusetts

87 Michigan

92 Minnesota

94 Mississippi

97 Missouri

100 Montana

103 Nebraska

107 Nevada

111 New Hampshire

113 New Jersey

118 New Mexico

120 New York

124 North Carolina

127 North Dakota

130 Ohio

133 Oklahoma

137 Oregon

140 Pennsylvania

142 Rhode Island

144 South Carolina

148 South Dakota

150 Tennessee

155 Texas

157 Utah

159 Vermont

161 Virginia

164 Washington

168 West Virginia

171 Wisconsin

173 Wyoming

176 D.C.

182 Handgun Instructors by State

This book surveys and summarizes the nation's gun laws to help keep you legal.

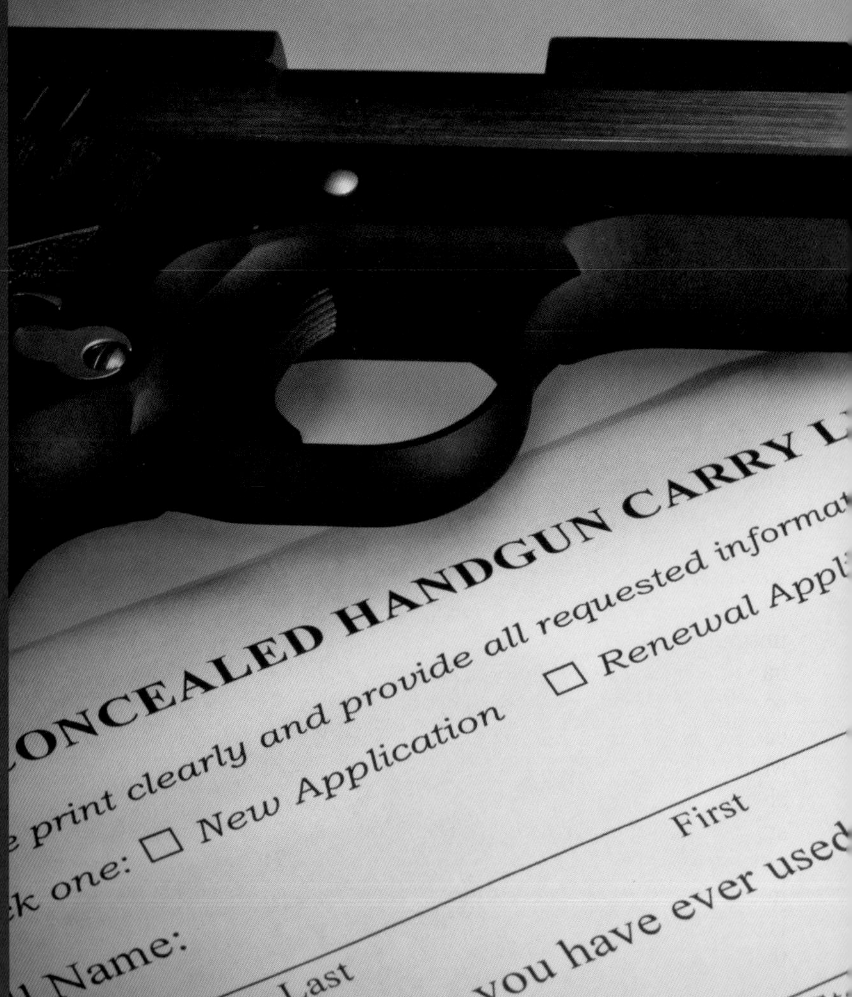

Introduction

For many Americans, the freedom to own, use, and carry firearms has remained one of the most cherished inalienable rights since our country's inception. When carefully and thoughtfully handled, firearms play an important and necessary role in our country. Citizens use them for sport, for hunting, and for personal safety. Personal safety extends outside the boundaries of individual homes and into the marketplace, as individuals carrying firearms in public are able to protect both themselves and others from those who would threaten human life. These armed citizens offer protection through the use of firearms, despite the claims of some skeptics that firearms exist only to cause harm. While firearms can present dangers if not handled properly, those in the hands of responsible, armed citizens only ever defend human life against those who would threaten it. The purpose of this book is to instill confidence in those who wish to legally obtain and carry a firearm in public and to outline how one should responsibly, safely, and legally carry a weapon in each of the 50 states and the District of Columbia.

The first portion of this book focuses on some of the overarching concerns and issues inherent in carrying a weapon, while the latter portion details carry law specific to each of the 50 states and D.C. Actual state law can be dense and difficult to understand, so this book seeks to simplify the basics and make key provisions for each state easily and quickly accessible for conscientious citizens who are vigilant about carrying their weapons responsibly and legally. The information in this book primarily addresses those citizens who have obtained concealed carry permits or are in the process of doing so. The editors of this book do not endorse or address the unlawful carry of a firearm and instead support validly permitted citizens who have navigated the permitting process through proper legal channels. This book is intended as a guide, but no area of law is static; that being said, laws in this area are continually being updated, amended, replaced, and repealed. For that reason, the best source of information for the most current governing law in any jurisdiction is the local police department or the attorney general presiding over that jurisdiction. Either of those offices can answer any questions concerning local carry laws and their exceptions and nuances.

Chapter 1: Concealed Carry Permit

How to Obtain a Handgun Carry Permit

Typically, a carry permit looks much like a driver's license and doubles as a proof of identification. Once you obtain a carry permit, you must abide by the laws of the issuing state while within its borders and the laws of any other state while within its borders. Those who have legally obtained a handgun carry permit will be referred to in these pages as "permit holders" or "permit carriers." Permit holders enjoy a wider latitude of freedoms associated with handling or carrying a firearm in public than individuals who are not permit holders, or "non–permit carriers," though some states still grant non-permit carriers extensive freedoms with firearms. Most states don't require residents to obtain permits before purchasing firearms, before using firearms on private lands for sporting purposes, or before keeping firearms in their homes. Individuals who wish to obtain a carry permit should consult state permit laws in the latter portion of this book and contact one of the permit instructors listed in the appendix or the legal authority listed as a contact for the issuing state.

Almost always, states require firearms training prior to the issuance of a carry permit, although the level of training varies. Local outdoor agencies—such as state wildlife agencies or game and fish commissions—often offer these classes, but many local gun shops and shooting ranges offer them as well. Regardless of location, class instructors should provide citizens with an in-depth look at the governing state's laws and should test students' levels of safety and proficiency with firearms. Information about carry permit class instruction is available from state wildlife agencies, state attorney general's offices, and, often, local gun dealers. Typically, once a student has completed the requirements of a firearm carry course, the student must submit a certificate of completion to the state office or agency responsible for issuance of the actual carry permit for that state. Often, the issuing office is the Department of Safety of the state, and the process for obtaining a permit is much akin to that for obtaining a driver's license.

There are some basic requirements for carry permit eligibility within each state, so ensure that these basic requirements are met before unnecessarily expending the money, time, and effort associated with a firearm carry course. For instance, most states require permit holders to be at least 21 years of age. Also, some states issue carry permits to non-residents working or visiting the state, but most only issue permits to residents. Before registering for a carry permit class, take special care to ensure that basic state-specific requirements for firearm carry are met.

Concealed and Open Carry

Firearms can be carried concealed or unconcealed ("open"). In public, a concealed firearm should remain out of sight and is usually concealed by clothing or in a purse or bag. Some states consider a firearm that reveals an obvious indention or impression of a gun through an article of clothing or bag to be an unconcealed weapon, even if the actual firearm is otherwise out of sight. Therefore, permit carriers should ensure that firearms remain as hidden as possible when in public and should determine how hidden their weapons must be to qualify as "concealed" in states where they carry. A discussion of the types of handguns that are ideal for concealed carry follows later in this book.

In contrast, carriers who opt for "open" carry wear firearms outside clothing and visible to onlookers, much like law enforcement officers. Individuals who open carry typically wear guns on belt holsters, under the arm, or on leg holsters. While most states permit some form of open carry, it is generally considered unwise in most contexts, as the practice usually draws unwanted attention. The mere sight of a person with a firearm, even a person who is not brandishing it or behaving threateningly, can be alarming for some people who are not comfortable around weapons. Additionally, open display of a handgun by a carrier may make that carrier an automatic target in the event a person decides to do harm to others. It is even possible that bystanders in public could mistake a person who is carrying openly as a member of law enforcement. While laws may permit open carry, extreme caution should be exercised when doing so. You should only opt for open carry with acute sensitivity for the context and cultural mores applicable to the situation and with an understanding and willingness to assume the risks that openly displaying a firearm may create out in the marketplace where you will randomly encounter what is often an unpredictable and vastly varied group of people.

A Situation: To Shoot or Not to Shoot

As you navigate the topics in these pages, consider the following scenario and try to determine the best course of action. Decide if a permit carrier has the right to discharge a firearm in self-defense or if doing so would be illegal. The scenario is as follows: Your young son wakes in the middle of the night with a cold. Not having appropriate medication available at home, you decide to drive to the neighborhood all-night pharmacy for cough syrup to help him sleep. The streets lay empty and still, but because it is so late at night, you take care to survey the surroundings and think to yourself how glad you are that you recently acquired your carry permit, which has allowed you the extra sense of security that the handgun in your front coat pocket is now providing. When you pull into the pharmacy, you choose a parking spot close to the door in order to minimize the amount of time you are most vulnerable—while walking through the darkened and sparsely filled lot. You make short work of your errand, finding and paying for the medicine quickly, and head back outside to your car. As you approach your driver side door, a stranger walks up to the far side of the vehicle, stops, and says, "I'm going to kill you." He's just across the hood of your sedan, and you can't tell if he has a weapon or not.

What should you do? Is your life in danger? Can you pull out your gun? Can you shoot him? These are all questions a permit holder must address in mere seconds before drawing or firing his weapon in self-defense.

Now consider if the assailant says nothing and, instead of standing by your car, he strikes the hood of it with a baseball bat. How does this change the scenario? Are you more or less justified in using your weapon? Again, more in-depth discussion follows in chapter 3, but as you read, try to determine how you should properly respond. Are you justified to use your weapon?

Before You Carry a Firearm

Carrying a firearm introduces a wealth of decisions, including what type of firearm to carry, where to carry, and what restrictions will likely be encountered. Carrying a weapon in public should not be a casual decision, and each of these issues and others should be considered and thoughtfully addressed before you make that choice. Additionally, the editors of this book urge readers who choose to obtain carry permits to carry their weapons frequently. A gun can't be used in defense of your life if it is always left at home or in a car's glove box. Though carrying a weapon may seem unnecessary in some contexts, no one can predict when a life-threatening situation may arise. Further, in the unfortunate event that a permit holder is forced to use a weapon in self-defense, the fact that the permit holder only carries sporadically may be misinterpreted by legal authorities who evaluate a shooting situation after the fact. For instance, officials in the justice system may argue that a shooting was premeditated based solely on the fact that it was unusual for a permit holder to actually carry a weapon. The best protection against this pitfall—and against any assailant who seeks to do you or others around you harm—is to regularly carry your firearm.

Best Firearm for Concealed Carry

The editors of this book would like to discourage readers from attempting to carry a shotgun or a rifle in public, since not only do state laws typically forbid both, but also, neither allows for discreet carry on one's person. Handguns, however, are ideal because their size allows for easy concealability. When making a decision about which handgun is best, several factors should instruct you and help determine which would best fit your specific habits and environment. While higher-caliber guns provide added firepower to more quickly and easily neutralize a life-threatening situation, these guns are typically larger and harder to conceal from public view. On the other hand, smaller-caliber weapons, such as a .22 caliber, might be a cinch to conceal due to their smaller designs, but they also lack the firepower necessary to neutralize a life-threatening situation without superior shot placement. Any gun, regardless of caliber, is capable of deterring an assailant, but some require much more precision. Permit holders must determine the right amount of firepower that allows for adequate concealment and effective self-defense.

Various models of handguns, aside from caliber, have their own benefits and drawbacks. Firearms experts have traditionallyconsidered revolvers, sometimes called "wheel-guns" for their wheel-shaped revolving cylinders, to be some of the most reliable handguns available. Revolvers seldom misfire and will shoot in almost any circumstance. However, revolvers lose some of their appeal when one considers that they offer a very limited number of shots; their cylinders generally only hold five or six rounds.While some shooters can neutralize a life-threatening situation in just a few rounds, others may find this limited number of shots to be insufficient to protect themselves. In contrast, semi-automatic pistols are magazine-fed, and magazines are offered in high-capacity and double-stacked varieties that hold upwards of 20 rounds. This type of handgun is widely carried by permit holders, law enforcement officers, and military personnel alike. In addition to higher-capacity magazines, semi-auto pistols also offer intricate designs with little compromise in reliability. However, some new shooters may find operating semi-autos a bit complicated and daunting.

Even with these differences and others in mind, most permit holders consider either option a good choice as a carry weapon, and final decisions usually come down to personal preference. In the event you purchase a firearm from an individual, always consult the local attorney general's office before making the purchase to determine and comply with applicable laws concerning the buying and selling of weapons in your jurisdiction.

Chapter 2: Restrictions on Permit Holders

General Commonalities

Although permit law and permit requirements do vary from state to state, there is a lot of common ground among most jurisdictions, allowing for several general assumptions that are reasonably safe to make.

Where You Can Carry

Each state restricts the carry of firearms in certain places. You should become familiar with these locations, which vary from state to state, and carry your firearm accordingly. Common restricted locations include courthouses, post offices, other government buildings, schools, parades, hospitals, public sporting events, daycares, airports, banks, casinos, amusement parks, polling places, bars, and some restaurants. Some states forbid carrying on college campuses, but even in states that do not forbid it by law, individual schools often have policies barring firearms from some or part of their campuses. The best practice is to consult the administration of the college in question to be sure you know where firearms are allowed.

Following is a list of other places where concealed carry is commonly restricted, so pay close attention to these areas in your jurisdiction, as laws concerning them vary from state to state.

• **National Parks**—Since 2010, visitors to national parks have been permitted to carry firearms in accordance with the carry laws of the state in which the park is located.

• **Vehicles**—Traveling with a loaded firearm in a passenger vehicle is addressed later for every state. When traveling through or in a state where carry laws are unfamiliar to you, behave like any non-permitted person. Take the appropriate actions to operate within the confines of the law by traveling with the firearm unloaded, separated from ammunition, disassembled, locked in a commercial grade case, and stored in a trunk or out of the reach of passengers. Do the same in states that do not recognize your permit, unless you are traveling within one of the extremely rare states that allow non-permitted carriers to travel with loaded firearms.

- **Motorhomes and RVs**—Firearm carry law is somewhat ambiguous as to motorhomes and RVs, since they function as both vehicles and residences. Courts in different states have ruled in favor of each of those characterizations, so erring on the side of caution, the safest approach for carriers is to adhere to state laws for *vehicles*, the stricter of the two.

- **Commercial Trucks**—Federal law permits the carry of firearms in commercial vehicles, as long as carriers adhere to each state's laws concerning storage of those firearms while within their borders. This federal protection allows interstate truck drivers to move from one state's legal regime to another without running afoul of any—so long as any firearm remains locked in a case and stored away appropriately. It is worth noting that, notwithstanding governmental clearance for firearms carry, many trucking companies implement their own policies that forbid employees to carry loaded firearms in company vehicles.

- **Motorcycles**—Motorcycles present an interesting set of problems when carrying a firearm. As state laws usually don't explicitly address carry on motorcycles, general rules for motor vehicles are typically applied to motorcyclists. That being the case, locked rear compartments of motorcycles are usually considered analogous to trunks or glove compartments of a car.

- **Restaurants**—Another somewhat vague area of carry law is that concerning restaurants. The state law section of this book addresses this issue for each jurisdiction, but as a general rule, permit holders should avoid bringing weapons into establishments that function primarily as bars—typically ones where over half of revenue generated results from the sales of alcohol. Indicators like the establishment's layout—whether more physical space is dedicated to a bar area than a dining area—or its name—"The Downtown Brewery & Bar," as opposed to "Smith's Steakhouse"—can be helpful for permit holders who need to make a judgment call about the appropriateness of carrying a weapon.

Note, however, that even if state law allows for concealed carry in restaurants, individual establishments may post notices banning firearms from their premises. In some states, those notices serve only as restaurant policies, and the worst repercussion of violating them is to be denied service or asked to leave. However, be aware that some state laws give such notices posted by individual establishments the force of law, meaning a violation of such a notice can result in criminal penalties. Upon entry at an unfamiliar restaurant, responsible carriers should consult restaurant management about concealed carry policies.

Alcohol Consumption

A permit carrier should never consume alcohol while in possession of a firearm, despite some state laws that allow for minimal consumption below the level of intoxication. Permit carriers should always leave firearms at home if there is a likelihood that they will drink while they are out. In the event that a carrier decides to consume alcohol while already in public with a firearm, the carrier should unload the firearm, remove rounds from the magazine, and place the gun and ammunition in separate locations that are as secure as possible. Ideally, each would be locked in separate compartments of a vehicle, rather than remaining on the carrier's person, but in some circumstances, that is not possible. These precautionary steps may be as good a course of action as is available in that predicament, but taking them still may not be adequate to protect against criminal liability in the event of an interaction with law enforcement. Do not wrongfully believe these measures will always suffice. Also, don't be fooled into thinking that by separating a weapon from its ammunition, the permit carrier essentially dispenses with the need for a permit to carry a firearm and, thus, begins to operate as a non-permit carrier. That may be true in some states, but it certainly is not always true and should not be generally relied upon to protect you in instances where you consume alcohol while carrying.

When a permit carrier is caught in possession of a loaded firearm while under the influence of alcohol, the punishments are usually severe. State sanctions vary, but possible outcomes include revocation of the carry permit, a lock-out period before the carrier is eligible to apply for a new permit, a lifetime ban from permit eligibility, significant fines, and even jail time. In the event the carrier is caught driving under the influence, the presence of a loaded firearm far compounds his problems. These problems are easily avoided. We strongly recommend not consuming alcohol at all while even in the proximity of firearms. Alcohol introduces an element of unpredictability into any situation, and that element can easily become dangerous when weapons are involved. We especially caution permit holders against consuming while carrying.

Traffic Stops

When dealing with law enforcement, permit holders must use clear communication to ensure that no misunderstanding arises that would make the situation dangerous to any party. Law enforcement officers are trained to be constantly vigilant for possible dangers, and the introduction of a firearm into an interaction with an officer has real potential for misinterpretation or false assumptions if not handled properly. A law enforcement officer's improper read on a situation can be dangerous or even fatal. Following the practices listed below can prevent unwanted tension and faulty conclusions when in contact with the law. These guidelines only apply to permit carriers and those legally allowed to transport a loaded firearm when they come into contact with police during routine interactions, most commonly traffic stops.

- During a traffic stop, a permit holder should keep hands held firmly around the steering wheel. Permit carriers should remain still, despite the inclination to go ahead and search for requisite documentation. Officers who see drivers moving around in the passenger compartment as they approach may mistakenly assume they are hiding contraband or even searching for a firearm, whereas drivers who are calm and still raise no suspicions. Always remain still with hands on the steering wheel as the officer approaches and wait for the officer's instructions before reaching for paperwork.

- Though mandatory in some states and not in others, best practice is for permit carriers to always disclose to law enforcement that a weapon is in the vehicle. By volunteering the information, the permit carrier establishes that no harm is intended, putting the officer at ease. Even if a permit holder doesn't generally disclose the presence of a firearm, disclosure is highly recommended if the gun is stored in a glove box along with documentation that the driver will need to retrieve for the officer. If the driver neglects to tell the officer, there is a risk that the officer may see the gun when the driver opens the glove box and reaches in for documentation. Serious problems can arise if the officer assumes the driver is reaching for the gun.

In most states, carry permits are linked to driver's licenses, which means that when a police officer runs a license during a stop, permit information is often also available. For this reason, even in states where carriers aren't required to divulge permit holder status or presence of a firearm, permit holders should still do so. If they do not, they run the risk of officers learning of their permit status and assume they withheld the information for nefarious purposes. In such a scenario, the officer could call for backup and instruct the permit carrier, typically via a loudspeaker, to exit the vehicle and lie down on the ground. The delay, discomfort, and embarrassment associated can easily be avoided by disclosing permit status and weapon possession from the beginning.

• Sometimes, though rarely, an officer will ask for a permit holder's firearm. If this occurs, the officer will most likely give very clear instruction as to how to surrender the weapon, but in the event the officer does not, the permit holder should ask how to proceed and follow the officer's instructions exactly. Again, a permit carrier with a firearm in possession should let an officer know exactly where the firearm is located. You should never reach for or reveal a firearm without an officer's instruction to do so.

Firearms in Vehicles: No Permit

Many states do not allow non–permit holders to carry loaded firearms in their vehicles at all. In states that do, any non–permit carrier transporting a firearm should follow the same rules when interacting with law enforcement as previously outlined. Carry laws differ for carriers with no permit, but a good rule of thumb when unsure of local laws is for non–permit carriers to travel with firearms unloaded, locked in a carry case, and locked in a trunk or rear storage compartment. Non–permit carriers should store ammunition separate from weapons. Be aware that many states don't consider a glove compartment or console the equivalent of a vehicle's trunk, in terms of storing a firearm.

Chapter 3: Firearms and Self-Defense

Discharging a Firearm in Self-Defense

Any permit carrier is subject to facing the extremely difficult decision of when the right and responsibility to discharge a weapon arises. Those with concealed carry permits should treat these situations with the utmost of careful scrutiny, as a trigger pull could end a life. Permit carriers should familiarize themselves with and think critically about the topics to follow before carrying a weapon in public for self-defense. State laws vary widely, but these general rules cover many of the overarching concerns related to firing a weapon and should be fairly universally applicable.

1. "Life-Threatening" Requirement

A permit carrier should only discharge a firearm when an assailant has placed someone's life in immediate danger and never for any other reason—such as preventing vandalism, destruction of property, or theft. Most states permit the use of deadly force only while the life-threatening circumstances exist; in other words, the moment a threat is neutralized—by an injury shot to the assailant, by the assailant's flight, etc.—a permit carrier no longer has the right to discharge a firearm. A permit carrier should never chase or follow an assailant to shoot or confront them after they have fled. Be aware that verbal threats are not considered life-threatening unless accompanied by other circumstances that heighten the threat in the words.

State law is nuanced, but three general qualifiers can help inform a permit holder whether a situation rises to the level of "life-threatening."

- **Means:** Does the assailant have the capability of seriously wounding or killing someone? Many juries tend to agree means exists when an assailant has a weapon or is possessed of significantly greater physical size and/or strength than the victim.

• **Position**: While an assailant may have the means to cause harm, has the assailant entered into a position that would allow them to actually inflict harm on another person? For example, an assailant with a knife wouldn't be in a position to cause harm from across a parking lot, but most juries would agree an assailant with a knife would be in a position to cause harm while within a conversational distance of another person. An assailant's range of position to cause harm obviously is much extended when the weapon involved is a firearm. Determining position is extremely subjective, so no real rules exist to definitively inform carriers as to what will qualify.

• **Intent**: Does the assailant actually plan on ending a person's life or causing serious bodily harm? A potential assailant in close proximity who is equipped to do harm may not necessarily plan to hurt anyone. For an actual threat to life to exist, an assailant must take overt and clear steps that confirm an intention of ending a person's life or causing serious bodily harm. Only after an assailant has made this intent clear can a permit carrier justifiably draw and discharge a weapon. Extreme caution must be exercised in making the decision to discharge a firearm at another person, not only because of the danger it introduces for the target, but also because any decision to fire will be examined later by law enforcement authorities.

2. Drawing Your Firearm

A permit carrier should never draw a firearm without being prepared to fire. In other words, a permit carrier should never draw a weapon only to intimidate another person or scare away a potential assailant. A firearm should never leave a holster until a threat becomes deadly and requires lethal force to neutralize. Examination by law enforcement and legal authorities does not afford sympathy or understanding to a carrier who drew a firearm out of cowardice or unjustified fear of a non-existent threat.

3. Responsibility for Each Bullet

A permit carrier should be well aware and ever mindful of the fact that any actions related to carry, and certainly discharge, of a firearm are subject to scrutiny in courts of law, even if criminal charges don't issue. Civil lawsuits are always a possibility, and in today's litigious society they are a probability. Any discharge of a weapon must be justified by a need for deadly force in defense of human life. Permit carriers should understand that discharging a firearm in self-defense is justified in only an incredibly small number of situations and should exercise extreme discretion before even drawing a weapon to ensure that all firearms handling will be defensible. Permit holders must also be aware that even if a situation justifies the discharge of a weapon, every carrier, just like every law enforcement officer, is held legally responsible for every bullet fired. That means that carriers are still civilly liable for any injury or any damage caused by the discharge of their weapons. If property damage is sustained due to a stray bullet, the carrier will likely have to pay for it; likewise, if an innocent bystander is killed by a stray bullet, the carrier will be subject to civil liability.

4. Castle Doctrine, Duty to Retreat, and Stand Your Ground

Every permit holder should be familiar with a few doctrines of law that apply to firearms use and ownership and whose basic principles are commonly embraced or rejected from state to state. Permit holders should know the concepts and the nuances within them and should familiarize themselves with which ones apply in their home jurisdictions and in those where they travel.

- **Castle Doctrine:** This area of law governs the use of deadly force against intruders in one's home. The doctrine originates in the belief that intruders into one's home have the means, the position, and likely the intent to do harm, thereby justifying the use of deadly force against them. This use of deadly force must often still be defended in court since shooters are always responsible for each round fired; however, this doctrine usually allows for a lower threshold of justification than a public discharge of a firearm would mandate. Castle doctrine laws are common among gun-friendly states, but they vary, sometimes significantly. Permit carriers should always research governing law in every jurisdiction where they carry.

- **Duty to Retreat**: This doctrine of law requires individuals to attempt retreat from a threat before resorting to the use of deadly force. Often, this means permit holders can only legally use deadly force when they cannot retreat or when they have reasonably attempted to retreat but were unsuccessful. Typically, states with stricter gun laws enact duty to retreat provisions to minimize usage of deadly force.

- **Stand Your Ground**: More common in gun-friendly states, stand your ground laws allow permit carriers to use deadly force when threatened in public, abandoning the requirement that they first attempt to retreat or escape the threat imposed. This doctrine supplies a legal defense for individuals who discharge firearms to protect themselves or others in public. Stand your ground and castle doctrine laws are often found together in gun-friendly states, as legislatures that embrace the philosophy of one tend to embrace the philosophy of the other.

In the portion of this book dedicated to specific states' laws, the presence of these doctrines within each given state is noted in the "Self-Defense Model" section. Bear in mind that each of these doctrines represent only a basic idea and that actual state laws incorporating those ideas can vary widely in detail. Do further research for exact requirements in jurisdictions that are of interest.

Situation Revisited: To Shoot or Not to Shoot

Recall the situation outlined in the first chapter of this book. In the scenario, an assailant approaches in a parking lot, stopping and standing on the opposite side of your sedan while verbally threatening your life. No one is around, it's late at night, and you can't tell if the assailant has a weapon or not. Can you lawfully discharge your firearm? Remember that a permit carrier should always assume that the discharge of a weapon will need to be defended in court. While likely an unsettling answer, a permit carrier probably could not legally discharge a firearm in this scenario. It would be difficult to convince a jury that an assailant placed your life in imminent danger if they didn't first draw a weapon or make an overt physical attempt against you. Before you can legally draw and discharge your firearm, the assailant needs to have the means, position, and intent to seriously injure or kill you or another person. That being said, the actual language in each state's self-defense laws differs, as do the leanings of the courts within each state, but even in the most gun-friendly states, this situation would likely not meet the threshold for justifying the use of deadly force. The situation drastically changes if the assailant draws a weapon or lunges at you with a baseball bat or similar blunt object. In those cases, most states and juries would condone the discharge of a weapon in self-defense. Being afraid isn't enough. There must be a real threat to life for the discharge of a weapon to be defensible and justifiable under the law. Permit carriers should never draw a firearm flippantly. Anyone considering carrying a weapon should first meditate on these realities and absorb the weight of the responsibilities associated before making that decision.

Chapter 4: Traveling with a Firearm

Travel in the United States

Our world gets smaller every day. People travel extensively and with ease, so crossing state lines has become a routine part of daily life for most Americans. As a concealed carrier, even a conscientious and law-abiding one who has a permit, that reality puts you at significant risk for criminal charges. That is why the information within these pages is vital to successful and responsible concealed carry.

It is fairly common for neighboring states to recognize one another's handgun carry permits, but this is DEFINITELY not always the case. For instance, both California and New Jersey recognize permits from NO states, meaning that permits from each of their respective three contiguous states are invalid within their borders. It is the responsibility of the permit holder to know which states offer reciprocity, and it is also that permit holder's responsibility to know the laws governing carry within those states, since the laws of the state where the firearm is being carried are always the ones that must be followed. In other words, a permit carrier who lives in and holds a permit from the state of Kentucky can travel to Tennessee knowing that his Kentucky permit is valid there, but while in Tennessee, he must follow Tennessee concealed carry law instead of carry law from Kentucky, his state of issuance. The same principal applies to anyone traveling with a firearm who doesn't have a carry permit. The laws of the state where the gun is being carried are the ones the carrier is responsible for knowing and following.

Note that even the strictest states allow carriers to travel through while transporting firearms, so long as the firearms remain secured in the manner outlined in federal law—firearms unloaded (and stored separately from ammunition), disassembled, and locked in a commercial firearms case with neither firearms nor ammunition readily accessible from the passenger compartment. In these states, keep on a direct route through the state and minimize the amount of time there as much as possible. If you are traveling with a firearm that is banned altogether in that state, take extra care not to make unnecessary stops unrelated to travel, as encounters with law enforcement during stops unrelated to travel through the state may result in charges for unlawful weapons possession.

In the latter portion of this book, you will find a section dedicated to each state and one dedicated to the District of Columbia. These law sections are not comprehensive, and due to space constraints, many provisions had to be redacted. Further research is necessary for a complete understanding of the nuances, caveats, and details within many of the laws included, but a good general understanding and working knowledge can be gleaned from the portions printed here.

Airplanes

The Transportation Security Administration Web site *(www.tsa.gov)*, in its portion dedicated to travel with firearms and ammunition, reads:

> *Travelers may only transport UNLOADED firearms in a locked, hard-sided container as checked baggage. The container must be completely secured from being accessed. All firearms, ammunition and firearm parts, including firearm frames, receivers, clips and magazines are prohibited in carry-on baggage.*

When traveling by air with a firearm, best practice is to thoroughly read all related information on the TSA Web site and all related information provided by the specific airline you will be utilizing. Note also that you must be in compliance with governing law not only in the place of your departure but also in the place of your destination. Travelers departing gun-friendly locations to arrive in stricter environs must familiarize themselves with the laws of the destination city and take measures to be in compliance at the outset. For example, travelers to New York City should be aware that visitors may only possess a locked, unloaded, and cased long arm within the city limits for 24 hours, at which point possession becomes illegal. Always consult airlines and airports for detailed information related to travel with firearms to and from metropolitan cities. Good travel tips include attaching a laminated tag with your name, address, and telephone number on it to your gun case before checking it with luggage at the airport. Also, before flying or traveling with a gun, photograph it and record its serial number in case it is lost in transit. Pack guns neatly and in their most compact forms. Long arms can be cumbersome while traversing an airport or even while traveling in a vehicle, so the process is often made easier if they are broken down. It is also advisable to orient a firearm within its case so that the sights or any accessories mounted on the gun are least likely to be damaged in the event the case is dropped.

Travel in Canada

To bring a handgun into Canada, a permit carrier must apply for an "Authorization to Transport" permit from the Chief Firearms Officer of the province where the firearm will enter the country. Unfortunately, these Canadian government officials issue very few ATT permits to Canadian citizens and even fewer to applicants from other countries, so the likelihood of obtaining one as an American traveler is extremely low. Penalties for entering the country with a handgun without such a permit include confiscation of the firearm, criminal prosecution, and detainment, and similar regulations and penalties apply to most military-style firearms as well.

Sporting arms can be introduced into Canada through a "Non-Resident Firearms Declaration Form," which applies to sporting rifles of at least 26 inches in overall length and with barrels of at least 18.5 inches. NRFD forms and information concerning them can be obtained online on the Royal Canadian Mounted Police Web site (*www.rcmp.gc.ca*) or by calling 800-731-4000. The form should be completed prior to travel with the exception of the required signature, which should be added once the traveler reaches Customs. Anyone transporting sporting rifles into the country may only do so for hunting or established target-shooting competitions; the firearms may not enter the country for self-defense purposes. Travelers should store guns unloaded, locked in cases, out of sight, and separated from ammunition.

Travel in Mexico

Traveling into Mexico with weapons of any sort is typically more difficult than the process for Canada, as the country forbids entirely the ownership and possession of most modern firearms and ammunition. Any traveling hunter seeking to introduce a firearm into Mexico should be prepared to purchase an expensive Consulate Gun Permit or Military Gun Permit and to pay hunting licensure fees. The process of obtaining the requisite permit can be daunting, but any experienced outfitter or hunting guide should be able to assist with the logistics, even down to arranging for trophies to be transferred to a U.S.D.A.-certified taxidermist. An easier alternative would be for hunters visiting Mexico to rent arms from a local outfitter or guide. Traveling into Mexico with a handgun is not recommended, but interested parties may contact the Mexican Consulate at 202-736-1000 for more information.

Chapter 5: Using *Legally Armed*

Navigating This Book

In state law sections that follow, you'll find basic information about carrying in those jurisdictions divided into four subsections. The first applies to permit holders, the second applies to non–permit holders, and the third is just general information about gun law in that jurisdiction that applies to all. These three sections cover very generally some common topics that a carrier should become familiar with before traveling into or through a state. Lastly, the fourth section for each state gives excerpts taken from actual gun laws for that jurisdiction. The actual excerpts printed were chosen most often because their contents are useful to carriers traveling within a jurisdiction. Sometimes, though, excerpts were included from certain laws because of their uniqueness; in an effort to keep traveling carriers from getting caught off guard, those laws were chosen to highlight unusual restrictions that they may not anticipate.

Readers should know that this book, while thoroughly researched, could never include every aspect of each state's gun law, given the sheer volume and level of detail that would require. Readers should also be aware that the landscape of firearms law is ever-changing, so unavoidably revisions are sometimes made in state laws just after the current edition of this book has gone to print. The following pages should be considered more of a quick reference to some of the most basic laws carriers are likely to encounter when traveling from state to state. For a more detailed analysis, for a deeper inquiry into a specific topic, or for absolute certainty that a certain provision remains in effect at any given time, you should contact the legal authorities for each jurisdiction. Contact information for those authorities has been provided for each state.

Before using this book, note that the phrases "glove compartment" and "vehicle storage compartment" have two distinct meanings; "vehicle storage compartment" refers to a compartment, such as a trunk, located outside the actual passenger compartment. Note also that a console between seats, a side door compartment, or a seat pocket cannot act as a substitute for a glove compartment; most laws do not consider these locations interchangeable in the context of firearm storage. Additionally, requirements that a firearm be "securely encased" or "cased" refer to storage of a firearm in a commercial-grade firearm case; a handbag, backpack, or duffle will not suffice.

Also be familiar with the difference between "may issue" and "shall issue" states, as each state is designated as one or the other. "Shall issue" refers to jurisdictions where a permit for firearm carry "shall issue" to an individual independent of the discretion of law enforcement officers. Usually this means that if an eligible individual goes through the proper avenues of pursuing a carry permit (such as completing a carry permit class, properly applying for a permit, and paying requisite fees), the government must grant them the right to carry a firearm regardless of the opinions of law enforcement officers. "May issue" refers to jurisdictions where issuance of a permit for firearm carry is not guaranteed, even to eligible applicants, because the issuing agency retains some discretion as to whom they will issue permits, e.g., local sheriff's offices may require those seeking a carry permit to provide just cause for carrying a firearm, may require an interview to assess the fitness of the applicant, etc. "May issue" laws are common among states with stricter gun laws, and their restrictiveness varies from state to state.

Another distinction to know relates to who is responsible for making carry law within a jurisdiction. Within the "General Info" portion of each state's section there is an entry indicating whether or not there is carry law uniformity throughout the jurisdiction. Some states have enacted laws reserving all law-making authority related to concealed carry for the state legislature, while other states have enacted laws stating that individual municipalities or counties may enact their own laws related to concealed carry, regardless of what the rest of the state has enacted. Knowing that state law "preempts," or "trumps," any laws enacted by localities is helpful for a traveling carrier, because the carrier then knows that only one set of laws— those enacted by the state—governs concealed carry throughout the entire state. In states where state law DOESN'T preempt that of localities, carriers BEWARE. Some states that allow different localities to enact their own laws for concealed carry are virtual minefields of criminal liability. In the state of New York, for example, literally every single county enacts its own carry laws, so moving around within the state amounts to traveling through a patchwork quilt of legal systems. What is legal in one county could very well put you in handcuffs in the next county. Even the most conscientious carrier would be hard-pressed to not only learn but to also stay current on the carry laws for every New York county, not to mention to memorize each county's borders in order to know which system was in effect at any given location.

In most states that allow localities to enact their own carry laws, travel is not as precarious as it is in New York. In most of those states, the only localities that take advantage of this right to legislate carry law are metropolitan areas. For instance, Colorado state carry law governs throughout most of that state, but Denver has enacted stricter carry laws that apply within the city limits. Be advised, though, that is not safe to rely on the assumption that only metro areas enact laws to further restrict carry. In some states that allow for local carry law, some smaller communities have also availed themselves of this right to restrict. Instances like this crop up for a few different reasons—sometimes as a result of the area having a liberal-leaning and politically proactive population, sometimes as a result of the area having a relatively high crime rate as compared to surrounding areas, and sometimes as a result of the area being an affluent one that is located very near a poorer area that is plagued with crime. Just be aware that there are no hard and fast rules about what areas within a state will choose to enact further restrictions, so you must educate yourself before traveling in these states while carrying, which gets at the point and purpose of this book.

The Purpose of This Book

The responsibility to know and abide by the law lies with the carrier, and ignorance of the law is no defense. By acquiring and exercising your rights under a carry permit, you accept the responsibilities attendant to carrying a loaded firearm in public. One area of responsibility includes safe handling and maintaining control of the firearm at all times. Another area of responsibility covers discharge of the firearm and ensuring that happens only in instances where it is legally justified. But, neither of those areas of responsibility will create problems for you as easily or as often as the third area of your responsibility as a concealed carry permit holder: always carrying within the parameters of the governing law. Once you are an experienced carrier, having a loaded firearm concealed on your person will become second nature to you. Being confident and comfortable with your weapon is a positive thing, but when that confidence or comfort level results in a relaxed attitude about where, when, and how you carry, legal issues are bound to arise. Stay cognizant. Stay informed. Keep this book in your glove compartment, so that it's accessible to you when you travel. Buy the new edition every year to stay abreast of the changing legal terrain. Make sure you are always *Legally Armed*.

Map and Legend

Each state has been given a letter grade and corresponding color designating the level of gun-friendliness of laws there. Permit holders will have greater freedoms with respect to where and how they may carry their weapons in states with more favorable grades (closer to A+).

- **A+ (Green):** These states allow permit holders great freedom as to how they may carry their weapons. Some of these states even allow citizens to carry concealed weapons without permits. Usually these states have enactedstand your ground and castle doctrine laws, and they issue permits on a "shall issue" basis. These states also usually recognize permits issued by many other states.

- **A (Light Green):** States with "A" ratings still have fairly relaxed gun laws but may restrict carry in more locations. Some of these states may also restrict issuance to a degree.

- **B (Blue):** While still fairly gun-friendly, these states' laws typically further restrict the use of firearms in self-defense through duty to

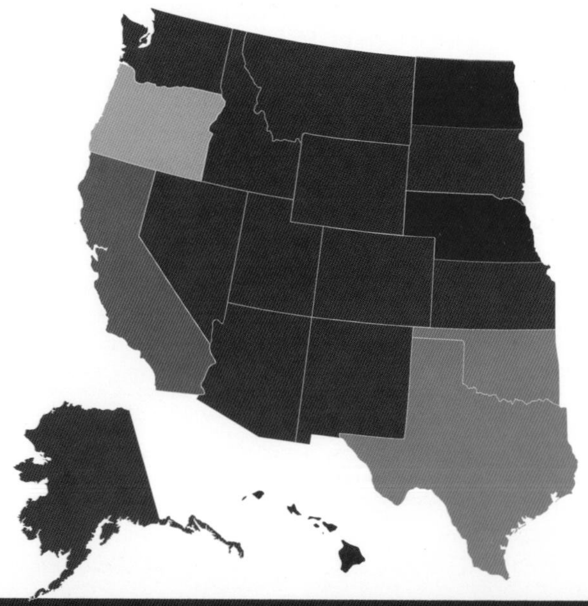

retreat laws, etc. They may also issue permits only on a "may issue" basis.

- **C (Yellow):** States with "C" grades impose relatively harsh limitations on gun ownership and carry. Usually they issue permits on a discretionary basis and don't have stand your ground or castle doctrine laws. Permit carriers should proceed with caution when traveling through these states.
- **D (Orange):** While these states may issue carry permits, they do so with extreme discretion. These states may also ban or heavily restrict the purchase and ownership of shotguns and rifles. These states don't typically recognize carry permits issued by other states. Again, those with carry permits or those who travel with firearms should proceed with extreme caution when in these states.
- **F (Red):** These states don't typically issue or recognize any carry permits. They also usually heavily restrict firearms of any sort and place extreme restrictions on their purchase. We generally suggest not bringing a firearm into one of these states at all.

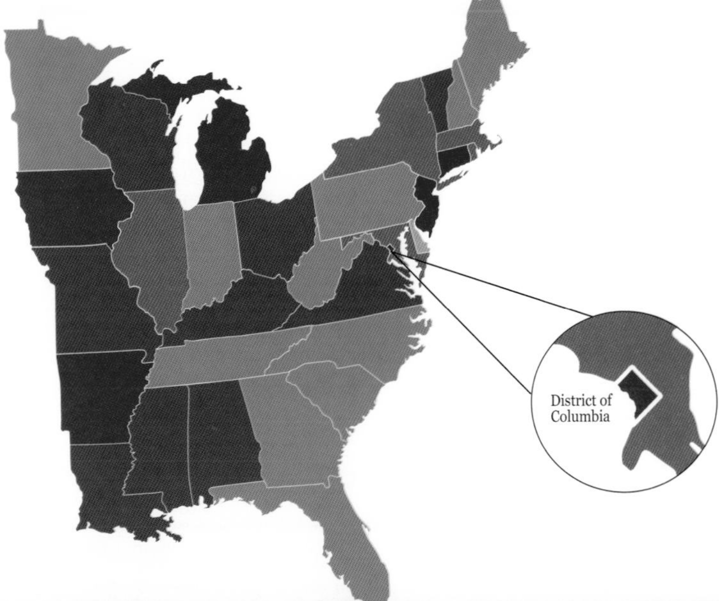

ALABAMA

Permit Holders

Permit: "Shall issue" state.

Open Carry: Permitted, with some exceptions.

Travel: Loaded handguns may be transported openly or concealed within a vehicle.

Disclose Presence of Handgun to Law Enforcement: Not mandatory unless asked by a law enforcement officer.

Restaurants: May carry if permit holder does not consume alcohol, must leave establishment if told to do so.

Recognizes Permits From: All states.

Non-Permit

Firearms Ownership: Permitted to all qualified citizens without license or permit.

Loaded Carry: All citizens of age (18+) may openly carry a loaded firearm in public.

Travel: Transporting a loaded handgun in a vehicle, without a concealed carry permit, is prohibited (unless you are on your own property). In transit, a firearm must be unloaded and locked within a container that is out of reach of the driver or any passengers.

General Info

State Parks: Restricted or prohibited.

Carry Law Uniformity: State law preempts that of local agencies/municipalities.

Self-Defense Model: Castle Doctrine, Stand Your Ground.

Notes: Though open carry is technically legal for both permitted and non-permitted citizens, it is not recommended. Alabama does not issue non-resident permits. Even if you have a concealed carry permit, you may not carry a firearm to any public gathering such as a sporting event, political rally, parade, demonstration, etc. "No Firearm" signs do not have force of law in Alabama, unless it is posted on property specifically mentioned in state law as off limits to permit holders. However, whether or not a sign is posted, if the property owner asks you to leave, you must to avoid the possibility of trespass charges. Ammunition designed to penetrate bullet-proof vests is illegal in AL.

Alabama Criminal Code § 13A-11-52 Carrying pistol on private property; who may carry pistol. Except as otherwise provided in this article, no person shall carry a pistol about his person on private property not his own or under his control unless the person possesses a valid concealed weapon permit or the person has the consent of the owner or legal possessor of the premises; but this section shall not apply to any law enforcement officer in the lawful discharge of the duties of his office, or to United States marshal or his deputies, rural free delivery mail carriers in the discharge of their duties as such, bonded constables in the discharge of their duties as such, conductors, railway mail clerks and express messengers in the discharge of their duties....

§ 13A-11-60 Possession or sale of brass or steel Teflon-coated handgun ammunition; applicability of section. (a) Except as provided in subsection (b) of this section, the possession or sale of brass or steel Teflon-coated handgun ammunition is illegal.... The possession or sale of said ammunition or any ammunition of like kind designed to penetrate bullet-proof vests, shall be unlawful and punishable as provided in subsection (c) of this section....

§ 13A-11-61.2 Possession of firearms in certain places. (a) In addition to any other place limited or prohibited by state or federal law, a person, including a person with a permit issued under Section 13A-11-75(a)(1) or recognized under Section 13A- 11-85, may not knowingly possess or carry a firearm in any of the following places without the express permission of a person or entity with authority over the premises: (1) Inside the building of a police, sheriff, or highway patrol station. (2) Inside or on the premises of a prison, jail, halfway house, community corrections facility, or other detention facility for those ... charged with or convicted of a criminal or juvenile offense. (3) Inside or on the premises of a facility which provides inpatient or custodial care of those with psychiatric, mental, or emotional disorders. (4) Inside a courthouse, courthouse annex, a building in which a District Attorney's office is located, or a building in which a county commission or city council is currently having a regularly scheduled or specially called meeting. (5) Inside any facility hosting an athletic event not related to or involving firearms which is sponsored by a private or public elementary or secondary school or any private or public institution of postsecondary education, unless the person has a permit ... (6) Inside any facility hosting a professional athletic event not related to or involving firearms, unless the person has a permit ... (b) Notwithstanding the provisions of subsection (a), a person, including a person with a permit ... may not, without the express permission of a person or entity with authority over the premises, knowingly possess or carry a firearm inside any building or facility to which access of unauthorized persons and prohibited articles is limited during normal hours of operation by the continuous posting of guards and the use of other security features... (c) The person or entity with authority over the premises set forth in subsections (a)(1)-(6) and subsection (b) shall place a notice at the public entrances of such premises or buildings alerting those entering that firearms are prohibited. (d) Except as provided in subsections (a)(5) and (a)(6), any firearm on the premises of any facility set forth in subsection

(a)(1), or subsections (a)(4)-(6), or subsection (b) must be kept from ordinary observation and locked within a compartment or in the interior of the person's motor vehicle or in a compartment or container securely affixed to the motor vehicle. (e) A violation of subsections (a) or (d) is a Class C misdemeanor....

Contact for Additional Information:
Attorney General of Alabama
P.O. Box 300152 • Montgomery, AL 36130
334-242-7300

FIREARM FRIENDLY: 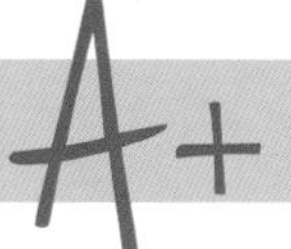  ALASKA

Permit: "Shall issue" state; a permit isn't necessary to carry concealed, but some residents acquire one to gain reciprocity rights in states that honor AK permits.

Open Carry: Permitted.

Travel: Loaded handguns may be transported anywhere in a vehicle.

Disclose Presence of Handgun to Law Enforcement: Required immediately on contact with law enforcement.

Restaurants: May carry if carrier does not consume alcohol, if establishment doesn't forbid firearms via a posting, AND if establishment earns less than 50% of its revenue from alcohol sales.

Recognizes Permits From: All states; however, for Idaho Alaska currently honors only its enhanced license.

Permit Holders

Firearms Ownership: Permitted to all qualified citizens without license or permit.

Loaded Carry: All citizens over 21 years of age may carry a loaded firearm in public, openly or concealed.

Travel: Loaded handguns may be transported anywhere in a vehicle.

Non-Permit

State Parks: Permissible unless posted.

Carry Law Uniformity: State law preempts that of local agencies/municipalities.

Self-Defense Model: Castle Doctrine, Stand Your Ground.

Notes: Castle Doctrine extends to any place a resident lays his head, be it a hotel room, an RV, or a tent. Firearms may not be carried in bars, unless the ammunition is removed. Posts forbidding firearms in restaurants, etc. do not carry the force of law; carriers will be denied admittance or service, but will not be subject to criminal penalties for violation. Carry is not permissible in National Parks, courthouses, or child care centers. Carry is permissible in state buildings unless posted.

General Info

Contact for Additional Information:

Alaskan State Police
5700 East Tudor Road • Anchorage, AK 99507
907-269-5511

ALASKA

Alaska Statutes § 11.61.195. Misconduct involving weapons in the second degree. (a) A person commits the crime of misconduct involving weapons in the second degree if the person knowingly (1) possesses a firearm during the commission of an offense under AS 11.71.010 - 11.71.040; (2) violates AS 11.61.200(a)(1) and is within the grounds of or on a parking lot immediately adjacent to (A) a public or private preschool, elementary, junior high, or secondary school without the permission of the chief administrative officer of the school or district or the designee of the chief administrative officer; or (B) an entity, other than a private residence, licensed as a child care facility under AS 47.32 or recognized by the federal government for the care of children.... (b) Misconduct involving weapons in the second degree is a class B felony.

Alaska Statutes § 11.61.210. Misconduct involving weapons in the fourth degree. (a) A person commits the crime of misconduct involving weapons in the fourth degree if the person (1) possesses on the person, or in the interior of a vehicle in which the person is present, a firearm when the person's physical or mental condition is impaired as a result of the introduction of an intoxicating liquor or a controlled substance into the person's body in circumstances other than described in AS 11.61.200 (a)(7)....

Alaska Statutes § 11.61.220. Misconduct involving weapons in the fifth degree. (a) A person commits the crime of misconduct involving weapons in the fifth degree if the person (1) is 21 years of age or older and knowingly possesses a deadly weapon, other than an ordinary pocket knife or a defensive weapon, (A) that is concealed on the person, and, when contacted by a peace officer, the person fails to (i) immediately inform the peace officer of that possession; or (ii) allow the peace officer to secure the deadly weapon, or fails to secure the weapon at the direction of the peace officer... (B) that is concealed on the person within the residence of another person unless the person has first obtained the express permission of an adult residing there to bring a concealed deadly weapon within ... (2) knowingly possesses a loaded firearm on the person in any place where intoxicating liquor is sold for consumption on the premises; ... (4) knowingly possesses a firearm (A) within the grounds of or on a parking lot immediately adjacent to an entity, other than a private residence, licensed as a child care facility ..., except that a person 21 years of age or older may possess an unloaded firearm in the trunk of a motor vehicle or encased in a closed container of a motor vehicle; (B) within a (i) courtroom or office of the Alaska Court System; or (ii) courthouse that is occupied only by the Alaska Court System and other justice related agencies; or (C) within a domestic violence or sexual assault shelter that receives funding from the state.... (6) is less than 21 years of age and knowingly possesses a deadly weapon, other than an ordinary pocket knife or a defensive weapon, that is concealed on the person. (b) In a prosecution under (a)(6) of this section, it is an affirmative defense that the defendant, at the time of possession, was (1) in the defendant's dwelling or on land owned or leased by the defendant appurtenant to the dwelling; or (2) actually engaged in lawful hunting, fishing, trapping, or other lawful outdoor activity that necessarily involves the carrying of a weapon for personal protection.....

FIREARM FRIENDLY:  ARIZONA

Permit: "Shall issue" state.

Open Carry: Permitted, constitutional carry state.

Travel: Loaded handguns may be transported openly or concealed in a vehicle.

Disclose Presence of Handgun to Law Enforcement: Required only if requested by officer on official business.

Restaurants: May carry in restaurants, including those that serve alcohol, unless posted, but may not consume alcohol.

Recognizes Permits From: All states.

Firearms Ownership: Permitted to all citizens without license or permit.

Loaded Carry: Permitted; constitutional carry state so non-permit holders may carry concealed.

Travel: Anyone 21 years of age or older may carry a concealed firearm in a vehicle.

State Parks: Permissible for permit holders, if not posted.

Carry Law Uniformity: State law preempts that of local agencies/municipalities.

Self-Defense Model: Castle Doctrine requires threat to life, Stand Your Ground.

Notes: Carry permits are not recognized on Native American reservation property, but firearms can be taken onto tribal land with permission from tribal authorities. Permit holders may generally carry in bars, as long as they are not posted. Posts forbidding firearms by private property owners carry force of law, and violations are punishable as criminal trespass. If an establishment serves alcohol, posts are displayed near liquor licenses on the wall, and carriers are allowed to enter the property for the limited purpose of inspecting for postings without violating the law. Carry is forbidden in any nuclear power generating station, all federal and state government buildings, school zones, and any posted private property.

Arizona Revised Statute § 13-3112. Concealed weapons; qualification; application; permit to carry; civil penalty; report; applicability

A. The department of public safety shall issue a permit to carry a concealed weapon to a person who is qualified under this section. The person shall carry the permit at all times when the person is in actual possession of the concealed weapon and is required by section 4-229 or 4-244 to carry the permit. If the person is in actual possession of the concealed weapon and is required by section 4-229 or 4-244 to carry the permit, the person shall present the permit for inspection to any law enforcement officer on request.

B. The permit of a person who is arrested or indicted for an offense that would make the person unqualified under section 13-3101, subsection A,

Arizona Revised Statute § 13-3112. Concealed weapons; qualification; application; permit to carry; civil penalty; report; applicability

A. The department of public safety shall issue a permit to carry a concealed weapon to a person who is qualified under this section. The person shall carry the permit at all times when the person is in actual possession of the concealed weapon and is required by section 4-229 or 4-244 to carry the permit. If the person is in actual possession of the concealed weapon and is required by section 4-229 or 4-244 to carry the permit, the person shall present the permit for inspection to any law enforcement officer on request.

B. The permit of a person who is arrested or indicted for an offense that would make the person unqualified under section 13-3101, subsection A, paragraph 7 or this section shall be immediately suspended and seized. The permit of a person who becomes unqualified on conviction of that offense shall be revoked. The permit shall be restored on presentation of documentation from the court if the permittee is found not guilty or the charges are dismissed. The permit shall be restored on presentation of documentation from the county attorney that the charges against the permittee were dropped or dismissed.

C. A permittee who carries a concealed weapon, who is required by section 4-229 or 4-244 to carry a permit and who fails to present the permit for inspection on the request of a law enforcement officer commits a violation of this subsection and is subject to a civil penalty of not more than three hundred dollars. The department of public safety shall be notified of all violations of this subsection and shall immediately suspend the permit. A permittee shall not be convicted of a violation of this subsection if the permittee produces to the court a legible permit that is issued to the permittee and that was valid at the time the permittee failed to present the permit for inspection.

D. A law enforcement officer shall not confiscate or forfeit a weapon that is otherwise lawfully possessed by a permittee whose permit is suspended pursuant to subsection C of this section, except that a law enforcement officer may take temporary custody of a firearm during an investigatory stop of the permittee.

E. The department of public safety shall issue a permit to an applicant who meets all of the following conditions:

1. Is a resident of this state or a United States citizen.

2. Is twenty-one years of age or older or is at least nineteen years of age and provides evidence of current military service or proof of honorable discharge or general discharge under honorable conditions from the United States armed forces, United States armed forces reserve or a state national guard.

3. Is not under indictment for and has not been convicted in any jurisdiction of a felony unless that conviction has been expunged, set aside or vacated or the applicant's rights have been restored and the applicant is currently not a prohibited possessor under state or federal law.

4. Does not suffer from mental illness and has not been adjudicated mentally incompetent or committed to a mental institution.

5. Is not unlawfully present in the United States.

6. Has ever demonstrated competence with a firearm as prescribed by subsection N of this section and provides adequate documentation that the person has satisfactorily completed a training program or demonstrated competence with a firearm in any state or political subdivision in the United States. For the purposes of this paragraph, "adequate documentation" means:

(a) A current or expired permit issued by the department of public safety pursuant to this section.

(b) An original or copy of a certificate, card or document that shows the applicant has ever completed any course or class prescribed by subsection N of this section or an affidavit from the instructor, school, club or organization that conducted or taught the course or class attesting to the applicant's completion of the course or class.

(c) An original or a copy of a United States department of defense form 214 (DD-214) indicating an honorable discharge or general discharge under honorable conditions, a certificate of completion of basic training or any other document demonstrating proof of the applicant's current or former service in the United States armed forces as prescribed by subsection N, paragraph 5 of this section.

(d) An original or a copy of a concealed weapon, firearm or handgun permit or a license as prescribed by subsection N, paragraph 6 of this section.

Contact for Additional Information:

Arizona Department of Public Safety

2102 West Encanto Boulevard • Phoenix, AZ 85009

602-223-2000

ARKANSAS

FIREARM FRIENDLY: B

Permit Holders

Permit: "Shall issue" state.

Open Carry: Prohibited, controversy surrounds this issue, but Arkansas State Government websites state open carry is not allowed at this time.

Travel: Loaded handguns may be transported concealed on your person or within a vehicle.

Disclose Presence of Handgun to Law Enforcement: Required immediately upon contact with a law enforcement officer.

Restaurants: May carry, unless posted, if permit holder does not consume alcohol; must not enter "bar" area or section designated for persons 21+ (if such a section exists within a restaurant).

Recognizes Permits From: All states.

Non-Permit

Firearms Ownership: Permitted to all qualified citizens without license or permit.

Loaded Carry: Non-permitted individuals may not carry a handgun in any fashion.

Travel: Transportation of a handgun is not allowed unless one is on a "journey," which state law defines as traveling beyond the county in which one lives.

General Info

State Parks: Permissible, some restrictions apply.

Carry Law Uniformity: State law does not preempt that of local agencies/municipalities.

Self-Defense Model: No Castle Doctrine, No Stand Your Ground,

Duty to Retreat.

Notes: If you enter the home of an AR resident while carrying, you must immediately disclose that you possess a firearm. "No Firearms" signs carry force of law in the state of Arkansas. Even with a permit, firearms cannot be carried at any athletic event not related to firearms, at any place licensed for alcohol consumption on the premises (unless it's a restaurant as defined by statute), or any institution of learning at any level (unless it is a K-12 school owned by a church and the church has given consent for carry).

Contact for Additional Information:

Arkansas State Police Headquarters

1 State Police Plaza Drive • Little Rock, AR 72209

501-618-8000

Arkansas Code Annotated § 5-73-119. Handguns -- Possession by minor or possession on school property.

(a) (1) No person in this state under eighteen (18) years of age shall possess a handgun.

(2) (A) A violation of subdivision (a)(1) of this section is a Class A misdemeanor.

(B) A violation of subdivision (a)(1) of this section is a Class D felony if the person has previously:

(i) Been adjudicated delinquent for a violation of subdivision (a)(1) of this section;

(ii) Been adjudicated delinquent for any offense that would be a felony if committed by an adult; or

(iii) Pleaded guilty or nolo contendere to or been found guilty of a felony in circuit court while under eighteen (18) years of age.

(b) (1) No person in this state shall possess a firearm:

(A) Upon the developed property of a public or private school, K-12;

(B) In or upon any school bus; or

(C) At a designated bus stop as identified on the route list published by a school district each year.

(2) (A) A violation of subdivision (b)(1) of this section is a Class D felony....

... (e) It is permissible to carry a handgun under this section if at the time of the act of possessing a handgun or firearm:

(1) The person is in his or her own dwelling or place of business or on property in which he or she has a possessory or proprietary interest, except upon the property of a public or private institution of higher learning;

(2) The person is a law enforcement officer, correctional officer, or member of the armed forces acting in the course and scope of his or her official duties;

(3) The person is assisting a law enforcement officer, correctional officer, or member of the armed forces acting in the course and scope of his or her official duties pursuant to the direction or request of the law enforcement officer, correctional officer, or member of the armed forces;

(4) The person is a registered commissioned security guard acting in the course and scope of his or her duties;

(5) The person is hunting game with a handgun or firearm that may be hunted with a handgun or firearm under the rules and regulations of the Arkansas State Game and Fish Commission or is en route to or from a hunting area for the purpose of hunting game with a handgun or firearm;

(6) The person is a certified law enforcement officer;

(7) The person is on a journey beyond the county in which the person lives, unless the person is eighteen (18) years of age or less;

(8) The person is participating in a certified hunting safety course sponsored by the commission or a firearm safety course recognized and approved by the commission or by a state or national nonprofit organization qualified and experienced in firearm safety;

(9) The person is participating in a school-approved educational course or sporting activity involving the use of firearms;

(10) The person is a minor engaged in lawful marksmanship competition or practice or other lawful recreational shooting under the supervision of his or her parent, legal guardian, or other person twenty-one (21) years of age or older standing in loco parentis or is traveling to or from a lawful marksmanship competition or practice or other lawful recreational shooting with an unloaded handgun or firearm accompanied by his or her parent, legal guardian, or other person twenty-one (21) years of age or older standing in loco parentis; or

(11) The person has a license to carry a concealed handgun under § 5-73-301 et seq. and is carrying a concealed handgun on the developed property of a kindergarten through grade twelve (K-12) private school operated by a church or other place of worship that:

(A) Is located on the developed property of the kindergarten through grade twelve (K-12) private school;

(B) Allows the person to carry a concealed handgun into the church or other place of worship under § 5-73-306; and

(C) Allows the person to possess a concealed handgun on the developed property of the kindergarten through grade twelve (K-12) private school.

§ 5-73-306. Prohibited places.

No license to carry a concealed handgun issued pursuant to this subchapter authorizes any person to carry a concealed handgun into:

(1) Any police station, sheriff's station, or Department of Arkansas State Police station;

(2) Any Arkansas Highway Police Division of the Arkansas State Highway and Transportation Department facility;

(3) (A) Any building of the Arkansas State Highway and Transportation Department or onto grounds adjacent to any building of the Arkansas State Highway and Transportation Department.

(B) However, subdivision (3)(A) of this section does not apply to a rest area or weigh station of the Arkansas State Highway and Transportation Department;

(4) Any detention facility, prison, or jail;

(5) Any courthouse;

(6) (A) Any courtroom.

(B) However, nothing in this subchapter precludes a judge from carrying a concealed weapon or determining who will carry a concealed weapon into his or her courtroom;

(7) Any polling place;

(8) Any meeting place of the governing body of any governmental entity;

(9) Any meeting of the General Assembly or a committee of the General Assembly;

(10) Any state office;

(11) Any athletic event not related to firearms;

(12) Any portion of an establishment, except a restaurant as defined in § 3-5-1202,

licensed to dispense alcoholic beverages for consumption on the premises;

(13) Any portion of an establishment, except a restaurant as defined in § 3-5-1202, where beer or light wine is consumed on the premises;

(14) (A) A school, college, community college, or university campus building or event, unless for the purpose of participating in an authorized firearms-related activity or otherwise provided for in § 5-73-322.

(B) However, subdivision (14)(A) of this section does not apply to a kindergarten through grade twelve (K-12) private school operated by a church or other place of worship that:

(i) Is located on the developed property of the kindergarten through grade twelve (K-12) private school;

(ii) Allows the licensee to carry a concealed handgun into the church or other place of worship under this section; and

(iii) Allows the licensee to possess a concealed handgun on the developed property of the kindergarten through grade twelve (K-12) private school under § 5-73-119(e);

(15) Inside the passenger terminal of any airport, except that no person is prohibited from carrying any legal firearm into the passenger terminal if the firearm is encased for shipment for purposes of checking the firearm as baggage to be lawfully transported on any aircraft;

(16) (A) Any church or other place of worship.

(B) However, this subchapter does not preclude a church or other place of worship from determining who may carry a concealed handgun into the church or other place of worship;

(17) Any place where the carrying of a firearm is prohibited by federal law;

(18) Any place where a parade or demonstration requiring a permit is being held, and the licensee is a participant in the parade or demonstration; or

(19) (A) (i) Any place at the discretion of the person or entity exercising control over the physical location of the place by placing at each entrance to the place a written notice clearly readable at a distance of not less than ten feet (10') that "carrying a handgun is prohibited".

(ii) (a) If the place does not have a roadway entrance, there shall be a written notice placed anywhere upon the premises of the place.

(b) In addition to the requirement of subdivision (19)(A)(ii)(a) of this section, there shall be at least one (1) written notice posted within every three (3) acres of a place with no roadway entrance.

(iii) A written notice as described in subdivision (19)(A)(i) of this section is not required for a private home.

(iv) Any licensee entering a private home shall notify the occupant that the licensee is carrying a concealed handgun.

(B) Subdivision (19)(A) of this section does not apply if the physical location is a public university, public college, or community college, as defined in § 5-73-322, and the licensee is carrying a concealed handgun as provided under § 5-73-322.

CALIFORNIA

FIREARM FRIENDLY: D

Permit Holders

Permit: "May issue" state.

Open Carry: Forbidden, on all but unposted National Forest property.

Travel: Loaded handguns may be transported anywhere in a vehicle but must remain concealed.

Disclose Presence of Handgun to Law Enforcement: Required only if requested by officer.

Restaurants: May carry if establishment earns less than 50% of its revenue from alcohol sales, unless posted.

Recognizes Permits From: No states.

Non-Permit

Firearms Ownership: Handguns must be registered within 90 days of arrival to the state. Any firearm purchased in CA is registered to the buyer forever or until registration is transferred to another person. Sales of firearms between private parties must involve transfer of the registration of the firearm from the seller to the buyer at an FFL.

Loaded Carry: Forbidden, unless on National Forest property not posted.

Travel: Handguns must be unloaded in locked containers (not glove box or console, even if they lock) with ammunition stored separately.

General Info

State Parks: Only permit holders.

Carry Law Uniformity: Local agencies/municipalities may further restrict state gun law.

Self-Defense Model: Castle Doctrine, Duty to Retreat in public.

Notes: The process and requirements for carry permit application are determined by the sheriff's office of each individual county as an autonomous body, so no state-wide application process or list of requirements exists. State law merely requires that each county sheriff offers some type of concealed carry permit program and gives a few general guidelines, i.e., that training requirements not exceed 16 hours, etc. Most counties require a one-on-one interview between a sheriff's deputy and the applicant for inquiry into character, regard for the law, and responsibility. Postings forbidding firearms on private property do not have the force of law; establishments may deny service or admittance to a carrier, but no criminal penalty will result from the carrier's possession of a firearm. Any semi-automatic with 2 or more "features" under CA law is banned as an assault weapon. High capacity magazines (over 10 rounds) are banned. Carry is forbidden in bars or any business whose primary purpose is to dispense alcoholic beverages for onsite consumption, and consumption of alcohol while carrying is forbidden. Concealed carry permits are not recognized on Native American reservation land. Printing or "flashing" (quickly and inadvertently exposing) a concealed firearm is not punishable as brandishing under the law, but it is heavily frowned upon and reports of it to issuing authorities could result in a sheriff's admonishment, permit revocation, required completion of a safety course to maintain carry privileges, or even surrender of the carrier's weapon.

CALIFORNIA PENAL CODE § 26150.

(a) When a person applies for a license to carry a pistol, revolver, or other firearm capable of being concealed upon the person, the sheriff of a county may issue a license to that person upon proof of all of the following:

(1) The applicant is of good moral character.

(2) Good cause exists for issuance of the license.

(3) The applicant is a resident of the county or a city within the county, or the applicant's principal place of employment or business is in the county or a city within the county and the applicant spends a substantial period of time in that place of employment or business.

(4) The applicant has completed a course of training as described in Section 26165.

(b) The sheriff may issue a license under subdivision (a) in either of the following formats:

(1) A license to carry concealed a pistol, revolver, or other firearm capable of being concealed upon the person.

(2) Where the population of the county is less than 200,000 persons according to the most recent federal decennial census, a license to carry loaded and exposed in only that county a pistol, revolver, or other firearm capable of being concealed upon the person.

§ 26155.

(a) When a person applies for a license to carry a pistol, revolver, or other firearm capable of being concealed upon the person, the chief or other head of a municipal police department of any city or city and county may issue a license to that person upon proof of all of the following:

(1) The applicant is of good moral character.

(2) Good cause exists for issuance of the license.

(3) The applicant is a resident of that city.

(4) The applicant has completed a course of training as described

in Section 26165.

(b) The chief or other head of a municipal police department may issue a license under subdivision (a) in either of the following formats:

(1) A license to carry concealed a pistol, revolver, or other firearm capable of being concealed upon the person.

(2) Where the population of the county in which the city is located is less than 200,000 persons according to the most recent federal decennial census, a license to carry loaded and exposed in only that county a pistol, revolver, or other firearm capable of being concealed upon the person.

(c) Nothing in this chapter shall preclude the chief or other head of a municipal police department of any city from entering an agreement with the sheriff of the county in which the city is located for the sheriff to process all applications for licenses, renewals of licenses, and amendments to licenses, pursuant to this chapter.

Contact for Additional Information:
California Bureau of Firearms
P.O. Box 820200 • Sacramento, CA 94203
916-227-7527

FIREARM FRIENDLY:   COLORADO

Permit: "Shall issue" state.

Open Carry: Permitted (but for some municipalities that regulate).

Travel: Loaded handguns may be transported in a vehicle for self-defense purposes and may be concealed on person or in glove box. Long arms may not have a round chambered while in transport in a vehicle.

Disclose Presence of Handgun to Law Enforcement: Only required if officer requests.

Restaurants: If carrier is not intoxicated, may carry (although those with posted anti-gun policies may refuse service/admittance).

Reciprocity: AL, AK, AZ, AR, DE, FL, GA, ID, IN, IA, KS, KY, LA, MI, MS, MO, MT, NE, NH, NM, NC, ND, OH, OK, PA, SD, TN, TX, UT, VA, WV, WI, WY

Firearms Ownership: Permitted to all citizens without license or permit, semi-autos included.

Loaded Carry: Only while hunting.

Travel: Loaded handguns may be transported in a vehicle for self-defense purposes and may be concealed on person or in glove box. Long arms may not have a round chambered while in transport in a vehicle.

State Parks: Permissible to conceal for permit holders but must be open for non-permit holders.

Carry Law Uniformity: Local agencies/municipalities may further regulate state law for open carry and types of loaded weapons permitted in vehicular travel. (See specific laws applying only in Denver.)

Self-Defense Model: Castle Doctrine, No Duty to Retreat.

Notes: Non-permitted residents and visitors (who are over 18, not prohibited possessors under other law, and not intoxicated) may keep concealed, loaded handguns anywhere inside vehicles for self-defense purposes; however, this law does not apply in Denver (where only permitted carriers may do so). Some communities have banned open carry, including Denver. Firearms transported on a motorized snow vehicle must be stored in a case and fully unloaded when transported, with rounds also removed from magazines.

Contact for Additional Information:

Colorado Bureau of Investigation
690 Kipling Street, Suite 3000 • Lakewood, CO 80215
303-239-4201

Colorado Revised Statutes § 18-12-203. Criteria for obtaining a permit

(1) Beginning May 17, 2003, except as otherwise provided in this section, a sheriff shall issue a permit to carry a concealed handgun to an applicant who:

(a) Is a legal resident of the state of Colorado. For purposes of this part 2, a person who is a member of the armed forces and is stationed pursuant to permanent duty station orders at a military installation in this state, and a member of the person's immediate family living in Colorado, shall be deemed to be a legal resident of the state of Colorado.

(b) Is twenty-one years of age or older;

(c) Is not ineligible to possess a firearm pursuant to section 18-12-108 or federal law;

(d) Has not been convicted of perjury under section 18-8-503, in relation to information provided or deliberately omitted on a permit application submitted pursuant to this part 2;

(e) (I) Does not chronically and habitually use alcoholic beverages to the extent that the applicant's normal faculties are impaired.

(II) The prohibition specified in this paragraph (e) shall not apply to an applicant who provides an affidavit, signed by a professional counselor or addiction counselor who is licensed pursuant to article 43 of title 12, C.R.S., and specializes in alcohol addiction, stating that the applicant has been evaluated by the counselor and has been determined to be a recovering alcoholic who has refrained from using alcohol for at least three years.

(f) Is not an unlawful user of or addicted to a controlled substance as defined in section 18-18-102

(5). Whether an applicant is an unlawful user of or addicted to a controlled substance shall be determined as provided in federal law and regulations.

(g) Is not subject to:

(I) A protection order issued pursuant to section 18-1-1001 or section 19-2-707, C.R.S., that is in effect at the time the application is submitted; or

(II) A permanent protection order issued pursuant to article 14 of title 13, C.R.S.; or(III) A temporary protection order issued pursuant to article 14 of title 13, C.R.S., that is in effect at the time the application is submitted;

(h) Demonstrates competence with a handgun by submitting:

(I) Evidence of experience with a firearm through participation in organized shooting competitions or current military service;

(II) Evidence that, at the time the application is submitted, the applicant is a certified instructor;

(III) Proof of honorable discharge from a branch of the United States armed forces within the three years preceding submittal of the application;

(IV) Proof of honorable discharge from a branch of the United States armed forces that reflects pistol qualifications obtained within the ten years preceding submittal of the application;

(V) A certificate showing retirement from a Colorado law enforcement agency that reflects pistol qualifications obtained within the ten years preceding submittal of the application; or

(VI) A training certificate from a handgun training class obtained within the ten years preceding submittal of the application. The applicant shall submit the original training certificate or a photocopy thereof that includes the original signature of the class instructor. To the extent permitted bysection 18-12-202 (5), in obtaining a training certificate from a handgun training class, the applicant shall have discretion in selecting which handgun training class to complete.

CONNECTICUT

Permit: "May issue" state, and only after prior acquisition of a permit to possess a firearm.

Open Carry: Permitted only with state permit.

Travel: Permissible; cannot be stored in glove box or console, but may be concealed on person or in locked container.

Disclose Presence of Handgun to Law Enforcement: Required only if requested by officer.

Restaurants: May carry in restaurants and bars unless posted.

Recognizes Permits From: No states.

Firearms Ownership: Permissible for any resident but must have a valid permit to possess for the firearm to leave the home.

Loaded Carry: Permissible open or concealed for those 21 and over, but only with valid permit to purchase and possess firearms outside the home.

Travel: Permissible for any resident 21 or over, but must have a valid permit to possess a firearm to travel with it outside the home; cannot be stored in glove box or console, but may be concealed on person or in locked container. For non-residents, federal requirements must be met, i.e., firearm must be unloaded, separated from ammunition, and in a locked container.

State Parks: Forbidden.

Carry Law Uniformity: State gun law preempts that of localities and municipalities.

Self-Defense Model: Castle Doctrine applies in instances of threat to serious bodily injury or death, Duty to Retreat in public.

Notes: Postings by private businesses carry force of law, and a violation of one is punishable as the felony of criminal trespass. Carriers may consume alcohol but may not be legally impaired. CT offers non-resident permits, which require applicants to hold valid permits from their state of domicile and to complete a safety course. An elaborate permit system is in place in CT in addition to the concealed carry permit process, requiring an 8-hour safety course for those 21 and over to purchase and possess a handgun, shotgun, rifle, or ammunition; a 14-hour safety course for those 18-21 years of age to purchase and possess long guns and ammunition; a hunter's safety course for anyone under 18 to possess a firearm only while in the presence of a permit-holder; and a background check to purchase ammunition. After the recent Sandy Hook tragedy, magazines with capacities over 10 rounds have been outlawed; residents who owned them at the time of the ban were forced to register them, and no new ones can legally be acquired.

CONNECTICUT

Connecticut General Statutes Sec. 29-35. Carrying of pistol or revolver without permit prohibited. Exceptions.

(a) No person shall carry any pistol or revolver upon his or her person, except when such person is within the dwelling house or place of business of such person, without a permit to carry the same issued as provided in section 29-28. The provisions of this subsection shall not apply to the carrying of any pistol or revolver by any parole officer or peace officer of this state, or parole officer or peace officer of any other state while engaged in the pursuit of official duties, or federal marshal or federal law enforcement agent, or to any member of the armed forces of the United States, as defined in section 27-103, or of this state, as defined in section 27-2, when on duty or going to or from duty, or to any member of any military organization when on parade or when going to or from any place of assembly, or to the transportation of pistols or revolvers as merchandise, or to any person transporting any pistol or revolver while contained in the package in which it was originally wrapped at the time of sale and while transporting the same from the place of sale to the purchaser's residence or place of business, or to any person removing such person's household goods or effects from one place to another, or to any person while transporting any such pistol or revolver from such person's place of residence or business to a place or individual where or by whom such pistol or revolver is to be repaired or while returning to such person's place of residence or business after the same has been repaired, or to any person transporting a pistol or revolver in or through the state for the purpose of taking part in competitions, taking part in formal pistol or revolver training, repairing such pistol or revolver or attending any meeting or exhibition of an organized collectors' group if such person is a bona fide resident of the United States and is permitted to possess and carry a pistol or revolver in the state or subdivision of the United States in which such person resides, or to any person transporting a pistol or revolver to and from a testing range at the request of the issuing authority, or to any person transporting an antique pistol or revolver, as defined in section 29-33. For the purposes of this subsection, "formal pistol or revolver training" means pistol or revolver training at a locally approved or permitted firing range or training facility, and "transporting a pistol or revolver" means transporting a pistol or revolver that is unloaded and, if such pistol or revolver is being transported in a motor vehicle, is not readily accessible or directly accessible from the passenger compartment of the vehicle or, if such pistol or revolver is being transported in a motor vehicle that does not have a compartment separate from the passenger compartment, such pistol or revolver shall be contained in a locked container other than the glove compartment or console. Nothing in this section shall be construed to prohibit the carrying of a pistol or revolver during formal pistol or revolver training or repair.

(b) The holder of a permit issued pursuant to section 29-28 shall carry such permit upon one's person while carrying such pistol or revolver.

Contact for Additional Information:

Connecticut State Police, Department of Emergency Services and Public Protection, Special Licensing and Firearms Unit

1111 Country Club Road • Middletown, CT 06457

860-685-8290

FIREARM FRIENDLY: C

DELAWARE

Permit: "May issue" state.

Open Carry: Unrestricted unless by local ordinance (See Dover, where must have signed letter from chief of police.)

Travel: Loaded handguns may be transported on seat or dashboard for self-defense purposes, but if the carrier is a DE resident, the permit must also be issued by DE.

Disclose Presence of Handgun to Law Enforcement: Required only if requested by officer.

Restaurants: May carry in restaurants and bars unless posted.

Recognizes Permits From: AK, AZ, AR, CO, FL, KY, ME, MI, MO, NM, NC, ND (Class 1 permit only), OH, OK, TN, TX, UT, WV

Firearms Ownership: Permitted to all qualified citizens without license or permit.

Loaded Carry: Permitted unless restricted by local ordinance (See Dover, where must have signed letter from chief of police.)

Travel: Firearm and ammunition must be stored in separate containers, and at least one must be locked.

State Parks: Forbidden.

Carry Law Uniformity: Local agencies/municipalities can restrict above and beyond state law.

Self-Defense Model: No Castle Doctrine, Duty to Retreat in public.

Notes: DE is a "may" issue state, but most of the very few denials result from past protection orders and violent crimes, commonly felony charges that were pled down to misdemeanor convictions in court. Carriers may consume alcohol, but possession of a firearm with over a 0.08% blood alcohol content is a crime. Carry is forbidden in school zones and in the three casinos in the state.

Delaware Criminal Code § 1441. License to carry concealed deadly weapons.

(a) A person of full age and good moral character desiring to be licensed to carry a concealed deadly weapon for personal protection or the protection of the person's property may be licensed to do so when the following conditions have been strictly complied with:

(1) The person shall make application therefor in writing and file the same with the Prothonotary of the proper county.... The person shall submit ... all

information necessary to conduct a criminal history background check....

(2) At the same time the person shall file, with the Prothonotary, a certificate of 5 respectable citizens of the county in which the applicant resides ... that the applicant is a person of full age, sobriety and good moral character, that the applicant bears a good reputation for peace and good order in the community ..., and that the carrying of a concealed deadly weapon by the applicant is necessary for the protection of the applicant or the applicant's property, or both. The certificate shall be signed with the proper signatures and in the proper handwriting of each such respectable citizen.

(3) Every such applicant shall file in the office of the Prothonotary of the proper county the application verified by oath or affirmation in writing taken before an officer authorized by the laws of this State to administer the same, and shall under such verification state that the applicant's certificate and recommendation were read to or by the signers thereof and that the signatures thereto are in the proper and genuine handwriting of each. Prior to the issuance of an initial license the person shall also file with the Prothonotary a notarized certificate signed by an instructor or authorized representative of a sponsoring agency, school, organization or institution certifying that the applicant: (i) has completed a firearms training course which contains at least the below described minimum elements; and (ii) is sponsored by a federal, state, county or municipal law enforcement agency, a college, a nationally recognized organization that customarily offers firearms training, or a firearms training school with instructors certified by a nationally recognized organization that customarily offers firearms training. The firearms training, course shall include the following elements:

a. Instruction regarding knowledge and safe handling of firearms; b. Instruction regarding safe storage of firearms and child safety; c. Instruction regarding knowledge and safe handling of ammunition; d. Instruction regarding safe storage of ammunition and child safety; e. Instruction regarding safe firearms shooting fundamentals; f. Live fire shooting exercises conducted on a range, including the expenditure of a minimum of 100 rounds of ammunition; g. Identification of ways to develop and maintain firearm shooting skills; h. Instruction regarding federal and state laws pertaining to the lawful purchase, ownership, transportation, use and possession of firearms; i. Instruction regarding the laws of this State pertaining to the use of deadly force for self defense; and j. Instruction regarding techniques for avoiding a criminal attack and how to manage a violent confrontation, including conflict resolution.

Contact for Additional Information:

Attorney General of Delaware
Delaware Department of Justice,
Carvel State Building
820 North French Street • Wilmington, DE 19801
302-577-8500

FIREARM FRIENDLY:  FLORIDA

Permit: "Shall issue" state.

Open Carry: Prohibited, with some exceptions.

Travel: Loaded handguns may be transported in a vehicle and concealed on your person.

Disclose Presence of Handgun to Law Enforcement: Not mandatory unless asked by a law enforcement officer.

Restaurants: May carry if permit holder does not consume alcohol, must leave establishment if told by ownership to do so.

Recognizes Permits From: The following states, but only if the permit holder is a resident there: AL, AK, AZ, AR, CO, DE, GA, ID, IN, IA, KS, KY, LA, ME, MI, MS, MO, MT, NE, NH, NM, NC, ND, NV, OH, OK, PA, SC, SD, TN, TX, UT, VA, WV, WY

Firearms Ownership: Permitted to all qualified citizens without license or permit.

Loaded Carry: Prohibited for anyone without a permit to do so in public, with some exceptions.

Travel: A handgun may be transported in a vehicle as long as it is securely encased and not available for immediate use. It is illegal to carry a gun on your person while in a vehicle without a concealed carry permit.

State Parks: Permissible, some restrictions apply.

Carry Law Uniformity: State law preempts that of local agencies/municipalities.

Self-Defense Model: Castle Doctrine, Stand Your Ground.

Notes: In Florida, an individual does not have a "duty to retreat" while in any place lawfully. It is legal for a concealed carry permit holder to briefly reveal their handgun to another person, as long as it is not done so in a threatening manner. Pepper spray and stun guns may be openly carried.

Contact for Additional Information:

Florida Department of Agriculture and Consumer Services (Division of Licensing), P.O. Box 6387 • Tallahassee, FL 32314-6387
850-245-5691

FLORIDA

Florida Statutes Title XLVI § 790.01 Carrying concealed weapons. —

(1) Except as provided in subsection (4), a person who carries a concealed weapon or electric weapon or device on or about his or her person commits a misdemeanor of the first degree, punishable as provided in s. 775.082 or s. 775.083.

(2) A person who carries a concealed firearm on or about his or her person commits a felony of the third degree, punishable as provided in s. 775.082, s. 775.083, or s. 775.084.

(3) This section does not apply to a person licensed to carry a concealed weapon or a concealed firearm pursuant to the provisions of s. 790.06....

§ 790.015 Nonresidents who are United States citizens and hold a concealed weapons license in another state; reciprocity.—

(1) Notwithstanding s. 790.01, a nonresident of Florida may carry a concealed weapon or concealed firearm while in this state if the nonresident:

(a) Is 21 years of age or older.

(b) Has in his or her immediate possession a valid license to carry a concealed weapon or concealed firearm issued to the nonresident in his or her state of residence.

(c) Is a resident of the United States.

(2) A nonresident is subject to the same laws and restrictions with respect to carrying a concealed weapon or concealed firearm as a resident of Florida who is so licensed....

§ 790.053 Open carrying of weapons.—

(1) Except as otherwise provided by law and in subsection (2), it is unlawful for any person to openly carry on or about his or her person any firearm or electric weapon or device. It is not a violation of this section for a person licensed to carry a concealed firearm as provided in s.790.06(1), and who is lawfully carrying a firearm in a concealed manner, to briefly and openly display the firearm to the ordinary sight of another person, unless the firearm is intentionally displayed in an angry or threatening manner, not in necessary self-defense....

§ 790.06 License to carry concealed weapon or firearm.—

...(12)(a) A license issued under this section does not authorize any person to openly carry a handgun or carry a concealed weapon or firearm into:

1. Any place of nuisance as defined in s. 823.05;

2. Any police, sheriff, or highway patrol station;

3. Any detention facility, prison, or jail;

4. Any courthouse;

5. Any courtroom, except that nothing in this section would preclude a judge from carrying a concealed weapon or determining who will carry a concealed weapon in his or her courtroom;

6. Any polling place;

7. Any meeting of the governing body of a county, public school district, municipality, or special district;

8. Any meeting of the Legislature or a committee thereof;

9. Any school, college, or professional athletic event not related to firearms;

10. Any elementary or secondary school facility or administration building;

11. Any career center;

12. Any portion of an establishment licensed to dispense alcoholic beverages for consumption on the premises, which portion of the establishment is primarily devoted to such purpose;

13. Any college or university facility unless the licensee is a registered student, employee, or faculty member of such college or university and the weapon is a stun gun or nonlethal electric weapon or device designed solely for defensive purposes and the weapon does not fire a dart or projectile;

14. The inside of the passenger terminal and sterile area of any airport, provided that no person shall be prohibited from carrying any legal firearm into the terminal, which firearm is encased for shipment for purposes of checking such firearm as baggage to be lawfully transported on any aircraft; or

15. Any place where the carrying of firearms is prohibited by federal law.

(b) A person licensed under this section shall not be prohibited from carrying or storing a firearm in a vehicle for lawful purposes.

(c) This section does not modify the terms or conditions of s. 790.251(7).

(d) Any person who knowingly and willfully violates any provision of this subsection commits a misdemeanor of the second degree, punishable as provided in s. 775.082 or s. 775.083....

GEORGIA

FIREARM FRIENDLY: 

Permit Holders

Permit: "Shall issue" state.

Open Carry: Permitted.

Travel: Loaded handguns may be transported in a vehicle for self-defense purposes, but they may not be in plain view.

Disclose Presence of Handgun to Law Enforcement: Required only if requested by officer.

Restaurants: May carry if establishment earns less than 50% of its revenue from alcohol sales and as long as firearms aren't forbidden by posting.

Recognizes Permits From: AL, AK, AZ, AR, CO, FL, ID, IN, IA, KS, KY, LA, MI, MS, MO, MT, NH, NC, ND, OH, OK, PA, SC, SD, TN, TX, UT, VA, WV, WI, WY

Non-Permit

Firearms Ownership: Permitted to all qualified citizens without license or permit.

Loaded Carry: As of July 2014, there is no open carry for residents without carry permits.

Travel: Loaded, concealed handguns may be transported in a vehicle for self-defense purposes as an extension of the Castle Doctrine.

General Info

State Parks: Only permit holders.

Carry Law Uniformity: State law preempts that of local agencies/municipalities.

Self-Defense Model: Castle Doctrine, Stand Your Ground.

Notes: Postings forbidding firearms on private property do not have the force of law; establishments may deny service or admittance if a carrier comes on the property, but no criminal penalty will result from the carrier's possession of a firearm on the property. Through a new law in 2014, carry is now permissible in bars, churches, some schools, colleges, communal areas in airports, and many state buildings. Anyone not specifically prohibited from carrying a firearm may possess a loaded firearm in a vehicle, residence, or business.

Contact for Additional Information:
Office of the Attorney General
40 Capitol Square, Southwest • Atlanta, GA 30334
404-656-3300

Official Code of Georgia Annotated § 16-11-126. Having or carrying handguns, long guns, or other weapons; license requirement; exceptions for homes, motor vehicles, private property, and other locations and conditions.

(a) Any person who is not prohibited by law from possessing a handgun or long gun may have or carry on his or her person a weapon or long gun on his or her property or inside his or her home, motor vehicle, or place of business without a valid weapons carry license.

(b) Any person who is not prohibited by law from possessing a handgun or long gun may have or carry on his or her person a long gun without a valid weapons carry license, provided that if the long gun is loaded, it shall only be carried in an open and fully exposed manner.

(c) Any person who is not prohibited by law from possessing a handgun or long gun may have or carry any handgun provided that it is enclosed in a case and unloaded.

(d) Any person who is not prohibited by law from possessing a handgun or long gun who is eligible for a weapons carry license may transport a handgun or long gun in any private passenger motor vehicle; provided, however, that private property owners or persons in legal control of private property through a lease, rental agreement, licensing agreement, contract, or any other agreement to control access to such private property shall have the right to exclude or eject a person who is in possession of a weapon or long gun on their private property in accordance with paragraph (3) of subsection (b) of Code Section 16-7-21, except as provided in Code Section 16-11-135.

(e) Any person licensed to carry a handgun or weapon in any other state whose laws recognize and give effect to a license issued pursuant to this part shall be authorized to carry a weapon in this state, but only while the licensee is not a resident of this state; provided, however, that such licensee shall carry the weapon in compliance with the laws of this state.

(f) Any person with a valid hunting or fishing license on his or her person, or any person not required by law to have a hunting or fishing license, who is engaged in legal hunting, fishing, or sport shooting when the person has the permission of the owner of the land on which the activities are being conducted may have or carry on his or her person a handgun or long gun without a valid weapons carry license while hunting, fishing, or engaging in sport shooting.

(g) Notwithstanding Code Sections 12-3-10, 27-3-1.1, 27-3-6, and 16-12-122 through 16-12-127, any person with a valid weapons carry license may carry a weapon in all parks, historic sites, or recreational areas, as such term is defined in Code Section 12-3-10, including all publicly owned buildings located in such parks, historic sites, and recreational areas, in wildlife management areas, and on public transportation; provided, however, that a person shall not carry a handgun into a place where it is prohibited by federal law.

(h) (1) No person shall carry a weapon without a valid weapons carry license unless he or she meets one of the exceptions to having such license as provided in subsections (a) through (g) of this Code section.

(2) A person commits the offense of carrying a weapon without a license when he or she violates the provisions of paragraph (1) of this subsection.

(i) Upon conviction of the offense of carrying a weapon without a valid weapons carry license, a person shall be punished as follows:

(1) For the first offense, he or she shall be guilty of a misdemeanor; and

(2) For the second offense within five years, as measured from the dates of previous arrests for which convictions were obtained to the date of the current arrest for which a conviction is obtained, and for any subsequent offense, he or she shall be guilty of a felony and, upon conviction thereof, shall be imprisoned for not less than two years and not more than five years.

§ 16-11-130.1. Allowing personnel to carry weapons within certain school safety zones and at school functions.

...(b) This Code section shall not be construed to require or otherwise mandate that any local board of education or school administrator adopt or implement a practice or program for the approval of personnel to possess or carry weapons within a school safety zone, at a school function, or on a bus or other transportation furnished by a school nor shall this Code section create any liability for adopting or declining to adopt such practice or program. Such decision shall rest with each individual local board of education. If a local board of education adopts a policy to allow certain personnel to possess or carry weapons as provided in paragraph (6) of subsection (c) of Code Section 16-11-127.1, such policy shall include approval of personnel to possess or carry weapons and provide for:

(1) Training of approved personnel prior to authorizing such personnel to carry weapons. ...

(2) An approved list of the types of weapons and ammunition and the quantity of weapons and ammunition authorized to be possessed or carried;

(3) The exclusion from approval of any personnel who has had an employment or other history indicating any type of mental or emotional instability as determined by the local board of education; and

(4) A mandatory method of securing weapons which shall include at a minimum a requirement that the weapon, if permitted to be carried concealed by personnel, shall be carried on the person and not in a purse, briefcase, bag, or similar other accessory which is not secured on the body of the person and, if maintained separate from the person, shall be maintained in a secured lock safe or similar lock box that cannot be easily accessed by students.

...(d) The selection of approved personnel to possess or carry a weapon within a school safety zone, at a school function, or on a bus or other transportation furnished by a school shall be done strictly on a voluntary basis. No personnel shall be required to possess or carry a weapon within a school safety zone, at a school function, or on a bus or other transportation furnished by a school and shall not be terminated or otherwise retaliated against for refusing to possess or carry a weapon.

§ 16-11-130.2. Carrying a weapon or long gun at a commercial service airport.

(a) No person shall enter the restricted access area of a commercial service airport, in or beyond the airport security screening checkpoint, knowingly possessing or knowingly having under his or her control a weapon or long gun. Such area shall not include an airport drive, general parking area, walkway, or shops and areas of the terminal that are outside the screening checkpoint and that are normally open to unscreened passengers or visitors to the airport. Any restricted access area shall be clearly indicated by prominent signs indicating that weapons are prohibited in such area...

HAWAII

FIREARM FRIENDLY: F

Permit Holders

Permit: "May issue" state, and HIGHLY restrictive; must show need for carry privileges, as evidenced by an active danger of some sort.

Open Carry: Forbidden.

Travel: Loaded handguns may be transported anywhere in a vehicle for self-defense purposes.

Disclose Presence of Handgun to Law Enforcement: Required only if requested by officer.

Restaurants: May carry unless posted.

Recognizes Permits From: No states.

Non-Permit

Firearms Ownership: Very restrictive. Firearms owned upon arrival to the state must be registered within 5 days of arrival, and purchase of new firearms requires a permit to acquire and registration of the firearms within 7 days of purchase. Violation of any of these registration requirements is punishable as a felony under Hawaii law.

Loaded Carry: Forbidden.

Travel: Heavily restricted. Firearms must be unloaded, locked in a commercially-produced case, and stored in a trunk or rear compartment separate from ammunition. They may only be transported while en route to and from a gun range, a gunsmith, or a gun dealer, etc., and no stops may be made at other destinations while in transit.

General Info

State Parks: Firearms must remain locked and stored in a vehicle.

Carry Law Uniformity: Localities and municipalities may enact restrictions above and beyond state law.

Self-Defense Model: Castle Doctrine but only protects against civil liability (not criminal liability), Stand Your Ground.

Notes: Concealed carry permit law is almost non-existent in the state, as it is largely unnecessary due to the very, very few active permits in place at this time. The legislature has not recognized a need for most of the nuances related to concealed carry to be captured in statutes or regulations; however, many laws are in place with regard to ownership and possession of firearms generally, and even ammunition transport is regulated by statute. Please note that HI explicitly equates ammunition with firearms in the statutes, so any rules applicable to a firearm also apply to ammunition. i.e., purchased ammunition must be taken straight home from the store with no intermediate stops, ammunition is banned where firearms are and must be handled in the same manner, etc.

Hawaii Revised Statutes § 134-9 Licenses to carry.

(a) In an exceptional case, when an applicant shows reason to fear injury to the applicant's person or property, the chief of police of the appropriate county may grant a license to an applicant who is a citizen of the United States of the age of twenty-one years or more or to a duly accredited official representative of a foreign nation of the age of twenty-one years or more to carry a pistol or revolver and ammunition therefor concealed on the person within the county where the license is granted. Where the urgency or the need has been sufficiently indicated, the respective chief of police may grant to an applicant of good moral character who is a citizen of the United States of the age of twenty-one years or more, is engaged in the protection of life and property, and is not prohibited under section 134-7 from the ownership or possession of a firearm, a license to carry a pistol or revolver and ammunition therefor unconcealed on the person within the county where the license is granted. The chief of police of the appropriate county, or the chief's designated representative, shall perform an inquiry on an applicant by using the National Instant Criminal Background Check System, to include a check of the Immigration and Customs Enforcement databases where the applicant is not a citizen of the United States, before any determination to grant a license is made. Unless renewed, the license shall expire one year from the date of issue.

(b) The chief of police of each county shall adopt procedures to require that any person granted a license to carry a concealed weapon on the person shall:

(1) Be qualified to use the firearm in a safe manner;

(2) Appear to be a suitable person to be so licensed;

(3) Not be prohibited under section 134-7 from the ownership or possession of a firearm; and

(4) Not have been adjudged insane or not appear to be mentally deranged.

(c) No person shall carry concealed or unconcealed on the person a pistol or revolver without being licensed to do so under this section or in compliance with sections 134-5(c) or 134-25.

(d) A fee of $10 shall be charged for each license and shall be deposited in the treasury of the county in which the license is granted.

§ 134-26 Carrying or possessing a loaded firearm on a public highway; penalty.

(a) It shall be unlawful for any person on any public highway to carry on the person, or to have in the person's possession, or to carry in a vehicle any firearm loaded with ammunition; provided that this section shall not apply to any person who has in the person's possession or carries a pistol or revolver in accordance with a license issued as provided in section 134-9.

(b) Any vehicle used in the commission of an offense under this section shall be forfeited to the State, subject to the notice and hearing requirements of chapter 712A.

(c) Any person violating this section shall be guilty of a class B felony.

§ 134-27 Place to keep ammunition; penalty.

(a) Except as provided in sections 134-5 and 134-9, all ammunition shall be confined to the possessor's place of business, residence, or sojourn; provided that it shall be lawful to carry ammunition in an enclosed container from the place of purchase to the purchaser's place of business, residence, or sojourn, or between these places upon change of place of business, residence, or sojourn, or between these places and the following:

(1) A place of repair;

(2) A target range;

(3) A licensed dealer's place of business;

(4) An organized, scheduled firearms show or exhibit;

(5) A place of formal hunter or firearm use training or instruction; or

(6) A police station.

"Enclosed container" means a rigidly constructed receptacle, or a commercially manufactured gun case, or the equivalent thereof that completely encloses the ammunition.

(b) Any person violating this section shall be guilty of a misdemeanor.

Contact for Additional Information:

Attorney General of Hawaii
425 Queen Street • Honolulu, HI 96813
808-586-1500

FIREARM FRIENDLY: 

 IDAHO

Permit: "Shall issue" state.

Open Carry: Permitted.

Travel: Loaded handguns may be transported openly or concealed within a vehicle.

Disclose Presence of Handgun to Law Enforcement: Required only if requested by a law enforcement officer.

Restaurants: May carry if permit holder does not consume alcohol, must leave establishment if told by ownership do so.

Recognizes Permits From: AL, AK, AZ, AR, CA, CO, CT, DE, FL, GA, HI, IL, IN, IA, KS, KY, LA, ME, MD, MA, MI, MN, MS, MO, MT, NE, NV, NH, NJ, NM, NY, NC, ND, OH, OK, OR, PA, RI, SC, SD, TN, TX, UT, VA, WA, WV, WI, WY

Firearms Ownership: Permitted to all qualified citizens without license or permit.

Loaded Carry: All citizens of age (18+) may openly carry a loaded firearm in public.

Travel: A loaded or unloaded handgun may be transported openly in a vehicle, but it may not be concealed. To transport a handgun in a concealed manner, the gun must be disassembled or unloaded.

State Parks: Permissible, unless otherwise posted.

Carry Law Uniformity: State law preempts that of local agencies/municipalities.

Self-Defense Model: Castle Doctrine.ww

Notes: In mid-2013, Idaho passed legislation to create an Enhanced Concealed Weapons License. This was done in order to meet requirements for reciprocal agreements with several other states. In mid-2014, Idaho passed a state law that gave Enhanced Concealed Weapons License holders or retired law enforcement officers the right to carry a concealed weapon on public college or university grounds. Some buildings on these campuses, such as dormitories, are exceptions to this rule and guns cannot be carried into them. Though the statutory age for a concealed carry permit is 21, sheriffs may elect to issue permits to residents 18-21 if they see fit.

Contact for Additional Information:

State of Idaho Office of the Attorney General
P.O. Box 83720 • Boise, ID 83720
208-334-2400

IDAHO

Idaho Statutes § 18-3302. Issuance of Licenses to Carry Concealed Weapons.

...(7) Except in the person's place of abode or fixed place of business, or on property in which the person has any ownership or leasehold interest, a person shall not carry a concealed weapon without a license to carry a concealed weapon. For the purposes of this section, a concealed weapon means any dirk, dirk knife, bowie knife, dagger, pistol, revolver or any other deadly or dangerous weapon. The provisions of this section shall not apply to any lawfully possessed shotgun or rifle...

...(9) While in any motor vehicle, inside the limits or confines of any city, a person shall not carry a concealed weapon on or about his person without a license to carry a concealed weapon. This shall not apply to any firearm located in plain view whether it is loaded or unloaded. A firearm may be concealed legally in a motor vehicle so long as the weapon is disassembled or unloaded....

...(11) The sheriff of a county may issue a license to carry a concealed weapon to those individuals between the ages of eighteen (18) and twenty-one (21) years who in the judgment of the sheriff warrant the issuance of the license to carry a concealed weapon. Such issuance shall be subject to limitations which the issuing authority deems appropriate. Licenses issued to individuals between the ages of eighteen (18) and twenty-one (21) years shall be easily distinguishable from regular licenses.

(12) The requirement to secure a license to carry a concealed weapon under this section shall not apply to the following persons:

(a) Officials of a county, city, state of Idaho, the United States, peace officers, guards of any jail, court appointed attendants or any officer of any express company on duty;

(b) Employees of the adjutant general and military division of the state where military membership is a condition of employment when on duty;

(c) Criminal investigators of the attorney general's office, criminal investigators of a prosecuting attorney's office, prosecutors and their deputies;

(d) Any person outside the limits of or confines of any city while engaged in lawful hunting, fishing, trapping or other lawful outdoor activity;

(e) Any publicly elected Idaho official;

(f) Retired peace officers or detention deputies with at least ten (10) years of service with the state or a political subdivision as a peace officer or detention deputy and who have been certified by the peace officer standards and training council;

(g) Any person who has a valid permit from a state or local law enforcement agency or court authorizing him to carry a concealed weapon. A permit issued in another state will only be considered valid if the permit is in the licensee's physical possession....

...(14) A person carrying a concealed weapon in violation of the provisions of this section shall be guilty of a misdemeanor....

Permit: "Shall issue" state; concealed carry legalized in 2013, so little interpretation of the law now exists.

Open Carry: Forbidden.

Travel: Loaded handguns may be transported anywhere in a vehicle for self-defense purposes.

Disclose Presence of Handgun to Law Enforcement: Only required if officer requests.

Restaurants: May carry in restaurants, as long as no more than 49% of receipts result from the sales of alcohol; duty of restaurant to post if alcohol sales exceed 49%. Carriers may not consume alcohol.

Recognizes Permits From: No states.

Firearms Ownership: Heavily regulated; requires issuance of a FOID (Firearm Owner's Identification) Card.

Loaded Carry: Forbidden.

Travel: With a valid FOID Card, non-permitted residents may travel with a firearm as long as the ammunition and the gun itself are in separated, locked compartments. Statutory language originally was intended to apply to glove boxes and consoles of motor vehicles, but a court has ruled that a holster fanny pack, where a gun was enclosed in one zippered compartment and ammunition was enclosed in another, was covered by it. IL State Police released a brochure detailing the case and explicitly stating that this type of carry is legal, as long as the resident has a FOID card. Residents without FOID cards should travel with firearms unloaded, disassembled, locked in cases, and stored in trunks or rear compartments. Permit holders from other states may travel with a loaded firearm in a vehicle while in IL, but the firearm must never leave the vehicle; the gun must be unloaded and the vehicle locked if the permit holder leaves the vehicle unattended.

State Parks: Permissible only for permit holders or while hunting.

Carry Law Uniformity: State law preempts that of localities.

Self-Defense Model: No Castle Doctrine, Duty to Retreat but only if you can retreat "in complete safety."

Notes: Residents must apply for and receive a FOID (Firearm Owner's Identification) card even to own a firearm, and issuance is a prerequisite for a carry permit. Prohibited places include: any place "under the control" of a public or private elementary or secondary school, pre-school, or child care facility; any place "under the control" of an officer of the executive or legislative branches of government; any courthouse; any building or portion thereof "under the control" of local government; any place under the control of an adult or juvenile detention or correctional institution; any place under the control of a public or private hospital, affiliate, mental health facility, or nursing home; any form of transportation financed in any amount by public funds and property associated with its function; any business that whose revenue is made up of over 50% in sales of alcohol; any public gathering that requires a governmentally-issued permit; any place issued a Special Event Retailer's license; any playground; any public park, athletic area, or athletic facility under the control of a municipality or park district; property under the control of the Cook County Forest Preserve District; any property under the control of a public or private college or university; any property under the control of a gaming facility; any stadium, arena, or parking area under the control of a collegiate or professional sporting event; public libraries; airports; amusement parks; zoos; museums; any property under the control of a nuclear energy storage or development site or regulated by the federal Nuclear Regulatory Commission; anywhere prohibited by federal law. "Safe harbor" provision allows permit carriers to possess loaded weapons in their cars even in prohibited places, as long as the loaded firearm never leaves the car; the only exception to the "safe harbor" provision is property used for storage or development of nuclear products or regulated by the federal Nuclear Regulatory Commission.

Illinois Compiled Statutes - 430 ILCS 66

§ Section 10. Issuance of licenses to carry a concealed firearm.

...(f) The Department shall deny the applicant a license if the applicant fails to meet the requirements under this Act or the Department receives a determination from the Board that the applicant is ineligible for a license. The Department must notify the applicant stating the grounds for the denial. The notice of denial must inform the applicant of his or her right to an appeal through administrative and judicial review.

§ Section 15. Objections by law enforcement agencies.

(a) Any law enforcement agency may submit an objection to a license applicant based upon a reasonable suspicion that the applicant is a danger to himself or herself or others, or a threat to public safety. The objection shall be made by the chief law enforcement officer of the law enforcement agency, or his or her designee, and must include any information relevant to the objection. If a law enforcement agency submits an objection within 30 days after the entry of an applicant into the database, the Department shall submit the objection and all information available to the Board under State and federal law related to the application to the Board within 10 days of completing all necessary background checks.

(b) If an applicant has 5 or more arrests for any reason, that have been entered into the Criminal History Records Information (CHRI) System, within the 7 years preceding the date of application for a license, or has 3 or more arrests within the 7 years preceding the date of application for a license for any combination of gang-related offenses, the Department shall object and submit the applicant's arrest record to the extent the Board is allowed to receive that information under State and federal law, the application materials, and any additional information submitted by a law enforcement agency to the Board....

§ Section 20. Concealed Carry Licensing Review Board.

(a) There is hereby created within the Department of State Police a Concealed Carry Licensing Review Board to consider any objection to an applicant's eligibility to obtain a license under this Act submitted by a law enforcement agency or the Department under Section 15 of this Act. The Board shall consist of 7 commissioners to be appointed by the Governor, with the advice and consent of the Senate, with 3 commissioners residing within the First Judicial District and one commissioner residing within each of the 4 remaining Judicial Districts. No more than 4 commissioners shall be members of the same political party. The Governor shall designate one commissioner as the Chairperson. The Board shall consist of:

(1) One commissioner with at least 5 years of service as a federal judge;

(2) 2 commissioners with at least 5 years of experience serving as an attorney with the United States Department of Justice;

(3) 3 commissioners with at least 5 years of experience as a federal agent or employee with investigative experience or duties related to criminal justice under the United States Department of Justice, Drug Enforcement Administration, Department of Homeland Security, or Federal Bureau of Investigation; and

(4) One member with at least 5 years of experience as a licensed physician or clinical psychologist with expertise in the diagnosis and treatment of mental illness ....

(e) In considering an objection of a law enforcement agency or the Department, the Board shall review the materials received with the objection from the law enforcement agency or the Department. By a vote of at least 4 commissioners, the Board may request additional information from the law enforcement agency, Department, or the applicant, or the testimony of the law enforcement agency, Department, or the applicant. The Board may require that the applicant submit electronic fingerprints to the Department for an updated background check where the Board determines it lacks sufficient information to determine eligibility. The Board may only consider information submitted by the Department, a law enforcement agency, or the applicant. The Board shall review each objection and determine by a majority of commissioners whether an applicant is eligible for a license.

§ Sec. 25. Qualifications for a license.

The Department shall issue a license to an applicant completing an application in accordance withSection 30 of this Act if the person:

(1) is at least 21 years of age;

(2) has a currently valid Firearm Owner's Identification Card and at the time of application meets the requirements for the issuance of a Firearm Owner's Identification Card and is not prohibited under the Firearm Owners Identification Card Act or federal law from possessing or receiving a firearm;

(3) has not been convicted or found guilty in this state or in any other state of:

(A) a misdemeanor involving the use or threat of physical force or violence to any person within the 5 years preceding the date of the license application; or

(B) 2 or more violations related to driving while under the influence of alcohol, other drug or drugs, intoxicating compound or compounds, or any combination thereof, within the 5 years preceding the date of the license application;

(4) is not the subject of a pending arrest warrant, prosecution, or proceeding for an offense or action that could lead to disqualification to own or possess a firearm;

(5) has not been in residential or court-ordered treatment for alcoholism, alcohol detoxification, or drug treatment within the 5 years immediately preceding the date of the license application; and

(6) has completed firearms training and any education component required under Section 75 of this Act.

Section 40. Non-resident license applications.

(e) Nothing in this Act shall prohibit a non-resident from transporting a concealed firearm within his or her vehicle in Illinois, if the concealed firearm remains within his or her vehicle and the non-resident:

(1) is not prohibited from owning or possessing a firearm under federal law;

(2) is eligible to carry a firearm in public under the laws of his or her state or territory of residence, as evidenced by the possession of a concealed carry license or permit issued by his or her state of residence, if applicable; and

(3) is not in possession of a license under this Act. If the non-resident leaves his or her vehicle unattended, he or she shall store the firearm within a locked vehicle or locked container within the vehicle in accordance with subsection (b) of Section 65 of this Act.

Sec. 90. Preemption.
The regulation, licensing, possession, registration, and transportation of handguns and ammunition for handguns by licensees are exclusive powers and functions of the State. Any ordinance or regulation, or portion thereof, enacted on or before the effective date of this Act that purports to impose regulations or restrictions on licensees or handguns and ammunition for handguns in a manner inconsistent with this Act shall be invalid in its application to licensees under this Act on the effective date of this Act. This Section is a denial and limitation of home rule powers and functions under subsection (h) of Section 6 of Article VII of the Illinois Constitution.

Contact for Additional Information:

Illinois State Police
801 South 7th Street • Springfield, IL 62703
217-782-7980

FIREARM FRIENDLY: A

INDIANA

Permit: "Shall issue" state.

Open Carry: Permitted.

Travel: Loaded handguns may be transported openly or concealed within a vehicle.

Disclose Presence of Handgun to Law Enforcement: Required only if requested by a law enforcement officer.

Restaurants: Permitted, alcohol can be consumed, though it is not encouraged. Must leave establishment if told by ownership to do so.

Recognizes Permits From: All states.

Permit Holders

Firearms Ownership: Permitted to all qualified citizens without license or permit.

Loaded Carry: Prohibited.

Travel: A handgun may not be transported in any vehicle without a license. A handgun can only be transported legally by a non-permitted individual if it is unloaded, not easily accessible, and secured within a case.

Non-Permit

State Parks: Generally permissible, some parks may not allow an individual to carry.

Carry Law Uniformity: State law preempts that of local agencies/municipalities.

Self-Defense Model: Castle Doctrine, Stand Your Ground.

Notes: All rules of law from a permitted individual's home state apply in Indiana. If the state that issued your permit places new restrictions upon it, then those same restrictions apply in Indiana. The state of Indiana issues both four-year and lifetime permits. Non-residents may only apply for a four-year permit.

General Info

Contact for Additional Information:

Firearms License Unit-Information Technology section/Criminal Justice Data Division-Indiana State Police

Indiana Government Center North-100 North Senate Avenue, Suite N302 • Indianapolis, IN 46204

(317)-232-8264

INDIANA

Indiana Code § 35-47-2-1 Carrying a handgun without being licensed; exceptions; person convicted of domestic battery

Sec. 1. (a) Except as provided in subsections (b) and (c) and section 2 of this chapter, a person shall not carry a handgun in any vehicle or on or about the person's body without being licensed under this chapter to carry a handgun.

(b) Except as provided in subsection (c), a person may carry a handgun without being licensed under this chapter to carry a handgun if:(1) the person carries the handgun on or about the person's body in or on property that is owned, leased, rented, or otherwise legally controlled by the person;(2) the person carries the handgun on or about the person's body while lawfully present in or on property that is owned, leased, rented, or otherwise legally controlled by another person, if the person:(A) has the consent of the owner, renter, lessor, or person who legally controls the property to have the handgun on the premises;(B) is attending a firearms related event on the property, including a gun show, firearms expo, gun owner's club or convention, hunting club, shooting club, or training course; or(C) is on the property to receive firearms related services, including the repair, maintenance, or modification of a firearm;(3) the person carries the handgun in a vehicle that is owned, leased, rented, or otherwise legally controlled by the person, if the handgun is:(A) unloaded;(B) not readily accessible; and(C) secured in a case;(4) the person carries the handgun while lawfully present in a vehicle that is owned, leased, rented, or otherwise legally controlled by another person, if the handgun is:(A) unloaded;(B) not readily accessible; and(C) secured in a case; or(5) the person carries the handgun:(A) at a shooting range (as defined in IC 14-22-31.5-3);(B) while attending a firearms instructional course; or(C) while engaged in a legal hunting activity.

(c) Unless the person's right to possess a firearm has been restored under IC 35-47-4-7, a person who has been convicted of domestic battery under IC 35-42-2-1.3 may not possess or carry a handgun.

....(e) A person who knowingly or intentionally violates this section commits a Class A misdemeanor. However, the offense is a Level 5 felony:(1) if the offense is committed:(A) on or in school property;(B) within five hundred (500) feet of school property; or(C) on a school bus; or(2) if the person:(A) has a prior conviction of any offense under:(i) this section; or(ii) section 22 of this chapter; or(B) has been convicted of a felony within fifteen (15) years before the date of the offense.

FIREARM FRIENDLY: B

IOWA

Permit: "Shall issue" state.

Open Carry: Permitted.

Travel: Loaded handguns may be transported openly or concealed within a vehicle.

Disclose Presence of Handgun to Law Enforcement: Required only if requested by a law enforcement officer.

Restaurants: May carry if permit holder does not consume alcohol, must leave establishment if told by ownership to do so.

Recognizes Permits From: All states.

Firearms Ownership: State issues a "Permit to Acquire" for handguns, a state-issued "Permit to Carry" can be used as a proper credential in the purchasing of a handgun.

Loaded Carry: Permitted open carry for non-permit holders ages 21+, heavy restrictions apply. Must have state-issued permit for loaded handgun to be carried within a vehicle.

Travel: A loaded handgun may not be transported in any vehicle without a license. A handgun can only be transported legally by a non-permitted individual if it is unloaded, not easily accessible to driver or any passengers, and secured within a case that is too large to be concealed on a person.

State Parks: Permissible, unless posted.

Carry Law Uniformity: State law preempts that of local agencies/municipalities.

Self-Defense Model: No Castle Doctrine, "Duty to Retreat."

Notes: Iowa also honors all non-resident permits from all of the states with which they have reciprocity agreements. Carrying a firearm on an ATV or snowmobile is prohibited, even if an individual has a carry permit. Consuming alcohol while carrying is forbidden.

Contact for Additional Information:

Weapon Permits, Program Services Bureau/
Administrative Services Division, Iowa Department of
Public Safety, Department of Public Safety Building
215 East 7th Street, 4th Floor • Des Moines, IA 50319
515-725-6230

IOWA

IOWA CODE TITLE XVI CRIMINAL LAW AND PROCEDURE § 724.4 Carrying weapons.

1. Except as otherwise provided in this section, a person who goes armed... with a pistol or revolver, or any loaded firearm of any kind, whether concealed or not, or who knowingly carries or transports in a vehicle a pistol or revolver, commits an aggravated misdemeanor....

...4. Subsections 1 through 3 do not apply to any of the following:

a. A person who goes armed with a dangerous weapon in the person's own dwelling or place of business, or on land owned or possessed by the person.

b. A peace officer, when the officer's duties require the person to carry such weapons.

c. A member of the armed forces of the United States....

d. A correctional officer....

e. A person who for any lawful purpose carries an unloaded pistol, revolver, or other dangerous weapon inside a closed and fastened container or securely wrapped package which is too large to be concealed on the person.

f. A person who for any lawful purpose carries or transports an unloaded pistol or revolver in a vehicle inside a closed and fastened container or securely wrapped package which is too large to be concealed on the person or inside a cargo or luggage compartment where the pistol or revolver will not be readily accessible to any person riding in the vehicle or common carrier.

g. A person while the person is lawfully engaged in target practice on a range designed for that purpose or while actually engaged in lawful hunting....

...i. A person who has in the person's possession and who displays to a peace officer on demand a valid permit to carry weapons which has been issued to the person, and whose conduct is within the limits of that permit....

j. A law enforcement officer from another state when the officer's duties require the officer to carry the weapon ....

k. A person engaged in the business of transporting prisoners under a contract with the Iowa department of corrections or a county sheriff, a similar agency from another state, or the federal government.

§ 724.4A Weapons free zones — enhanced penalties.

1. As used in this section, "weapons free zone" means the area in or on, or within one thousand feet of, the real property comprising a public or private elementary or secondary school, or in or on the real property comprising a public park. A weapons free zone shall not include that portion of a public park designated as a hunting area under section 461A.42.

2. Notwithstanding sections 902.9 and 903.1, a person who commits a public offense involving a firearm or offensive weapon, within a weapons free zone, in violation of this or any other chapter shall be subject to a fine of twice the maximum amount which may otherwise be imposed for the public offense.

§ 724.4C Possession or carrying of firearms while under the influence.

A permit issued under this chapter is invalid if the person to whom the permit is issued is intoxicated as provided in section 321J.2, subsection 1.

KANSAS

Permit: "Shall issue" state.

Open Carry: Permitted.

Travel: Loaded handguns may be transported anywhere in a vehicle.

Disclose Presence of Handgun to Law Enforcement: Only required if requested.

Restaurants: May carry as long as 1) no posting forbids it, 2) alcohol is not consumed, AND 3) restaurant generates less than 50% of revenue from alcohol sales.

Recognizes Permits From: All states.

Firearm Ownership: Permitted to all qualified citizens without license or permit.

Loaded Carry: Residents may openly carry a loaded firearm.

Travel: May travel with loaded firearm in vehicle.

State Parks: Only permit holders; parks cannot post.

Carry Law Uniformity: State law preempts that of local agencies/municipalities.

Self-Defense Model: Castle Doctrine, Stand Your Ground.

Notes: Alcohol cannot be consumed while carrying. Carry is not permitted in bars. Interestingly, the state is entertaining a "constitutional carry" bill in the legislature at the time of printing of this book; if passed, the law will allow anyone in the state to carry a concealed weapon (See Senate Bill 45). Recent changes to K.S.A. 21-6332 (Possession of a Firearm Under the Influence) may be worth looking into if you frequent the state and are unaware of them.

Contact for Additional Information:

Attorney General of Kansas
120 Southwest 10th Avenue 2nd Floor • Topeka, KS 66612
785-296-2215

KANSAS

Kansas Statutes Annotated § 75-7c04. License to carry a concealed firearm; qualifications; weapons safety and training course.

(a) The attorney general shall not issue a license pursuant to this act if the applicant: (1) Is not a resident of the county where application for licensure is made or is not a resident of the state; (2) is prohibited from shipping, transporting, possessing or receiving a firearm or ammunition under 18 U.S.C. 922(g) or (n), and amendments thereto, or K.S.A. 21-4204, prior to its repeal, or subsection (a)(10) through (a)(13) of K.S.A. 2014 Supp. 21-6301 or subsections (a)(1) through (a)(3) of K.S.A. 2014 Supp. 21-6304, and amendments thereto; or (3) has been convicted of or was adjudicated a juvenile offender because of the commission of an act which if done by an adult would constitute the commission of any of the offenses described in subsections (a)(1) and (a)(3)(A) of K.S.A. 2014 Supp. 21-6304, and amendments thereto; or (4) is less than 21 years of age.

§ 75-7c10. Same; places where carrying concealed weapon not authorized; penalties for violations.

Subject to the provisions of K.S.A. 2014 Supp. 75-7c20, and amendments thereto: (a) Provided that the building is conspicuously posted in accordance with rules and regulations adopted by the attorney general a building where carrying a concealed handgun is prohibited, no license issued or recognized pursuant to this act shall authorize the licensee to carry a concealed handgun into any building.

(b) Nothing in this act shall be construed to prevent: (1) any public or private employer from restricting or prohibiting by personnel policies persons licensed under this act from carrying a concealed handgun while on the premises of the employer's business or while engaged in the duties of the person's employment by the employer, except that no employer may prohibit possession of a handgun in a private means of conveyance, even if parked on the employer's premises; or (2) any private business or city, county or political subdivision from restricting or prohibiting persons licensed under this act from carrying a concealed handgun within a building or buildings of such entity, provided that the building is posted, in accordance with rules and regulations adopted by the attorney general pursuant to this section, as a building where carrying a concealed handgun is prohibited;

(c)(1) Any private entity which provides adequate security measures in a private building and which conspicuously posts signage in accordance with this section prohibiting the carrying of a concealed handgun in such building as authorized by the personal and family protection act shall not be liable for any wrongful act or omission relating to actions of persons licensed to carry a concealed handgun concerning acts or omissions regarding such handguns. (2) Any private entity which does not provide adequate security measures in a private building and which allows the carrying of a concealed handgun as authorized by the personal and family protection act shall not be liable for any wrongful act or omission relating to actions of persons licensed to carry a concealed handgun concerning acts or omissions regarding such handguns. (3) Nothing in this act shall be deemed to increase the liability of any private entity where liability would have existed under the personal and family protection act prior to the effective date of this act.

(d) The governing body or the chief administrative officer, if no governing body exists, of any of the following institutions may permit any employee, who is licensed to carry a concealed handgun as authorized by the provisions of K.S.A. 75-7c01 et seq., and amendments thereto, to carry a concealed handgun in any building of such institution, if the employee meets such institution's own policy requirements regardless of whether such building is conspicuously posted in accordance with the provisions of this section: (1) a unified school district; (2) a postsecondary educational institution, as defined in K.S.A. 74-3201b, and amendments thereto; (3) a state or municipal-owned medical care facility, as defined in K.S.A. 65-425, and amendments thereto; (4) a state or municipal-owned adult care home, as defined in K.S.A. 39-923, and amendments thereto; (5) a community mental health center organized pursuant to K.S.A. 19-4001 et seq., and amendments thereto; or (6) an indigent health care clinic, as defined by K.S.A. 2014 Supp. 65-7402, and amendments thereto.

(e)(1) It shall be a violation of this section to carry a concealed handgun in violation of any restriction or prohibition allowed by subsection (a) or (b) if the building is posted in accordance with rules and regulations adopted by the attorney general pursuant to subsection (i). Any person who violates this section shall not be subject to a criminal penalty but may be subject to denial to such premises or removal from such premises....

...(f) On and after July 1, 2014, provided that the provisions of K.S.A. 2014 Supp. 75-7c21, and amendments thereto, are in full force and effect, the provisions of this section shall not apply to the carrying of a concealed handgun in the state capitol.

(g) For the purpose of this section: (1) "Adequate security measures" shall have the same meaning as the term is defined in K.S.A. 2014 Supp. 75-7c20, and amendments thereto; (2) "building" shall not include any structure, or any area of a structure, designed for the parking of motor vehicles.

(h) Nothing in this act shall be construed to authorize the carrying or possession of a handgun where prohibited by federal law.

(i) The attorney general shall adopt rules and regulations prescribing the location, content, size, and other characteristics of signs to be posted on a building where carrying a concealed handgun is prohibited pursuant to subsections (a) and (b). Such regulations shall prescribe, at a minimum, that: (1) The signs be posted at all exterior entrances to the prohibited buildings; (2) the signs be posted at eye level of adults using the entrance and not more than 12 inches to the right or left of such entrance; (3) the signs not be obstructed or altered in any way; and (4) signs which become illegible for any reason be immediately replaced.

KENTUCKY FIREARM FRIENDLY: A+

Permit Holders

Permit: "Shall issue" state.

Open Carry: Permitted.

Travel: Loaded handguns may be transported anywhere in a vehicle for self-defense purposes.

Disclose Presence of Handgun to Law Enforcement: Required only if requested by officer.

Restaurants: May carry if establishment earns less than 50% of its revenue from alcohol sales.

Recognizes Permits From: All states.

Non-Permit

Firearms Ownership: Permitted to all citizens without license or permit.

Loaded Carry: All citizens over 21 years of age may carry a loaded firearm in public, openly or concealed.

Travel: Loaded firearms are permissible as long as they are within a factory-installed compartment of a vehicle, such as a console or glove box.

General Info

State Parks: Only permit holders and only in parks (not while inside structures on park property).

Law Uniformity: State law preempts that of local agencies/municipalities.

Self-Defense Model: Castle Doctrine, Stand Your Ground.

Notes: Postings forbidding firearms on private property do not have the force of law; establishments may deny service or admittance if a carrier comes on the property, but no criminal penalty will result from the carrier's possession of a firearm on the property. Carry is not permissible in bars. Permit holders may not consume alcohol while carrying; doing so is punishable as the first degree felony of wanton endangerment. Employees whose places of employment post forbidding firearms may still carry as long as firearms are left in the car while on the property. Carry is not permissible in courthouses or hospitals but is permissible in state buildings unless posted.

Contact for Additional Information:

Kentucky State Police
919 Versailles Road • Frankfort, KY 40601
502-782-1800

Kentucky Revised Statutes § 237.110 License to carry concealed deadly weapon.

...(4) The Department of Kentucky State Police shall issue an original or renewal license if the applicant: ...(f) Does not owe a child support arrearage which equals or exceeds the cumulative amount which would be owed after one (1) year of nonpayment, if the Department of Kentucky State Police has been notified of the arrearage by the Cabinet for Health and Family Services; (g) Has complied with any subpoena or warrant relating to child support or paternity proceedings. If the Department of Kentucky State Police has not been notified by the Cabinet for Health and Family Services that the applicant has failed to meet this requirement, the Department of Kentucky State Police shall assume that paternity and child support proceedings are not an issue;

...(13)...(k) When a domestic violence order or emergency protective order is issued pursuant to the provisions of KRS Chapter 403 against a person holding a license issued under this section, the holder of the permit shall surrender the license to the court or to the officer serving the order. The officer to whom the license is surrendered shall forthwith transmit the license to the court issuing the order. The license shall be suspended until the order is terminated, or until the judge who issued the order terminates the suspension prior to the termination of the underlying domestic violence order or emergency protective order, in writing and by return of the license, upon proper motion by the license holder. Subject to the same conditions as above, a peace officer against whom an emergency protective order or domestic violence order has been issued shall not be permitted to carry a concealed deadly weapon when not on duty, the provisions of KRS 527.020 to the contrary notwithstanding.

...(16) Except as provided in KRS 527.020, no license issued pursuant to this section shall authorize any person to carry a concealed firearm into: (a) Any police station or sheriff's office; (b) Any detention facility, prison, or jail; (c) Any courthouse, solely occupied by the Court of Justice courtroom, or court proceeding; (d) Any meeting of the governing body of a county, municipality, or special district; or any meeting of the General Assembly or a committee of the General Assembly, except that nothing in this section shall preclude a member of the body, holding a concealed deadly weapon license, from carrying a concealed deadly weapon at a meeting of the body of which he or she is a member; (e) Any portion of an establishment licensed to dispense beer or alcoholic beverages for consumption on the premises, which portion of the establishment is primarily devoted to that purpose; (f) Any elementary or secondary school facility without the consent of school authorities as provided in KRS 527.070, any child-caring facility as defined in KRS 199.011, any day-care center as defined in KRS 199.894, or any certified family child-care home as defined in KRS 199.8982, except however, any owner of a certified child-care home may carry a concealed firearm into the owner's residence used as a certified child-care home; (g) An area of an airport to which access is controlled by the inspection of persons and property; or (h) Any place where the carrying of firearms is prohibited by federal law.

LOUISIANA  FIREARM FRIENDLY: 

Permit Holders

Permit: "Shall issue" state.

Open Carry: Permitted.

Travel: Loaded handguns may be transported anywhere in a vehicle for self-defense purposes.

Disclose Presence of Handgun to Law Enforcement: Must disclose immediately upon contact.

Restaurants: May carry in restaurants but not in bars, unless posted otherwise.

Recognizes Permits From: AL, AK, AZ, AR, CO, FL, GA, ID, IN, IA, KS, KY, ME, MI, MN, MS, MO, MT, NE, NH, NM, NC, ND, NV, OH, OK, PA, SC, SD, TN, TX, UT, VA, WA, WV, WI, WY

Non-Permit

Firearms Ownership: Permitted to all qualified citizens without license or permit.

Loaded Carry: All citizens over 21 years of age may openly carry a loaded firearm in public.

Travel: Even non-permitted carriers may conceal a loaded weapon in a car.

General Info

State Parks: May open carry unless posted.

Carry Law Uniformity: State law preempts that of local agencies/municipalities.

Self-Defense Model: Castle Doctrine, Stand Your Ground.

Notes: Postings forbidding firearms on private property have the force of law, and violations are punishable as criminal offenses. Carry is permissible in schools with written permission from the principal; without permission, firearms are restricted to parking areas only. Carry is forbidden in governmental buildings, police stations, penal institutions, churches, parades, and airports. Carriers may consume alcohol up to a blood alcohol content of 0.04%; beyond that level is punishable as a felony.

Contact for Additional Information:

Louisiana State Police/ CHP Unit
P.O. Box 66375 • Baton Rouge, LA 70896
225-925-4867

LOUISIANA

Louisiana Revised Statutes § 1379.3. Statewide permits for concealed handguns; application procedures; definitions.

...C. To qualify for a concealed handgun permit, a Louisiana resident shall:

(1)(a) Make sworn application to the ... Department of Public Safety and Corrections. ....

(b) In the case of an applicant who is not a United States citizen, the applicant shall provide any alien or admission number issued by the United States Bureau of Immigration and Customs Enforcement and any basis, if applicable, for an exception to the prohibitions of 18 U.S.C. 922(g)(5)(B).

(2) Agree in writing to hold harmless and indemnify the department, the state, or any peace officer for any and all liability arising out of the issuance or use of the concealed handgun permit.

(3) Be a resident of the state.

(4) Be twenty-one years of age or older.

(5) Not suffer from a mental or physical infirmity due to disease, illness, or intellectual disability which prevents the safe handling of a handgun.

(6) Not be ineligible to possess a firearm by virtue of having been convicted of a felony.

(7) Not have been committed, either voluntarily or involuntarily, for the abuse of a controlled dangerous substance, as defined by R.S. 40:961 and 964, or been found guilty of, or entered a plea of guilty or nolo contendere to a misdemeanor under the laws of this state or similar laws of any other state relating to a controlled dangerous substance within a five-year period immediately preceding ..., or be presently charged under indictment or a bill of information for such an offense.

(8) Not chronically and habitually use alcoholic beverages to the extent that his normal faculties are impaired. It shall be presumed that an applicant or permittee chronically and habitually uses alcoholic beverages ... if the applicant has been found guilty of, or entered a plea of guilty or nolo contendere to operating a vehicle while intoxicated, or has been admitted, either voluntarily or involuntarily, for treatment as an alcoholic, within the five-year period immediately preceding the date on which the application is submitted, or at any time after the application has been submitted.

(9) Not have entered a plea of guilty or nolo contendere to or been found guilty of a crime of violence as defined in R.S. 14:2 at the misdemeanor level, unless five years have elapsed since completion of sentence or any other conditions set by the court have been fulfilled, or unless the conviction was set aside and the prosecution dismissed, prior to the date on which the application is submitted.

(10) Not have been convicted of, have entered a plea of guilty or nolo contendere to, or not be charged under indictment or a bill of information for any crime of violence or any crime punishable by imprisonment for a term of one year or greater. ...this Paragraph shall include an expungement of such conviction or a dismissal and conviction set-aside under the provisions of Code of Criminal Procedure Article 893. However, a person who has been convicted of a violation of 18 U.S.C. 491(a) shall be permitted to qualify for a concealed handgun permit if fifteen or more years has elapsed between the date of application and the successful completion or service of any sentence, deferred adjudication, or period of probation or parole.

(11) Not be a fugitive from justice.

(12) Not be an unlawful user of, or addicted to, marijuana, depressants, stimulants, or narcotic drugs.

(13) Not have been adjudicated to be mentally deficient or been committed to a mental institution, unless the resident's right to possess a firearm has been restored pursuant to R.S. 28:57.

(14) Not be an illegal alien in the United States.

(15) Not have been discharged from the Armed Forces of the United States with a discharge characterized as "Under Other than Honorable Conditions", a "Bad Conduct Discharge", or a "Dishonorable Discharge"....

(16) Not have a history of engaging in violent behavior. There shall be a rebuttable presumption that an applicant has a history of engaging in violent behavior upon proof that, within a ten-year period immediately preceding the date of the application, the applicant has been arrested or charged on three or more occasions for any crime of violence as defined in R.S. 14:2(B), or has been arrested or charged on two or more occasions for any crime of violence that may be punished by death.

(17) Not be ineligible to possess or receive a firearm under 18 U.S.C. 922(g) or (n).

(18) Not have had a permit denied within one year prior to the most recent application.

(19) Not have had a permit revoked within four years prior to the most recent application.

....

N. No concealed handgun may be carried into and no concealed handgun permit issued pursuant to this Section shall authorize or entitle a permittee to carry a concealed handgun in any of the following:

(1) A law enforcement office, station, or building.

(2) A detention facility, prison, or jail.

(3) A courthouse or courtroom, provided that a judge may carry such a weapon in his own courtroom.

(4) A polling place.

(5) A meeting place of the governing authority of a political subdivision.

(6) The state capitol building.

(7) Any portion of an airport facility where the carrying of firearms is prohibited under federal law, except that ... the firearm is encased for shipment, for the purpose of checking such firearm as lawful baggage.

(8) Any church, synagogue, mosque, or other similar place of worship, eligible for qualification as a tax-exempt organization under 26 U.S.C. 501, except as provided for in Subsection U of this Section.

(9) A parade or demonstration for which a permit is issued by a governmental entity.

(10) Any portion of the permitted area of an establishment that has been granted a Class A-General retail permit ... to sell alcoholic beverages for consumption on the premises.

(11) Any school, school campus, or school bus as defined in R.S. 14:95.6.

FIREARM FRIENDLY: 

MAINE

Permit: "Shall issue" state.

Open Carry: Permitted.

Travel: Loaded handguns may be transported openly or concealed within a vehicle.

Disclose Presence of Handgun to Law Enforcement: Required only if requested by a law enforcement officer.

Restaurants: May carry if permit holder does not consume alcohol, must leave establishment if told by ownership to do so. "No Firearms" signs do have rule of law in Maine, so a permit holder may not carry their gun into an establishment that forbids it via legal posting.

Recognizes Permits From: The following states, but only if the permit holder is a resident there: AR, DE, FL, GA, LA, MI, ND, NH, SD, VA, WY

Firearms Ownership: All qualified citizens may own firearms without a license or permit to do so.

Loaded Carry: Open carry for non-permitted citizens 18+ is generally permissible. However, to open carry within a motor vehicle, a concealed carry permit must be obtained.

Travel: Non-permitted individuals may only transport an unloaded handgun. The handgun may either be in plain view or concealed within a trunk, as long as the gun's chamber and magazine are clear of ammunition.

State Parks: Generally permissible, some restrictions apply and some parks may prohibit carrying.

Carry Law Uniformity: State law preempts that of local agencies/municipalities.

Self-Defense Model: Castle Doctrine, Duty to Retreat.

Notes: ME issues permits to applicants 18 years of age and over as a matter of course, a few years lower than the typical 21.

Contact for Additional Information:

Maine State Police

State House Station 164 • Augusta, ME 04333

207-624-7210

MAINE

Maine Revised Statutes 25-5-252 § 2003. Permits to carry concealed handguns.

...11. Permit to be in permit holder's immediate possession. Every permit holder shall have the holder's permit in the holder's immediate possession at all times when carrying a concealed handgun and shall display the same on demand of any law enforcement officer. A person charged with violating this subsection may not be adjudicated as having committed a civil violation if that person produces in court the concealed handgun permit that was valid at the time of the issuance of a summons to court or, if the holder exhibits the permit to a law enforcement officer designated by the summonsing officer not later than 24 hours before the time set for the court appearance, a complaint may not be issued....

§ 2011. State Preemption.

...5. Restrictions on firearms and ammunition prohibited during state of emergency. The provisions of this subsection apply to restrictions on firearms and ammunition during a state of emergency, as declared by the Governor pursuant to Title 37-B, section 742, subsection 1.

A. During a state of emergency, notwithstanding any provision of law to the contrary, a person acting on behalf or under the authority of the State or a political subdivision of the State may not:

(1) Prohibit or restrict the otherwise lawful possession, use, carrying, transfer, transportation, storage or display of a firearm or ammunition. The provisions of this paragraph regarding the lawful transfer of a firearm or ammunition do not apply to the commercial sale of a firearm or ammunition if an authorized person has ordered an evacuation or general closure of businesses in the area of the business engaged in the sale of firearms or ammunition;

(2) Seize or confiscate, or authorize the seizure or confiscation of, an otherwise lawfully possessed firearm or ammunition unless the person acting on behalf of or under the authority of the State is:

(a) Acting in self-defense against an assault;

(b) Defending another person from an assault;

(c) Arresting a person in actual possession of a firearm or ammunition for a violation of law; or

(d) Seizing or confiscating the firearm or ammunition as evidence of a crime; or

(3) Require registration of a firearm or ammunition for which registration is not otherwise required by state law....

Permit: "May issue" state.

Open Carry: Permissible only with a valid permit, restrictions apply.

Travel: Loaded handguns may be transported openly or concealed within a vehicle.

Disclose Presence of Handgun to Law Enforcement: Not mandatory unless asked by a law enforcement officer.

Restaurants: May carry if permit holder does not consume alcohol, must leave establishment if told by ownership to do so. May not carry if posted.

Recognizes Permits From: No states.

Firearms Ownership: Must obtain permit to purchase firearms. Many regulations and restrictions in place. All handgun purchases or transfers of ownership must be registered with the Maryland State Police.

Loaded Carry: Not allowed without a permit.

Travel: For the purposes of traveling within and through Maryland, handguns must be unloaded, in a carrying case or holster with a flap, and the ammunition must be separated from the firearm. It is advised to keep the unloaded weapon in the trunk, where it cannot be easily accessed. There are more regulations, but essentially, you can only transport a handgun between residence, to and from a repair shop, a shooting sporting event, between a residence and place of business if substantially owned and operated by the person.

State Parks: Prohibited.

Carry Law Uniformity: Most State law preempts that of local agencies/municipalities in regard to firearms.

Self-Defense Model: Castle Doctrine, Duty to Retreat.

Notes: If you travel through Maryland with a firearm unloaded, secured within a case or holster, and kept in a place where it is not easily accessible, you are covered under Federal law. If you stop or interrupt your travel through the state, then you immediately fall under state jurisdiction. Also, several bans on various "types" of handguns and magazines exist.

Contact for Additional Information:

Maryland State Police (Licensing Division)
1201 Reisterstown Road • Pikesville, MD 21208
410-653-4200

Maryland Criminal Law Code Annotated
§ 4-110. Restricted firearm ammunition.

(a) "Restricted firearm ammunition" defined. -- In this section, "restricted firearm ammunition" means a cartridge, a shell, or any other device that:

(1) contains explosive or incendiary material designed and intended for use in a firearm; and

(2) has a core constructed, excluding traces of other substances, entirely from one or a combination of:

(i) tungsten alloys;

(ii) steel;

(iii) iron;

(iv) brass;

(v) beryllium copper;

(vi) depleted uranium; or

(vii) an equivalent material of similar density or hardness.

(b) Possession prohibited. -- A person may not, during and in relation to the commission of a crime of violence as defined in § 14-101 of this article, possess or use restricted firearm ammunition.

(c) Penalty. -- A person who violates this section is guilty of a misdemeanor and on conviction is subject to imprisonment not exceeding 5 years or a fine not exceeding $ 5,000 or both.

§ 4-203. Wearing, carrying, or transporting handgun

(a) Prohibited. --
(1) Except as provided in subsection (b) of this section, a person may not:

(i) wear, carry, or transport a handgun, whether concealed or open, on or about the person;

(ii) wear, carry, or knowingly transport a handgun, whether concealed or open, in a vehicle traveling on a road or parking lot generally used by the public, highway, waterway, or airway of the State;

(iii) violate item (i) or (ii) of this paragraph while on public school property in the State; or

(iv) violate item (i) or (ii) of this paragraph with the deliberate purpose of injuring or killing another person.

(2) There is a rebuttable presumption that a person who transports a handgun under paragraph (1)(ii) of this subsection transports the handgun knowingly.

(b) Exceptions. -- This section does not prohibit:

(1) the wearing, carrying, or transporting of a handgun by a person who is authorized at the time and under the circumstances to wear, carry, or transport the handgun as part of the person's official equipment, and is:

(i) a law enforcement official of the United States, the State, or a county or city of the State;

(ii) a member of the armed forces of the United States or of the National Guard on duty or traveling to or from duty;

(iii) a law enforcement official of another state or subdivision of another state temporarily in this State on official business;

(iv) a correctional officer or warden of a correctional facility in the State;

(v) a sheriff or full-time assistant or deputy sheriff of the State; or

(vi) a temporary or part-time sheriff's deputy;

(2) the wearing, carrying, or transporting of a handgun, in compliance with any limitations imposed under § 5-307 of the Public Safety Article, by a person to whom a permit to wear, carry, or transport the handgun has been issued under Title 5, Subtitle 3 of the Public Safety Article;

(3) the carrying of a handgun on the person or in a vehicle while the person is transporting the handgun to or from the place of legal purchase or sale, or to or from a bona fide repair shop, or between bona fide residences of the person, or between the bona fide residence and place of business of the person, if the business is operated and owned substantially by the person if each handgun is unloaded and carried in an enclosed case or an enclosed holster;

(4) the wearing, carrying, or transporting by a person of a handgun used in connection with an organized military activity, a target shoot, formal or informal target practice, sport shooting event, hunting, a Department of Natural Resources-sponsored firearms and hunter safety class, trapping, or a dog obedience training class or show, while the person is engaged in, on the way to, or returning from that activity if each handgun is unloaded and carried in an enclosed case or an enclosed holster;

(5) the moving by a bona fide gun collector of part or all of the collector's gun collection from place to place for public or private exhibition if each handgun is unloaded and carried in an enclosed case or an enclosed holster;

(6) the wearing, carrying, or transporting of a handgun by a person on real estate that the person owns or leases or where the person resides or within

the confines of a business establishment that the person owns or leases;

(7) the wearing, carrying, or transporting of a handgun by a supervisory employee:

(i) in the course of employment;

(ii) within the confines of the business establishment in which the supervisory employee is employed; and

(iii) when so authorized by the owner or manager of the business establishment;

(8) the carrying or transporting of a signal pistol or other visual distress signal approved by the United

States Coast Guard in a vessel on the waterways of the State or, if the signal pistol or other visual distress signal is unloaded and carried in an enclosed case, in a vehicle; or

(9) the wearing, carrying, or transporting of a handgun by a person who is carrying a court order requiring the surrender of the handgun, if:

(i) the handgun is unloaded;

(ii) the person has notified the law enforcement unit, barracks, or station that the handgun is being transported in accordance with the court order; and

(iii) the person transports the handgun directly to the law enforcement unit, barracks, or station.

(c) Penalty. --
(1) A person who violates this section is guilty of a misdemeanor and on conviction is subject to the penalties provided in this subsection.

(2) If the person has not previously been convicted under this section, § 4-204 of this subtitle, or § 4- 101 or § 4-102 of this title:

(i) except as provided in item (ii) of this paragraph, the person is subject to imprisonment for not less than 30 days and not exceeding 3 years or a fine of not less than $ 250 and not exceeding $ 2,500 or both; or

(ii) if the person violates subsection (a)(1)(iii) of this section, the person shall be sentenced to imprisonment for not less than 90 days.

(3) (i) If the person has previously been convicted once under this section, § 4-204 of this subtitle, or §4-101 or § 4-102 of this title:

1. except as provided in item 2 of this subparagraph, the person is subject to imprisonment for not less than 1 year and not exceeding 10 years; or

2. if the person violates subsection (a)(1)(iii) of this section, the person is subject to imprisonmentfor not less than 3 years and not exceeding 10 years.

(ii) The court may not impose less than the applicable minimum sentence provided under subparagraph (i) of this paragraph.

(4) (i) If the person has previously been convicted more than once under this section, § 4-204 of this subtitle, or § 4-101 or § 4-102 of this title, or of any combination of these crimes:

1. except as provided in item 2 of this subparagraph, the person is subject to imprisonment for not less than 3 years and not exceeding 10 years; or

2. A. if the person violates subsection (a)(1)(iii) of this section, the person is subject to imprisonment for not less than 5 years and not exceeding 10 years; or

B. if the person violates subsection (a)(1)(iv) of this section, the person is subject to imprisonment for not less than 5 years and not exceeding 10 years.
(ii) The court may not impose less than the applicable minimum sentence provided under subparagraph (i)....

MASSACHUSETTS

Permit Holders

Permit: "May issue" state.

Open Carry: No statute in the law prevents open carry, but it is extremely discouraged and could result in the loss of an individual's license to carry. Some areas of the state may be more open carry friendly than others.

Travel: Loaded handguns may be transported in a vehicle, as long as they are under the direct control of the permit holder and the appropriate permit for the weapon possessed is acquired.

Disclose Presence of Handgun to Law Enforcement: Required only if requested by a law enforcement officer.

Restaurants: Permissible, with restrictions.

Recognizes Permits From: No states.

Non-Permit

Firearms Ownership: Must obtain a state issued "License to Carry" or "Firearm Identification Card" before purchase.

Loaded Carry: Non-permitted carry of any kind is illegal in the state of Massachusetts.

Travel: No firearm of any kind may be transported by a citizen in a motor vehicle without a "License to Carry" issued by the state of Massachusetts. However, non-residents, with permits issued from their home state, may travel to or through Massachusetts with a pistol or revolver in their vehicle, as long as they are traveling to a collector's meeting, exhibition/competition, or carrying for hunting purposes.

General Info

State Parks: Generally permissible, some restrictions apply.

Carry Law Uniformity: Generally, state law does not preempt that of local municipalities/agencies, but there are a few exceptions.

Self-Defense Model: Castle Doctrine, Duty to Retreat.

Notes: There are several types of carry licenses in Massachusetts, and they often vary between different parts of the state. Massachusetts State Law on concealed carry and matters concerning it tend to be ambiguous. The laws that are clear remain strictly implemented. Please be especially careful if your firearms or magazines/feeding devices exceed 10 rounds or 5 shells for semi-automatics and shotguns, respectively; MA issues two different licenses—Classes A and B—correlative to the feed capacity of the weapons carried. If you plan to travel to Massachusetts, please contact local authorities there beforehand with any questions you may have.

General Laws of Massachusetts Title XX, Public Safety and Good Order, Chapter 140 Licenses

§ Section 121 Firearms sales; definitions; antique firearms; application of law; exceptions.

As used in sections 122 to 131P, inclusive, the following words shall, unless the context clearly requires otherwise, have the following meanings...

..."Large capacity feeding device", (i) a fixed or detachable magazine, box, drum, feed strip or similar device capable of accepting, or that can be readily converted to accept, more than ten rounds of ammunition or more than five shotgun shells; or (ii) a large capacity ammunition feeding device as defined in the federal Public Safety and Recreational Firearms Use Protection Act, 18 U.S.C. section 921(a)(31) as appearing in such section on September 13, 1994. The term "large capacity feeding device" shall not include an attached tubular device designed to accept, and capable of operating only with,.22 caliber ammunition.

"Large capacity weapon", any firearm, rifle or shotgun: (i) that is semiautomatic with a fixed large capacity feeding device; (ii) that is semiautomatic and capable of accepting, or readily modifiable to accept, any detachable large capacity feeding device; (iii) that employs a rotating cylinder capable of accepting more than ten rounds of ammunition in a rifle or firearm and more than five shotgun shells in the case of a shotgun or firearm; or (iv) that is an assault weapon. The term "large capacity weapon" shall be a secondary designation and shall apply to a weapon in addition to its primary designation as a firearm, rifle or shotgun and shall not include: (i) any weapon that was manufactured in or prior to the year 1899; (ii) any weapon that operates by manual bolt, pump, lever or slide action; (iii) any weapon that is a single-shot weapon; (iv) any weapon that has been modified so as to render it permanently inoperable or otherwise rendered permanently unable to be designated a large capacity weapon; or (v) any weapon that is an antique or relic, theatrical prop or other weapon that is not capable of firing a projectile and which is not intended for use as a functional weapon and cannot be readily modified through a combination of available parts into an operable large capacity weapon....

§ Section 131. Licenses to carry firearms; Class A and B; conditions and restrictions.

All licenses to carry firearms shall be designated Class A or Class B, and the issuance and possession of any such license shall be subject to the following conditions and restrictions:

(a) A Class A license shall entitle a holder thereof to purchase, rent, lease, borrow, possess and carry: (i) firearms, including large capacity firearms, and feeding devices and ammunition therefor, for all lawful purposes, subject to such restrictions relative to the possession, use or carrying of firearms as the licensing authority deems proper; and (ii) rifles and shotguns, including large capacity weapons, and feeding devices and ammunition therefor, for all lawful purposes; provided, however, that the licensing authority may impose such restrictions relative to the possession, use or carrying of large capacity rifles and shotguns as it deems proper. A violation of a restriction imposed by the licensing authority under the provisions of this paragraph

shall be cause for suspension or revocation and shall, unless otherwise provided, be punished by a fine of not less than $1,000 nor more than $10,000; provided, however, that the provisions of section 10 of chapter 269 shall not apply to such violation....

...(b) A Class B license shall entitle a holder thereof to purchase, rent, lease, borrow, possess and carry: (i) non-large capacity firearms and feeding devices and ammunition therefor, for all lawful purposes, subject to such restrictions relative to the possession, use or carrying of such firearm as the licensing authority deems proper; provided, however, that a Class B license shall not entitle the holder thereof to carry or possess a loaded firearm in a concealed manner in any public way or place; and provided further, that a Class B license shall not entitle the holder thereof to possess a large capacity firearm, except under a Class A club license issued under this section or under the direct supervision of a holder of a valid Class A license at an incorporated shooting club or licensed shooting range; and (ii) rifles and shotguns, including large capacity rifles and shotguns, and feeding devices and ammunition therefor, for all lawful purposes; provided, however, that the licensing authority may impose such restrictions relative to the possession, use or carrying of large capacity rifles and shotguns as he deems proper. A violation of a restriction provided under this paragraph, or a restriction imposed by the licensing authority under the provisions of this paragraph, shall be cause for suspension or revocation and shall, unless otherwise provided, be punished by a fine of not less than $1,000 nor more than $10,000; provided, however, that the provisions of section 10 of chapter 269 shall not apply to such violation.

A Class B license shall not be a valid license for the purpose of complying with any provision under this chapter governing the purchase, sale, lease, rental or transfer of any weapon or ammunition feeding device if such weapon is a large capacity firearm or if such ammunition feeding device is a large capacity feeding device for use with a large capacity firearm, both as defined in section 121.

(c) Either a Class A or Class B license shall be valid for the purpose of owning, possessing, purchasing and transferring non-large capacity rifles and shotguns....

Contact for Additional Information:

Firearms Records Bureau

200 Arlington Street, Suite 220 • Chelsea, MA 02150

617-660-4782

FIREARM FRIENDLY:   MICHIGAN

Permit: "Shall issue" state.

Open Carry: Generally permitted.

Travel: A handgun may be transported openly or concealed by a permit holder.

Disclose Presence of Handgun to Law Enforcement: Must inform immediately upon making contact with an officer.

Restaurants: Permissible unless a "No Firearms" sign is posted, must not consume alcohol.

Recognizes Permits from: All states, but only if the permit holder is a resident there.

Firearm Ownership: Must have permit to purchase or even possess handguns.

Loaded Carry: It is illegal to carry a handgun in any capacity without a permit.

Travel: A non-permitted person may transport a handgun they own in a vehicle, but the firearm must be unloaded, securely encased, and placed in the trunk of the vehicle. If your vehicle does not have a trunk, then you may place the securely encased handgun within a passenger compartment, as long as it is not readily accessible to anyone in the vehicle.

State Parks: Permissible, some restrictions may apply.

Carry Law Uniformity: State law preempts most local municipality/agency implemented laws regarding firearms.

Self-Defense Model: Castle Doctrine, Stand Your Ground.

Notes: To even possess a handgun at all in MI, one must acquire a license. Several changes in MI gun law went into effect December 2015, including changes as to where concealed firearms may be carried, so be sure to update your familiarity with MI law if you travel.

Contact for Additional Information:

Michigan State Police
P.O. Box 30634 • Lansing, MI 48909
517-332-2521

Michigan Firearms Act 372 § 28.422. License to purchase, carry, possess, or transport pistol; issuance; qualifications; applications; sale of pistol; exemptions; nonresidents; forging application as felony; implementation during business hours.

Sec. 2.

(1) Except as otherwise provided in this act, a person shall not purchase, carry, possess, or transport a pistol in this state without first having obtained a license for the pistol as prescribed in this section.

(2) A person who brings a pistol into this state who is on leave from active duty with the armed forces of the United States or who has been discharged from active duty with the armed forces of the United States shall obtain a license for the pistol within 30 days after his or her arrival in this state.

(3) The commissioner or chief of police of a city, township, or village police department that issues licenses to purchase, carry, possess, or transport pistols, or his or her duly authorized deputy, or the sheriff or his or her duly authorized deputy, in the parts of a county not included within a city, township, or village having an organized police department, in discharging the duty to issue licenses shall with due speed and diligence issue licenses to purchase, carry, possess, or transport pistols to qualified applicants unless he or she has probable cause to believe that the applicant would be a threat to himself or herself or to other individuals, or would commit an offense with the pistol that would violate a law of this or another state or of the United States. An applicant is qualified if all of the following circumstances exist:

(a) The person is not subject to an order or disposition for which he or she has received notice and an opportunity for a hearing, and which was entered into the law enforcement information network under any of the following:

(i) Section 464a of the mental health code, 1974 PA 258, MCL 330.1464a.

(ii) Section 5107 of the estates and protected individuals code, 1998 PA 386, MCL 700.5107, or section 444a of former 1978 PA 642.

(iii) Section 2950 of the revised judicature act of 1961, 1961 PA 236, MCL 600.2950.

(iv) Section 2950a of the revised judicature act of 1961, 1961 PA 236, MCL 600.2950a.

(v) Section 14 of 1846 RS 84, MCL 552.14.

(vi) Section 6b of chapter V of the code of criminal procedure, 1927 PA 175, MCL 765.6b, if the order has a condition imposed under section 6b(3) of chapter V of the code of criminal procedure, 1927 PA 175, MCL 765.6b.

(vii) Section 16b of chapter IX of the code of criminal procedure, 1927 PA 175, MCL 769.16b.

(b) The person is 18 years of age or older or, if the seller is licensed under 18 USC 923, is 21 years of age or older.

(c) The person is a citizen of the United States or an alien lawfully

admitted into the United States and is a legal resident of this state. ...

(d) A felony charge or a criminal charge listed in section 5b against the person is not pending at the time of application.

(e) The person is not prohibited from possessing, using, transporting, selling, purchasing, carrying, shipping, receiving, or distributing a firearm under section 224f of the Michigan penal code, 1931 PA 328, MCL 750.224f.

(f) The person has not been adjudged insane in this state or elsewhere unless he or she has been adjudged restored to sanity by court order.

(g) The person is not under an order of involuntary commitment in an inpatient or outpatient setting due to mental illness.

(h) The person has not been adjudged legally incapacitated in this state or elsewhere. This subdivision does not apply to a person who has had his or her legal capacity restored by order of the court.

... (8) An individual who is not a resident of this state is not required to obtain a license under this section if all of the following conditions apply:

(a) The individual is licensed in his or her state of residence to purchase, carry, or transport a pistol.

(b) The individual is in possession of the license described in subdivision (a).

(c) The individual is the owner of the pistol he or she possesses, carries, or transports.

(d) The individual possesses the pistol for a lawful purpose as that term is defined in section 231a of the Michigan penal code, 1931 PA 328, MCL 750.231a.

(e) The individual is in this state for a period of 180 days or less and does not intend to establish residency in this state.

(9) An individual who is a nonresident of this state shall present the license described in subsection (8)(a) upon the demand of a police officer. An individual who violates this subsection is guilty of a misdemeanor punishable by imprisonment for not more than 90 days or a fine of not more than $100.00, or both....

§ 28.425f. Concealed pistol license; possession; disclosure to peace officer; violation; penalty; notice to department and issuing board; seizure; forfeiture; "peace officer" defined.

Sec. 5f.

(1) An individual who is licensed under this act to carry a concealed pistol shall have his or her license to carry that pistol in his or her possession at all times he or she is carrying a concealed pistol...

...(3) An individual licensed under this act to carry a concealed pistol and who is carrying a concealed pistol ... and who is stopped by a peace officer shall immediately disclose to the peace officer that he or she is carrying a pistol ... concealed upon his or her person or in his or her vehicle.

(4) An individual who violates subsection (1) or (2) is responsible for a state civil infraction and may be fined not more than $100.00.

(5) An individual who violates subsection (3) is responsible for a state civil infraction and may be fined as follows:

(a) For a first offense, by a fine of not more than $500.00 or by the individual's license to carry a concealed pistol being suspended for 6 months, or both.

(b) For a subsequent offense within 3 years of a prior offense, by a fine of not more than $1,000.00 and by the individual's license to carry a concealed pistol being revoked....

§ 28.4250. Premises on which carrying concealed weapon or portable device that uses electro-muscular disruption technology prohibited; "premises" defined; exceptions to subsections (1) and (2); violation; penalties.

Sec. 50.

(1) Subject to subsection (5), an individual licensed under this act to carry a concealed pistol, or who is exempt from licensure under section 12a(1)(h), shall not carry a concealed pistol on the premises of any of the following:

(a) A school or school property except that a parent or legal guardian of a student of the school is not precluded from carrying a concealed pistol while in a vehicle on school property, if he or she is dropping the student off at the school or picking up the student from the school....

(b) A public or private child care center or day care center, public or private child caring institution, or public or private child placing agency.

(c) A sports arena or stadium.

(d) A bar or tavern licensed under the Michigan liquor control code of 1998, 1998 PA 58, MCL 436.1101 to 436.2303, where the primary source of income of the business is the sale of alcoholic liquor by the glass and consumed on the premises. This subdivision does not apply to an owner or employee of the business. The Michigan liquor control commission shall develop and make available to holders of licenses under the Michigan liquor control code of 1998, 1998 PA 58, MCL 436.1101 to 436.2303, an appropriate sign stating that "This establishment prohibits patrons from carrying concealed weapons". The owner or operator of an establishment licensed under the Michigan liquor control code of 1998, 1998 PA 58, MCL 436.1101 to 436.2303, may, but is not required to, post the sign developed under this subdivision.

(e) Any property or facility owned or operated by a church, synagogue, mosque, temple, or other place of worship, unless the presiding official or officials of the church, synagogue, mosque, temple, or other place of worship permit the carrying of concealed pistol on that property or facility.

(f) An entertainment facility with a seating capacity of 2,500 or more individuals

that the individual knows or should know has a seating capacity of 2,500 or more individuals or that has a sign above each public entrance stating in letters not less than 1-inch high a seating capacity of 2,500 or more individuals.

(g) A hospital.

(h) A dormitory or classroom of a community college, college, or university....

...(4) As used in subsection (1), "premises" does not include parking areas of the places identified under subsection (1).

(5) Subsections (1) and (2) do not apply to any of the following:

(a) An individual licensed under this act who is a retired police officer or retired law enforcement officer....

(b) An individual who is licensed under this act and who is employed or contracted by an entity described under subsection (1) to provide security services and is required by his or her employer or the terms of a contract to carry a concealed firearm....

(c) An individual who is licensed as a private investigator or private detective....

(d) An individual who is licensed under this act and who is a corrections officer of a county sheriff's department.

(e) An individual who is licensed under this act and who is a motor carrier officer or capitol security officer of the department of state police.

(f) An individual who is licensed under this act and who is a member of a sheriff's posse.

(g) An individual who is licensed under this act and who is an auxiliary officer or reserve officer of a police or sheriff's department.

(h) An individual who is licensed under this act and who is a parole or probation officer of the department of corrections.

(i) A state court judge or state court retired judge who is licensed under this act....

(j) An individual who is licensed under this act and who is a court officer.

(6) An individual who violates this section is responsible for a state civil infraction or guilty of a crime as follows:

(a) Except as provided in subdivisions (b) and (c), the individual is responsible for a state civil infraction and may be fined not more than $500.00. The court shall order the individual's license to carry a concealed pistol suspended for 6 months.

(b) For a second violation, the individual is guilty of a misdemeanor punishable by a fine of not more than $1,000.00. The court shall order the individual's license to carry a concealed pistol revoked.

(c) For a third or subsequent violation, the individual is guilty of a felony punishable by imprisonment for not more than 4 years or a fine of not more than $5,000.00, or both. The court shall order the individual's license to carry a concealed pistol revoked.

MINNESOTA

FIREARM FRIENDLY: A

Permit Holders

Permit: "Shall issue" state.

Open Carry: Permitted.

Travel: Loaded handguns may be transported anywhere in a vehicle for self-defense purposes.

Disclose Presence of Handgun to Law Enforcement: Required only if requested by officer.

Restaurants: May carry in restaurants and bars unless posted.

Recognizes Permits From: DE, IL, KS, KY, LA, MI, MO, NJ, NV, NM, RI, SC, TX, UT, WY

Non-Permit

Firearms Ownership: Must acquire a permit to purchase; concealed carry permit suffices.

Loaded Carry: Only permitted residents can carry openly.

Travel: Handguns must be unloaded, cased, and placed in the trunk or rear compartment.

General Info

State Parks: Only permit holders.

Law Uniformity: State law preempts that of local agencies/municipalities.

Self-Defense Model: Castle Doctrine requires commission of a felony by invader or fear of great bodily harm or death, Duty to Retreat in public.

Notes: Postings forbidding firearms on private property do not have the immediate force of law; in fact, a posting must be followed by a demand for compliance by the owner of the property. Only if a carrier refuses after such a demand to comply does the offense become punishable as a misdemeanor. Carriers may consume alcohol while carrying but a blood alcohol content of 0.04% or greater will result in a suspension of a permit; a blood alcohol content of 0.10% or higher will result in revocation for a year. Governmental properties may not post unless statute explicitly states that firearms are forbidden. Carriers may carry in daycares with owner's permission and in schools with principal or superintendent's permission. On school property, carrier may have a firearm in a vehicle and may get it out only for the limited purpose of placing it into the trunk of the car. Carriers may carry in courthouses and the state capitol if they notify the local sheriff or the state police they intend to do so prior to arrival; prior notification exempts carrier from bar on firearms for these places. (Note, however, that some judges will hold carriers in contempt of court if they carry into the confines of their courtrooms.) Between publication of the third and fourth editions of this book, Minnesota dropped recognition of permits from Alaska, Arkansas, Ohio, Oklahoma, and Tennessee.

Contact for Additional Information:

Minnesota Dept. of Public Safety

445 Minnesota Street • St. Paul, MN 55101

651-215-1328

Minnesota Statutes § 624.714

Carrying of Weapons Without Permits; Penalties.
Subd. 1a.Permit required; penalty.

A person, other than a peace officer, as defined in section 626.84, subdivision 1, who carries, holds, or possesses a pistol in a motor vehicle, snowmobile, or boat, or on or about the person's clothes or the person, or otherwise in possession or control in a public place, as defined in section624.7181, subdivision 1, paragraph (c), without first having obtained a permit to carry the pistol is guilty of a gross misdemeanor. A person who is convicted a second or subsequent time is guilty of a felony.

Subd. 1b.Display of permit; penalty.

(a) The holder of a permit to carry must have the permit card and a driver's license, state identification card, or other government-issued photo identification in immediate possession at all times when carrying a pistol and must display the permit card and identification document upon lawful demand by a peace officer, as defined in section 626.84, subdivision 1. A violation of this paragraph is a petty misdemeanor. The fine for a first offense must not exceed $25. Notwithstanding section 609.531, a firearm carried in violation of this paragraph is not subject to forfeiture.

(b) A citation issued for violating paragraph (a) must be dismissed if the person demonstrates, in court or in the office of the arresting officer, that the person was authorized to carry the pistol at the time of the alleged violation.

(c) Upon the request of a peace officer, a permit holder must write a sample signature in the officer's presence to aid in verifying the person's identity.

(d) Upon the request of a peace officer, a permit holder shall disclose to the officer whether or not the permit holder is currently carrying a firearm.

....

Subd. 17.Posting; trespass.

(a) A person carrying a firearm on or about his or her person or clothes under a permit or otherwise who remains at a private establishment knowing that the operator of the establishment or its agent has made a reasonable request that firearms not be brought into the establishment may be ordered to leave the premises. A person who fails to leave when so requested is guilty of a petty misdemeanor. The fine for a first offense must not exceed $25. Notwithstanding section 609.531, a firearm carried in violation of this subdivision is not subject to forfeiture.

....

(c) The owner or operator of a private establishment may not prohibit the lawful carry or possession of firearms in a parking facility or parking area.

(d) This subdivision does not apply to private residences. The lawful possessor of a private residence may prohibit firearms, and provide notice thereof, in any lawful manner.

(e) A landlord may not restrict the lawful carry or possession of firearms by tenants or their guests....

MISSISSIPPI — FIREARM FRIENDLY: A+

Permit Holders

Permit: "Shall issue" state.

Open Carry: Permissible.

Travel: A permitted individual may transport a loaded handgun either openly or concealed within their vehicle.

Disclose Presence of Handgun to Law Enforcement: Required only if requested by a law enforcement officer.

Restaurants: Permissible unless otherwise posted, no alcohol may be consumed.

Recognizes Permits From: All states

Non-Permit

Firearms Ownership: No license or permit required for purchase.

Loaded Carry: All qualified citizens 18+ years of age may openly carry a loaded handgun.

Travel: It is permissible to travel with a wholly concealed or openly carried handgun. The firearm may be loaded as well.

General Info

State Parks: Permissible, some restrictions may apply.

Carry Law Uniformity: State law preempts most local municipality laws regarding firearms.

Self-Defense Model: Castle Doctrine, Stand Your Ground.

Notes: MS prohibits carry in any "place of nuisance," which MS law defines as a place where "lewdness, assignation, or prostitution is conducted, permitted, continued, or exists" or any place where drugs are "used, sold, or delivered." Residents may apply for a permit under the required age of 21 if they are at least 18 and are active members or veterans of the military.

Contact for Additional Information:

Mississippi Highway Patrol / Gun Permits
P.O. Box 958 • Jackson, MS 39205
601-987-1212

MISSISSIPPI

Mississippi Code Annotated § 45-9-51. Prohibition against adoption of certain ordinances

(1) Subject to the provisions of Section 45-9-53, no county or municipality may adopt any ordinance

that restricts the possession, carrying, transportation, sale, transfer or ownership of firearms or ammunition or their components.

(2) No public housing authority operating in this state may adopt any rule or regulation restricting a lessee or tenant of a dwelling owned and operated by such public housing authority from lawfully possessing firearms or ammunition or their components within individual dwelling units or the transportation of such firearms or ammunition or their components to and from such dwelling.

§ 45-9-55. Employer not permitted to prohibit transportation or storage of firearms on employer property; exceptions; certain immunity for employer

(1) Except as otherwise provided in subsection (2) of this section, a public or private employer may not establish, maintain, or enforce any policy or rule that has the effect of prohibiting a person from transporting or storing a firearm in a locked vehicle in any parking lot, parking garage, or other designated parking area.

(2) A private employer may prohibit an employee from transporting or storing a firearm in a vehicle in a parking lot, parking garage, or other parking area the employer provides for employees to which access is restricted or limited through the use of a gate, security station or other means of restricting or limiting general public access onto the property.

(3) This section shall not apply to vehicles owned or leased by an employer and used by the employee in the course of his business.

(4) This section does not authorize a person to transport or store a firearm on any premises where the possession of a firearm is prohibited by state or federal law....

§ 45-9-101. License to carry stun gun, concealed pistol or revolver

(1) (a) The Department of Public Safety is authorized to issue licenses to carry ... concealed pistols or revolvers to persons qualified as provided in this section....

(b) The licensee must carry the license, together with valid identification, at all times in which the licensee is carrying a stun gun, concealed pistol or revolver and must display both the license and proper identification upon demand by a law enforcement officer. A violation of the provisions of this paragraph

(b) shall constitute a noncriminal violation with a penalty of Twenty-five Dollars ($ 25.00) and shall be enforceable by summons....

MISSISSIPPI

...(13) No license issued pursuant to this section shall authorize any person to carry a stun gun, concealed pistol or revolver into any place of nuisance as defined in Section 95-3-1, Mississippi Code of 1972; any police, sheriff or highway patrol station; any detention facility, prison or jail; any courthouse; any courtroom, except that nothing in this section shall preclude a judge from carrying a concealed weapon or determining who will carry a concealed weapon in his courtroom; any polling place; any meeting place of the governing body of any governmental entity; any meeting of the Legislature or a committee thereof; any school, college or professional athletic event not related to firearms; any portion of an establishment, licensed to dispense alcoholic beverages for consumption on the premises, that is primarily devoted to dispensing alcoholic beverages; any portion of an establishment in which beer or light wine is consumed on the premises, that is primarily devoted to such purpose; any elementary or secondary school facility; any junior college, community college, college or university facility unless for the purpose of participating in any authorized firearms-related activity; inside the passenger terminal of any airport, except that no person shall be prohibited from carrying any legal firearm into the terminal if the firearm is encased for shipment, for purposes of checking such firearm as baggage to be lawfully transported on any aircraft; any church or other place of worship; or any place where the carrying of firearms is prohibited by federal law. In addition to the places enumerated in this subsection, the carrying of a stun gun, concealed pistol or revolver may be disallowed in any place in the discretion of the person or entity exercising control over the physical location of such place by the placing of a written notice clearly readable at a distance of not less than ten (10) feet that the "carrying of a pistol or revolver is prohibited." No license issued pursuant to this section shall authorize the participants in a parade or demonstration for which a permit is required to carry a stun gun, concealed pistol or revolver....

Permit: "Shall issue" state.

Open Carry: Permissible for individuals with permits. Open carry was only recently made legal in the state of Missouri.

Travel: Loaded handguns may be transported openly or concealed within a vehicle.

Disclose Presence of Handgun to Law Enforcement: Required only when requested by a law enforcement officer.

Restaurants: May carry if permit holder does not consume alcohol, must leave establishment if told by ownership to do so.

Recognizes Permits From: All states.

Firearms Ownership: Permitted to all qualified citizens without license or permit.

Loaded Carry: Non-permitted individuals may not carry a loaded handgun in public.

Travel: Non-permitted citizens (ages 19+ or 18 if a member of the Armed Forces or honorably discharged from the Armed Forces) may carry a loaded handgun in a vehicle openly or concealed. It may even be concealed upon one's person, as long as they do not step outside of their vehicle. This aligns with Missouri's "peaceable journey" law.

State Parks: Permissible, some restrictions may apply.

Carry Law Uniformity: State law preempts that of local agencies/municipalities.

Self-Defense Model: Castle Doctrine, No Duty to Retreat.

Notes: Open carry with a valid permit in Missouri has been legalized since October of 2014. It is advised that you research and understand these laws before travel. Contact local authorities if you have any questions or concerns.

Missouri Revised Statutes Open display of firearm permitted, when.
§ 571.037. Any person who has a valid concealed carry endorsement issued prior to August 28, 2013, or a valid concealed carry permit, and who is lawfully carrying a firearm in a concealed manner, may briefly and openly display the firearm to the ordinary sight of another person, unless the firearm is intentionally displayed in an angry or threatening manner, not in necessary self defense.

Permit does not authorize concealed firearms, where--penalty for violation.
§ 571.107. 1. A concealed carry permit issued pursuant to sections 571.101 to 571.121, a valid concealed carry endorsement issued prior to August 28, 2013, or a concealed carry endorsement or permit issued by another state or political subdivision of another state shall authorize the person in whose name the permit or endorsement is issued to

carry concealed firearms on or about his or her person or vehicle throughout the state. No concealed carry permit...shall authorize any person to carry concealed firearms into:

(1) Any police, sheriff, or highway patrol office or station without the consent of the chief law enforcement officer in charge....;

(2) Within twenty-five feet of any polling place on any election day.;

(3) The facility of any adult or juvenile detention or correctional institution, prison or jail. Possession of a firearm in a vehicle on the premises...shall not be a criminal offense so long as the firearm is not removed from the vehicle or brandished while the vehicle is on the premises;

(4) Any courthouse solely occupied by the circuit, appellate or supreme court, or any courtrooms, administrative offices, libraries or other rooms of any such court whether or not such court solely occupies the building in question.;

(5) Any meeting of the governing body of a unit of local government;... except that nothing in this subdivision shall preclude a member of the body holding a valid concealed carry permit or endorsement from carrying a concealed firearm at a meeting of the body which he or she is a member.;

(6) The general assembly, supreme court, county or municipality may by rule, administrative regulation, or ordinance prohibit or limit the carrying of concealed firearms by permit or endorsement holders in that portion of a building owned, leased or controlled by that unit of government. Any portion of a building in which the carrying of concealed firearms is prohibited or limited shall be clearly identified by signs posted at the entrance to the restricted area. The statute, rule or ordinance shall exempt any building used for public housing by private persons, highways or rest areas, firing ranges, and private dwellings owned, leased, or controlled by that unit of government from any restriction on the carrying or possession of a firearm. The statute, rule or ordinance shall not specify any criminal penalty ... but may specify that persons violating ... may be denied entrance to the building, ordered to leave the building and if employees of the unit of government, be subjected to disciplinary measures for violation .... The provisions of this subdivision shall not apply to any other unit of government;

(7) Any establishment licensed to dispense intoxicating liquor for consumption on the premises, which portion is primarily devoted to that purpose, without the consent of the owner or manager. The provisions of this subdivision shall not apply to the licensee of said establishment. The provisions of this subdivision shall not apply to any bona fide restaurant open to the general public having dining facilities for not less than fifty persons and that receives at least fifty-one percent of its gross annual income from the dining facilities by the sale of food. This subdivision does not prohibit the possession of a firearm in a vehicle on the premises of the establishment...;

(8) Any area of an airport to which access is controlled by the inspection of persons and property.;

(9) Any place where the carrying of a firearm is prohibited by federal law;

(10) Any higher education institution or elementary or secondary school facility without the consent of the governing body of the higher education institution or a school official or the district school board, unless the person with the concealed carry endorsement or permit is a teacher or administrator of an elementary or secondary school who has been designated by his or her school district as a school protection officer and is carrying a firearm in a school within that district, in which case no consent is required.;

(11) Any portion of a building used as a child care facility without the consent of the manager...;

(12) Any riverboat gambling operation accessible by the public without the consent of the owner or manager pursuant to rules promulgated by the gaming commission.;

(13) Any gated area of an amusement park.;

(14) Any church or other place of religious worship without the consent of the minister.... Possession of a firearm in a vehicle on the premises shall not be a criminal offense so long as the firearm is not removed...;

(15) Any private property whose owner has posted the premises as being off-limits to concealed firearms by means of one or more signs displayed in a conspicuous place of a minimum size of eleven inches by fourteen inches with the writing thereon in letters of not less than one inch. The owner...may prohibit persons holding a concealed carry permit or endorsement from carrying concealed firearms on the premises and may prohibit employees, not authorized by the employer, holding a concealed carry permit or endorsement from carrying concealed firearms on the property of the employer. If the building or the premises are open to the public, the employer of the business enterprise shall post signs on or about the premises if carrying a concealed firearm is prohibited...An employer may prohibit employees or other persons holding a concealed carry permit or endorsement from carrying a concealed firearm in vehicles owned by the employer;

(16) Any sports arena or stadium with a seating capacity of five thousand or more.;

(17) Any hospital accessible by the public...;

Contact for Additional Information:

Attorney General of Missouri
P.O. Box 899 • Jefferson City, MO 65102
573-751-3321

MONTANA FIREARM FRIENDLY:

Permit Holders

Permit: "Shall issue" to residents only.

Open Carry: Generally permitted in all areas not specifically prohibiting firearms.

Travel: Montana has no prohibitions against carrying a weapon in a motor vehicle. Montana forbids carrying firearms on a train.

Disclose Presence of Handgun to Law Enforcement: Only required if requested by officer

Restaurants: May carry unless establishment has posted signs noting otherwise. May not carry concealed in any establishment in which alcoholic beverages are sold, dispensed, and consumed on the premises.

Recognizes Permits From: AL, AK, AR, AZ, CA, CO, CT, FL, GA, ID, IL, IN, IA, KS, KY, LA, MA, MD, MI, MN, MO, MS, NC, ND, NE, NJ, NM, NV, NY, OH, OK, OR, PA, SC, SD, TN, TX, UT, VA, WA, WV, WI, WY

Non-Permit

Firearms Ownership: Permitted to all law abiding citizens without license or permit.

Loaded Carry: Generally, law-abiding citizens 14 years of age or older may openly carry a loaded firearm in public, openly without a permit. Citizens may carry concealed without a permit while lawfully engaged in hunting, fishing, trapping, camping, hiking, backpacking, farming, ranching, or other outdoor activity in which weapons are often carried for recreation or protection. Generally, citizens may carry concealed if they are outside the official boundaries of a city or town or the confines of a logging, lumbering, mining, or railroad camp.

Travel: Montana makes no prohibitions against carrying weapons in a motor vehicle. Montana forbids carrying firearms on a train.

General Info

State Parks: Permitted with exceptions in certain posted buildings.

Carry Law Uniformity: Generally, state law preempts that of local agencies/ municipalities. For public safety purposes, however, a county, city, town, or any local government unit has power prevent or repress concealed or open carry of weapons in specific public areas or buildings and may place additional restrictions on felons, the mentally ill, illegal aliens, and minors.

Self-Defense Model: Castle Doctrine, Stand Your Ground, No Duty to Retreat.

Notes: Postings forbidding firearms on private property do not have force of law. No weapons are allowed in school buildings in Montana. National parks in Montana are now governed by Montana state laws with respect to concealed and open carry of a firearm. Even with a permit, concealed weapons are not permitted in federal, state, or local government buildings, financial institutions, or any place where alcoholic beverages are sold, dispensed, and consumed. For residents, permits can be obtained in the county of permanent residence and issued by the sheriff of that county.

Montana Code Annotated § 45-8-327. Carrying concealed weapon while under influence. A person commits the offense of carrying a concealed weapon while under the influence if the person purposely or knowingly carries a concealed weapon while under the influence of an intoxicating substance. It is not a defense that the person had a valid permit to carry a concealed weapon. A person convicted of the offense shall be imprisoned in the county jail for a term not to exceed 6 months or be fined an amount not to exceed $500, or both.

§ 45-8-328. Carrying concealed weapon in prohibited place -- penalty. (1) Except for legislative security officers authorized to carry a concealed weapon in the state capitol as provided in 45-8-317(1)(k), a person commits the offense of carrying a concealed weapon in a prohibited place if the person purposely or knowingly carries a concealed weapon in: (a) portions of a building used for state or local government offices and related areas in the building that have been restricted; (b) a bank, credit union, savings and loan institution, or similar institution during the institution's normal business hours. It is not an offense under this section to carry a concealed weapon while: (i) using an institution's drive-up window, automatic teller machine, or unstaffed night depository; or (ii) at or near a branch office of an institution in a mall, grocery store, or other place unless the person is inside the enclosure used for the institution's financial services or is using the institution's financial services. (c) a room in which alcoholic beverages are sold, dispensed, and consumed under a license issued under Title 16 for the sale of alcoholic beverages for consumption on the premises.

(2) It is not a defense that the person had a valid permit to carry a concealed weapon. A person convicted of the offense shall be imprisoned in the county jail for a term not to exceed 6 months or fined an amount not to exceed $500, or both.

§ 45-8-351. Restriction on local government regulation of firearms. (1) Except as provided in subsection (2), a county, city, town, consolidated local government, or other local government unit may not prohibit, register, tax, license, or regulate the purchase, sale or other transfer (including delay in purchase, sale, or other transfer), ownership, possession, transportation, use, or unconcealed carrying of any weapon, including a rifle, shotgun, handgun, or concealed handgun.

(2) (a) For public safety purposes, a city or town may regulate the discharge of rifles, shotguns, and handguns. A county, city, town, consolidated local government, or other local government unit has power to prevent and suppress the carrying of concealed or unconcealed weapons to a public assembly, publicly owned building, park under its jurisdiction, or school, and the possession of firearms by convicted felons, adjudicated mental incompetents, illegal aliens, and minors. (b) Nothing contained in this section allows any government to prohibit the legitimate display of firearms at shows or other public occasions by collectors and others or to prohibit the legitimate transportation of firearms through any jurisdiction, whether in airports or otherwise. (c) A local ordinance enacted pursuant to this section may not prohibit a legislative security officer who has been issued a concealed weapon permit from carrying a concealed weapon in the state capitol as provided in 45-8-317.

MONTANA

§ 45-8-361. Possession or allowing possession of weapon in school building -- exceptions -- penalties -- seizure and forfeiture or return authorized -- definitions. (1) A person commits the offense of possession of a weapon in a school building if the person purposely and knowingly possesses, carries, or stores a weapon in a school building.

(2) A parent or guardian of a minor commits the offense of allowing possession of a weapon in a school building if the parent or guardian purposely and knowingly permits the minor to possess, carry, or store a weapon in a school building.

(3) (a) Subsection (1) does not apply to law enforcement personnel. (b) The trustees of a district may grant persons and entities advance permission to possess, carry, or store a weapon in a school building.

(4) (a) A person convicted under this section shall be fined an amount not to exceed $500, imprisoned in the county jail for a term not to exceed 6 months, or both. The court shall consider alternatives to incarceration that are available in the community. (b) (i) A weapon in violation of this section may be seized and, upon conviction of the person possessing or permitting possession of the weapon, may be forfeited to the state or returned to the lawful owner. (ii) If a weapon seized under the provisions of this section is subsequently determined to have been stolen or otherwise taken from the owner's possession without permission, the weapon must be returned to the lawful owner.

(5) As used in this section: (a) "school building" means all buildings owned or leased by a local school district that are used for instruction or for student activities. The term does not include a home school provided for in 20-5-109. (b) "weapon" means any type of firearm, a knife with a blade 4 or more inches in length, a sword, a straight razor, a throwing star, nun-chucks, or brass or other metal knuckles. The term also includes any other article or instrument possessed with the purpose to commit a criminal offense.

Contact for Additional Information:

Montana Department of Justice
Division of Criminal Investigation
22225 11th Avenue / P.O. Box 201417
Helena, MT 59620
406-444-3874

FIREARM FRIENDLY: B NEBRASKA

Permit: "Shall issue" state. Law only pertains to carrying concealed handguns.

Open Carry: Generally permitted, but local agencies may regulate.

Travel: Concealed handguns may be transported in a vehicle or on the person. NE prohibits loaded shotguns in vehicles.

Disclose Presence of Handgun to Law Enforcement: Must inform officer of the concealed handgun immediately upon making contact.

Restaurants: May carry if establishment earns less than 50% of its revenue from alcohol sales.

Recognizes Permits From: AK, AZ, AR, CO, CT, DC, FL, HI, ID, IL, KS, KY, LA, MI, MN, MO, NV, NJ, NM, NC, ND (class 1), OH, OK, OR, RI, SC, TN, UT, VA, WI, WY

**Also, these states if carrier is 21 years of age: CA, ME, MT, ND (class 2), TX*

Firearms Ownership: Permitted to all citizens without license or permit, but must obtain a certificate to purchase a handgun.

Loaded Carry: May open carry a loaded firearm in public in most areas, but local agencies may regulate. Must have a permit to conceal. Lincoln and Omaha require a permit to open carry.

Travel: Firearms are permissible in a vehicle as long as they are clearly visible. Firearms may not be concealed without a permit. NE prohibits loaded shotguns in vehicles.

State Parks: Permitted, but with some restrictions.

Carry Law Uniformity: State law preempts that of local agencies/municipalities enacted after September 1991; however, local agencies may ban the open carry of handguns.

Self-Defense Model: Duty to Retreat.

Notes: Firearms are not permitted on any school grounds or in any school buildings. Signs prohibiting firearms in establishments have the force of law. The legal obligation for a carrier to immediately notify law enforcement personnel of possession of a concealed firearm also applies to emergency services personnel; similarly, just like law enforcement personnel, emergency services personnel have the right to disarm a carrier out of concerns for safety.

Contact for Additional Information:

Nebraska State Patrol Criminal Investigation Division (CID)
3800 Northwest 12th Street • Lincoln, NE 68521
402-479-4971

Nebraska Revised Statutes § 69-2425. City or village ordinance; not preempted. Any city or village ordinance existing on September 6, 1991, shall not be preempted by sections 69-2401 to 69-2425.

§ 69-2440. Permitholder; duties; contact with peace officer or emergency services personnel; procedures for securing handgun.

(1) A permitholder shall carry his or her permit to carry a concealed handgun and his or her Nebraska driver's license, Nebraska-issued state identification card, or military identification card any time he or she carries a concealed handgun. The permitholder shall display both ... when asked to do so by a peace officer or by emergency services personnel.

(2) Whenever a permitholder who is carrying a concealed handgun is contacted by a peace officer or by emergency services personnel, the permitholder shall immediately inform the peace officer or emergency services personnel that the permitholder is carrying a concealed handgun.

(3)(a) During contact with a permitholder, a peace officer or emergency services personnel may secure the handgun or direct that it be secured during the duration of the contact if the peace officer or emergency services personnel determines that it is necessary for the safety of any person present, including the peace officer or emergency services personnel. The permitholder shall submit to the order to secure the handgun.

(b)(i) When the peace officer has determined that the permitholder is not a threat to the safety of any person present, including the peace officer, and the permitholder has not committed any other violation that would result in his or her arrest or the suspension or revocation of his or her permit, the peace officer shall return the handgun to the permitholder before releasing the permitholder from the scene and breaking contact.

(ii) When emergency services personnel have determined that the permitholder is not a threat to the safety of any person present, including emergency services personnel, and if the permitholder is physically and mentally capable of possessing the handgun, the emergency services personnel shall return the handgun to the permitholder before releasing the permitholder from the scene and breaking contact. If the permitholder is transported for treatment to another location, the handgun shall be turned over to any peace officer. The peace officer shall provide a receipt which includes the make, model, caliber, and serial number of the handgun.

(4) For purposes of this section, contact with a peace officer means any time a peace officer personally stops, detains, questions, or addresses a permitholder for an official purpose or in the course of his or her official duties, and contact with

with emergency services personnel means any time emergency services personnel provide treatment to a permitholder in the course of their official duties.

§ 69-2441. Permitholder; locations; restrictions; posting of prohibition; consumption of alcohol; prohibited.

(1)(a) A permitholder may carry a concealed handgun anywhere in Nebraska, except any: Police, sheriff, or Nebraska State Patrol station or office; detention facility, prison, or jail; courtroom or building which contains a courtroom; polling place during a bona fide election; meeting of the governing body of a county, public school district, municipality, or other political subdivision; meeting of the Legislature or a committee of the Legislature; financial institution; professional or semiprofessional athletic event; building, grounds, vehicle, or sponsored activity or athletic event of any public, private, denominational, or parochial elementary, vocational, or secondary school, a private postsecondary career school as defined in section 85-1603, a community college, or a public or private college, junior college, or university; place of worship; hospital, emergency room, or trauma center; political rally or fundraiser; establishment having a license issued under the Nebraska Liquor Control Act that derives over one-half of its total income from the sale of alcoholic liquor; place where the possession or carrying of a firearm is prohibited by state or federal law; a place or premises where the person, persons, entity, or entities in control of the property or employer in control of the property has prohibited permitholders from carrying concealed handguns into or onto the place or premises; or into or onto any other place or premises where handguns are prohibited by state law....

...(2) If a person, persons, entity, or entities in control of the property or an employer in control of the property prohibits a permitholder from carrying a concealed handgun into or onto the place or premises and such place or premises are open to the public, a permitholder does not violate this section unless the person, persons, entity, or entities in control of the property or employer in control of the property has posted conspicuous notice that carrying a concealed handgun is prohibited in or on the place or premises or has made a request, directly or through an authorized representative or management personnel, that the permitholder remove the concealed handgun from the place or premises.

(3) A permitholder carrying a concealed handgun in a vehicle or on his or her person while riding in or on a vehicle into or onto any parking area, which is open to the public, used by any location listed in subdivision (1)(a) of this section, does not violate this section if, prior to exiting the vehicle, the handgun is locked inside the glove box, trunk, or other compartment of the vehicle, a storage box securely attached to the vehicle, or, if the vehicle is a motorcycle, a hardened compartment securely attached to the motorcycle. This subsection

does not apply to any parking area used by such location when the carrying of a concealed handgun into or onto such parking area is prohibited by federal law.

(4) An employer may prohibit employees or other persons who are permitholders from carrying concealed handguns in vehicles owned by the employer.

(5) A permitholder shall not carry a concealed handgun while he or she is consuming alcohol or while the permitholder has remaining in his or her blood, urine, or breath any previously consumed alcohol or any controlled substance as defined in section 28-401. A permitholder does not violate this subsection if the controlled substance in his or her blood, urine, or breath was lawfully obtained and was taken in therapeutically prescribed amounts.

FIREARM FRIENDLY:   NEVADA

Permit: "Shall issue" state.

Open Carry: Permit holders are forbidden from open carry in public, unless hunting.

Travel: Permit holders must conceal firearms while they are in the vehicle.

Disclose Presence of Handgun to Law Enforcement: Only required if requested by officer.

Restaurants: May carry in bars and restaurants unless posted.

Recognizes Permits From: AK, AZ, AR, DE, FL, IL, KS, KY, LA, MA, MI, MN, MT, NE, NC, ND, OH, OK, RI, SC, SD, TN, TX, UT, VA, WV, WI, WY

Firearm Ownership: Permitted to all citizens without license or permit; Las Vegas is an exception and requires registration of firearms by new residents within three days of arrival.

Loaded Carry: Open carry is permissible in most jurisdictions, but some have banned it (see Las Vegas).

Travel: Traveling with a loaded firearm is permissible, but the firearm must be in a compartment of the vehicle, such as a glove box or trunk. Las Vegas is an exception to this rule. Long guns may be in the vehicle if the carrier is over 18, but no round may be in the chamber; if the carrier is under 18, the long arm must be completely unloaded.

State Parks: Only permit holders.

Carry Law Uniformity: Local jurisdictions may promulgate gun restrictions that apply only within their borders. North Las Vegas, for instance, bans all carry, irrespective of permit status.

Self-Defense Model: No Castle Doctrine, Stand Your Ground; justifiable homicide law permits defense of self or others in your presence as long as you are in a place where you may lawfully be.

Notes: Carriers may consume alcohol but may not consume to the point of legal intoxication, which is a blood alcohol content of 0.10. Posts forbidding firearms on private property have the force of law, and violation is punishable as an A misdemeanor; establishments must post at every entrance open to the public. Firearms are not permitted on any campus under the authority of the Nevada system of higher education.

Contact for Additional Information:

Nevada Department of Public Safety
55 Wright Way • Carson City, NV 89711
775-684-4808

NEVADA

Nevada Administrative Code 202.020 Application for permit. (Nevada Revised Statutes 202.369)

1. In addition to the requirements of subsection 2, the application form for a permit to carry a concealed firearm must contain the following sections, which must be in substantially the following form:

GENERAL INFORMATION

The sheriff shall issue or renew a permit to carry a concealed firearm for no more than two specific firearms to any person who is qualified to possess a firearm under state and federal law.

A permittee shall carry the permit together with proper identification whenever he or she is in actual possession of a concealed firearm. Both the permit and proper identification must be presented to a peace officer upon request.

Except as otherwise provided in NRS 202.265 and subsections 2 and 3 of NRS 202.3673, a permittee shall not carry a concealed firearm into:

1. Any facility of a law enforcement agency;

2. A prison, county or city jail or detention facility;

3. A courthouse or courtroom;

4. Any facility of a public or private school;

5. Any facility of a vocational or technical school, or of the Nevada System of Higher Education;

6. Any other building owned or occupied by the Federal Government, the State or a local government; or

7. Any other place in which the carrying of a concealed firearm is prohibited by state or federal law.

Unless suspended or revoked by the sheriff, a permit expires on the fifth anniversary of the permittee's birthday, measured from the birthday nearest the date of issuance or renewal. If the date of birth of a permittee is on February 29 in a leap year, for the purposes of NRS 202.3653 to 202.369, inclusive, his or her date of birth shall be deemed to be on February 28.

A permittee shall notify the sheriff who issued the permit, in writing, within 30 days if his or her permanent address changes or if the permit is lost, stolen or destroyed.

ELIGIBILITY

The sheriff shall conduct an investigation of an applicant, including a check of the applicant's fingerprints, to determine if the person is eligible for a permit.

Except as otherwise provided in NRS 202.3657, a person is eligible to carry a concealed firearm if he or she:

1. Is a resident of the State of Nevada and of the county in which the permit is sought;

2. Is 21 years of age or older;

3. Is not prohibited from possessing a firearm pursuant to NRS 202.360; and

4. Demonstrates competence with a firearm by presenting a certificate or other documentation which shows that the applicant has successfully completed a course approved by the sheriff, or successfully completed a course in firearm safety offered by a federal, state or local law enforcement agency, community college, university or national organization that certifies instructors in firearm safety. Any such course must include instruction in the use of each firearm to which the application pertains and in the laws of the State of Nevada relating to the proper use of a firearm.

The sheriff shall deny an application or revoke a permit to carry a concealed firearm if the sheriff determines that the applicant or permittee:

1. Has an outstanding warrant for his or her arrest.

2. Has been judicially declared incompetent or insane.

3. Has been voluntarily or involuntarily admitted to a mental health facility during the immediately preceding 5 years.

4. Has been habitually using intoxicating liquor or a controlled substance to the extent that his or her normal faculties are impaired. Such use is presumed if, during the immediately preceding 5 years, the applicant or permittee has been convicted of driving under the influence of intoxicating liquor or a controlled substance pursuant to NRS 484C.110, or has been ordered by a court to enter a program for treatment of drug or alcohol abuse pursuant to NRS 458.290 to 458.350, inclusive.

5. Has been convicted of a crime involving the use or threatened use of force or violence punishable as a misdemeanor under the laws

of this State or any other state, territory or possession of the United States at any time during the immediately preceding 3 years.

6. Has been convicted of a felony in this State or under the laws of any state, territory or possession of the United States.

7. Has been convicted of a crime involving domestic violence or stalking, or is currently subject to a restraining order, injunction or other order for protection against domestic violence.

8. Is currently on parole or probation from a conviction obtained in this State or in any other state or territory or possession of the United States.

9. Has, within the immediately preceding 5 years, been subject to any requirements imposed by a court of this State or any other state or territory or possession of the United States, as a condition to the court's withholding the entry of judgment for a conviction of a felony or the court's suspending a sentence for the conviction of a felony.

10. Has made a false statement on any application for a permit or for the renewal of a permit.

The sheriff may deny an application or revoke a permit if he or she receives a sworn affidavit stating articulable facts based upon personal knowledge from any natural person who is 18 years of age or older that the applicant or permittee has or may have committed an offense or engaged in any other activity specified in subsection 3 of NRS 202.3657 which would preclude the issuance of a permit to the applicant or require the revocation of a permit pursuant to NRS 202.3657....

FIREARM FRIENDLY: A NEW HAMPSHIRE

Permit: "Shall issue" state.

Open Carry: Generally permitted.

Travel: Loaded pistols or revolvers may be transported in a vehicle with a permit. Long guns must be unloaded.

Disclose Presence of Handgun to Law Enforcement: Not required.

Restaurants: May carry in establishments that do not have posted signs noting otherwise and as long as alcohol is not consumed.

Recognizes Permits From: AL, AK, AZ, AR, CO, FL, GA, ID, IN, IA, KS, KY, LA, ME, MI, MO, MS, NC, ND, OH, OK, PA, SD, TN, UT, VA, WV, WY

**NH only recognizes these permits if the carrier is 21 years of age or older.*

Permit Holders

Firearm Ownership: Permitted to all law abiding citizens without license or permit.

Loaded Carry: Generally, citizens over 21 years of age may carry a loaded firearm in public openly. Concealed carry requires a permit. Non-permit holders may not carry loaded firearms in a vehicle.

Travel: Firearms must be unloaded to carry in a vehicle without a permit.

Non-Permit

State Parks: Permitted.

Carry Law Uniformity: State law preempts that of local agencies/municipalities.

Self-Defense Model: Stand Your Ground, No Duty to Retreat.

Notes: NH issues concealed carry pistol/revolver permits to residents and non-residents. "No Guns" signs are enforceable by law.

General Info

New Hampshire Revised Statutes Annotated Title XII Public Safety and Welfare § 159:4 Carrying Without License. –

No person shall carry a loaded pistol or revolver in any vehicle or concealed upon his person, except in his dwelling, house or place of business, without a valid license therefor as hereinafter provided. A loaded pistol or revolver shall include any pistol or revolver with a magazine, cylinder, chamber or clip in which there are loaded cartridges. Whoever violates the provisions of this section shall, for the first such offense, be guilty of a misdemeanor. For the second and for each subsequent violation of the provisions of this section, such person shall be guilty of a class B felony, provided such second or subsequent violation has occurred within 7 years of the previous conviction.

§159:19 Courthouse Security. –

I. No person shall knowingly carry a loaded or unloaded pistol, revolver, or firearm or any other deadly weapon as defined in RSA 625:11, V, whether open or concealed or whether licensed or unlicensed, upon the person or within any of the person's possessions owned or within the person's control in a courtroom or area used by a court. Whoever violates the provisions of this paragraph shall be guilty of a class B felony.

II. Firearms may be secured at the entrance to a courthouse by courthouse security personnel.

III. For purposes of paragraph I, "area used by a court" means:

(a) In a building dedicated exclusively to court use, the entire building exclusive of the area between the entrance and the courthouse security.

(b) In any other building which includes a court facility, courtrooms, jury assembly rooms, deliberation rooms, conference and interview rooms, the judge's chambers, other court staff facilities, holding facilities, and corridors, stairways, waiting areas, and elevators directly connecting these rooms and facilities.

IV. The provisions of this section shall not apply to marshals, sheriffs, deputy sheriffs, police or other duly appointed or elected law enforcement officers, bailiffs and court security officers, or persons with prior authorization of the court for the purpose of introducing weapons into evidence and as otherwise provided for in RSA 159:5.

V. It shall be an affirmative defense to any prosecution under paragraph I that there was no notice of the provisions of paragraph I posted in a conspicuous place at each public entrance to the court building.

Contact for Additional Information:

Department of Safety
Division of State Police
Permits and Licensing Unit
33 Hazen Drive • Concord, NH 03305
603-223-3873

FIREARM FRIENDLY: F NEW JERSEY

Permit: "May issue" state.

Open Carry: Forbidden.

Travel: Permissible but must be concealed.

Disclose Presence of Handgun to Law Enforcement: Required only if requested by officer.

Restaurants: Permissible, unless posted.

Recognizes Permits From: No states.

Permit Holders

Firearm Ownership: No person may even hold a handgun without first acquiring a permit to carry.

Loaded Carry: Forbidden.

Travel: For carriers who travel through NJ, firearms must be in compliance with federal law (unloaded, with neither firearm nor ammunition accessible to the passenger compartment or, if no rear compartment, in a locked container other than a glove box or console). For carriers who travel within NJ, firearms should be unloaded, in a closed container or locked in the trunk with the ammunition stored in a separate container and locked in the trunk; if there is no trunk, the firearm and ammunition must be locked in a container other than a glove box or console.

Non-Permit

State Parks: Forbidden.

Carry Law Uniformity: Localities and municipalities may enact stricter carry laws than the state.

Self-Defense Model: Duty to Retreat in public, Castle Doctrine with threat of death or serious bodily injury.

Notes: NJ has some of the strictest firearms laws in the country, and they are extremely strictly enforced. Permits are only issued with a showing of justifiable need, and in some jurisdictions, even require the signatures of a prosecutor, a judge, AND a chief of police. Issuing judges may limit the type of permit issued as to type of handgun and where and for what purpose they may be carried. If traveling to NJ, be aware there are also requirements for permits to be in place before transferring or receiving ammunition through any means. Firearms are forbidden at any learning institution of any level and at casinos.

General Info

Contact for Additional Information:

New Jersey State Police
P.O. Box 7068 • W. Trenton, NJ 08628
609-882-2000

New Jersey Administrative Code § 13:54-2.2 Permit required.

No person, except as provided in N.J.S.A. 2C:39-6, shall carry, hold or possess a handgun without first having obtained a permit to carry the same in accordance with the provisions of this chapter.

New Jersey Revised Statutes § 2C:39-5 Unlawful possession of weapons.

...b. Handguns. Any person who knowingly has in his possession any handgun, including any antique handgun, without first having obtained a permit to carry the same as provided in N.J.S.2C:58-4, is guilty of a crime of the third degree if the handgun is in the nature of an air gun, spring gun or pistol or other weapon of a similar nature in which the propelling force is a spring, elastic band, carbon dioxide, compressed or other gas or vapor, air or compressed air, or is ignited by compressed air, and ejecting a bullet or missile smaller than three-eighths of an inch in diameter, with sufficient force to injure a person. Otherwise it is a crime of the second degree....

... e. Firearms or other weapons in educational institutions.

(1) Any person who knowingly has in his possession any firearm in or upon any part of the buildings or grounds of any school, college, university or other educational institution, without the written authorization of the governing officer of the institution, is guilty of a crime of the third degree, irrespective of whether he possesses a valid permit to carry the firearm or a valid firearms purchaser identification card....

§ 2C:39-6 Exemptions.

a. Provided a person complies with the requirements of subsection j. of this section, N.J.S.2C:39-5 does not apply to:

(1) Members of the Armed Forces;

(2) Federal law enforcement officers;

(3) Members of the State Police;

(4) A sheriff, undersheriff, sheriff's officer, county prosecutor, assistant prosecutor, prosecutor's detective or investigator, deputy attorney general or State investigator employed by the Division of Criminal Justice of the Department of Law and Public Safety, investigator employed by the State Commission of Investigation, inspector of the Alcoholic Beverage Control Enforcement Bureau of the Division of State Police in the Department of Law and Public Safety authorized to carry such weapons by the Superintendent of State Police, State park police officer, or State conservation officer;

(5) ... warden of any penal institution in this State or his deputies, or an employee of the Department of Corrections;

(6) A civilian employee of the United States Government...;

(7) (a) A regularly employed member, including a detective, of the police department...;

(b) A special law enforcement officer authorized to carry a weapon...;

(c) An airport security officer or a special law enforcement officer appointed by the governing body of any county or municipality, except as provided in subsection (b) of this section, or by the commission, board or other body having control of a county park or airport or boulevard police force, while engaged in the actual performance of his official duties and when specifically authorized by the governing body to carry weapons;

(8) A full-time, paid member of a paid or part-paid fire department or force of any

...municipality who is assigned full-time or part-time to an arson investigation unit ...;

(9) A juvenile corrections officer...;

(10) A designated employee or designated licensed agent for a nuclear power plant under license of the Nuclear Regulatory Commission, while in the actual performance of his official duties...;

(11) A county corrections officer... ;

... e. Nothing in subsections b., c. and d. of N.J.S.2C:39-5 shall be construed to prevent a person keeping or carrying about his place of business, residence, premises or other land owned or possessed by him, any firearm, or from carrying the same, in the manner specified in subsection g. of this section, from any place of purchase to his residence or place of business, between his dwelling and his place of business, between one place of business or residence and another when moving, or between his dwelling or place of business and place where such firearms are repaired, for the purpose of repair...

f. Nothing in subsections b., c. and d. of N.J.S.2C:39-5 shall be construed to prevent:

(1) A member of any rifle or pistol club organized in accordance with the rules prescribed by the National Board for the Promotion of Rifle Practice, in going to or from a place of target practice, carrying such firearms as are necessary for said target practice,...;

(2) A person carrying a firearm...for the purpose of hunting, target practice or fishing, provided that the firearm...is legal and appropriate for hunting ...and he has in his possession a valid hunting license,...;

(3) A person transporting any firearm or knife while traveling:

(a) Directly to or from any place for the purpose of hunting or fishing...

(b) Directly to or from any target range, or other authorized place for the purpose of practice, match, target, trap or skeet shooting exhibitions,...; or

(c) In the case of a firearm, directly to or from any exhibition or display of firearms which is sponsored by any law enforcement agency, any rifle or pistol club, or any firearms collectors club, for the purpose of displaying the firearms to the public or to the members of the organization or club,...

...(g). All weapons being transported under paragraph (2) of subsection b., subsection e., or paragraph (1) or (3) of subsection f. of this section shall be carried unloaded and contained in a closed and fastened case, gunbox, securely tied package, or locked in the trunk of the automobile in which it is being transported, and in the course of travel shall include only such deviations as are reasonably necessary under the circumstances....

§ 2C:39-7 Certain persons not to have weapons.

6. Certain Persons Not to Have Weapons.

a. Except as provided in subsection b. of this section, any person, having been convicted in this State or elsewhere of the crime of aggravated assault, arson, burglary, escape, extortion, homicide, kidnapping, robbery, aggravated sexual assault, sexual assault, bias intimidation in violation of N.J.S.2C:16-1 or endangering the welfare of a child pursuant to N.J.S.2C:24-4, whether or not armed with or having in his possession any weapon enumerated in subsection r. of N.J.S.2C:39-1, or any person convicted of a crime pursuant to the provisions of N.J.S.2C:39-3, N.J.S.2C:39-4 or N.J.S.2C:39-9, or any person who has ever been committed for a mental disorder to any hospital, mental institution or sanitarium unless he possesses a certificate of a medical doctor or psychiatrist licensed to practice in New Jersey or other satisfactory proof that he is no longer suffering from a mental disorder which interferes with or handicaps him in the handling of a firearm, or any person who has been convicted of other than a disorderly persons or petty disorderly persons offense for the unlawful use, possession or sale of a controlled dangerous substance as defined in N.J.S.2C:35-2 who purchases, owns, possesses or controls any of the said weapons is guilty of a crime of the fourth degree.

... (b)(2) A person having been convicted in this State or elsewhere of a disorderly persons offense involving domestic violence...who purchases, owns, possesses or controls a firearm is guilty of a crime of the third degree.

...c. Whenever any person shall have been convicted in another state, territory, commonwealth or other jurisdiction of the United States, or any country in the world, in a court of competent jurisdiction, of a crime which in said other jurisdiction or country is comparable to one of the crimes enumerated in subsection a. or b. of this section, then that person shall be subject to the provisions of this section.

§ 2C:39-9 Manufacture, transport, disposition and defacement of weapons and dangerous instruments and appliances.

... f. (1) Any person who manufactures, causes to be manufactured, transports, ships, sells, or disposes of any bullet, which is primarily designed for use in a handgun, and which is comprised of a bullet whose core or jacket, if the jacket is thicker than .025 of an inch, is made of tungsten carbide, or hard bronze, or other material which is harder than a rating of 72 or greater on the Rockwell B. Hardness Scale, and is therefore capable of breaching or penetrating body armor and which is intended to be used for any purpose other than for authorized military or law enforcement purposes by duly authorized military or law enforcement personnel, is guilty of a crime of the fourth degree.

(2) Nothing in this subsection shall be construed to prevent a licensed collector of ammunition as defined in paragraph (2) of subsection f. of N.J.S.2C:39-3 from transporting the bullets defined in paragraph (1) of this subsection from (a) any licensed retail or wholesale firearms dealer's place of business to the collector's dwelling, premises, or other land owned or possessed by him, or (b) to or from the collector's dwelling, premises or other land owned or possessed by him to any gun show for the purposes of display, sale, trade, or transfer between collectors, or (c) to or from the collector's dwelling, premises or other land owned or possessed by him to any rifle or pistol club organized in accordance with the rules prescribed by the National Board for the Promotion of Rifle Practice; provided that the club has filed a copy of its charter with the superintendent of the State Police and annually submits a list of its members to the superintendent, and provided further that the ammunition being transported shall be carried not loaded in any firearm and contained in a closed and fastened case, gun box, or locked in the trunk of the automobile in which it is being transported, and the course of travel shall include only such deviations as are reasonably necessary under the circumstances.

g. Assault firearms. Any person who manufactures, causes to be manufactured, transports, ships, sells or disposes of an assault firearm without being registered or licensed to do so pursuant to N.J.S.2C:58-1 et seq. is guilty of a crime of the third degree.

h. Large capacity ammunition magazines. Any person who manufactures, causes to be manufactured, transports, ships, sells or disposes of a large capacity ammunition magazine which is intended to be used for any purpose other than for authorized military or law enforcement purposes by duly authorized military or law enforcement personnel is guilty of a crime of the fourth degree.

i. Transporting firearms into this State for an unlawful sale or transfer. Any person who knowingly transports, ships or otherwise brings into this State any firearm for the purpose of unlawfully selling, transferring, giving, assigning or otherwise disposing of that firearm to another individual is guilty of a crime of the second degree. Any motor vehicle used by a person to transport, ship, or otherwise bring a firearm into this State for unlawful sale or transfer shall be subject to forfeiture in accordance with the provisions of N.J.S.2C:64-1 et seq.; provided however, this forfeiture provision shall not apply to innocent owners, nor shall it affect the rights of a holder of a valid lien.

The temporary transfer of a firearm shall not constitute a violation of this subsection if that firearm is transferred:

(1) while hunting or target shooting in accordance with the provisions of section 1 of P.L.1992, c.74 (C.2C:58-3.1);

(2) for shooting competitions sponsored by a licensed dealer, law enforcement agency, legally recognized military organization, or a rifle or pistol club which has filed a copy of its charter with the superintendent in accordance with the provisions of section 1 of P.L.1992, c.74 (C.2C:58-3.1); or

(3) for participation in a training course conducted by a certified instructor in accordance with the provisions of section 1 of P.L.1997, c.375 (C.2C:58-3.2)....

§ 2C:58-3.3 "Handgun ammunition" defined; sale, purchase, etc., regulated; violation, fourth degree crime.

...b. No person shall sell, give, transfer, assign or otherwise dispose of, or receive, purchase, or otherwise acquire handgun ammunition unless the purchaser, assignee, donee, receiver or holder is licensed as a manufacturer, wholesaler, or dealer under this chapter or is the holder of and possesses a valid firearms purchaser identification card, a valid copy of a permit to purchase a handgun, or a valid permit to carry a handgun and first exhibits such card or permit to the seller, donor, transferor or assignor.

c. No person shall sell, give, transfer, assign or otherwise dispose of handgun ammunition to a person who is under 21 years of age.

d. The provisions of this section shall not apply to a collector of firearms or ammunition as curios or relics who purchases, receives, acquires, possesses, or transfers handgun ammunition which is recognized as being historical in nature or of historical significance.

e. A person who violates this section shall be guilty of a crime of the fourth degree, except that nothing contained herein shall be construed to prohibit the sale, transfer, assignment or disposition of handgun ammunition to or the purchase, receipt or acceptance of ammunition by a law enforcement agency or law enforcement official for law enforcement purposes...

...g. Nothing in this section shall be construed to prohibit the sale of a de minimis amount of handgun ammunition at a firearms range operated by a licensed dealer; a law enforcement agency; a legally recognized military organization; or a rifle or pistol club which has filed a copy of its charter with the superintendent for immediate use at that range.

NEW MEXICO  FIREARM FRIENDLY: 

Permit Holders

Permit: "Shall issue" state.

Open Carry: Permitted (except in some localities that regulate).

Travel: Loaded handguns may be transported anywhere in a vehicle for self-defense purposes.

Disclose Presence of Handgun to Law Enforcement: Only required if officer requests.

Restaurants: May carry if carrier does not consume alcohol, if restaurant doesn't forbid firearms via a posting, AND if restaurant does not serve liquor (beer/wine service ok).

Recognizes Permits From: AK, AZ, AR, CO, DE, FL, KS, LA, MI, MS, MO, NE, NV, NC, ND, OH, OK, SC, TN, TX, VA, WV, WY

Non-Permit

Firearm Ownership: Permitted to all citizens without license or permit.

Loaded Carry: All citizens over 21 years of age may openly carry a loaded, holstered firearm in public.

Travel: Same as rule above for permit holders.

General Info

State Parks: Permissible only for permit holders.

Carry Law Uniformity: Local agencies/municipalities may not further tighten most state gun law.

Self-Defense Model: No Castle Doctrine, No Duty to Retreat, Stand Your Ground in public.

Notes: Open or concealed firearms may be carried in state buildings as long as the building has not posted otherwise. Concealed weapons are permitted on commuter trains but not on public buses. Carry, open or concealed, is not allowed in any establishment that sells alcohol, whether loaded or not and whether in a case or not; violation is a fourth degree felony. No firearms permitted on Native American reservations even with permit, unless while traveling on a state or federal road that runs through property.

Contact for Additional Information:

New Mexico Department of Public Safety

6301 Indian School Road Northeast Street, Suite 310 • Albuquerque, NM 87110

505-841-8053

New Mexico Administrative Code § 10-8-2-16

TERMS AND CONDITIONS OF LICENSE:

A. Carrying only handguns listed on license. No person shall carry a concealed handgun of a different category or higher caliber than is indicated on the license issued to that person by the department. A licensee shall only carry one (1) concealed handgun at any given time.

B. Consumption of alcohol prohibited. No person shall consume alcohol while carrying a concealed handgun.

C. Carrying while impaired. Pursuant to NMSA 1978 Section 30-7-4, no person shall carry a concealed handgun while impaired by the use of alcohol, controlled substances, or over-the-counter or prescribed medications.

D. Display of license on demand. A licensee carrying a concealed handgun on or about his person in public shall, upon demand by a peace officer, display his license to carry a concealed handgun.

E. Prohibited acts. A licensee shall not deface, alter, mutilate, reproduce, lend, transfer, or sell a license. A licensee shall adhere to NMSA 1978 Section 30-7-4 as it pertains to negligent use of a deadly weapon.

F. Carrying prohibited on private property. In addition to other limitations stated in the act, a licensee may not carry a concealed handgun on or about his person on private property that has signs posted prohibiting the carrying of concealed weapons or when verbally told so by a person lawfully in possession of the property.

G. Carrying prohibited in preschools. As used in Subsection C of NMSA 1978 Section 29-19-8, preschool means a child care facility, whether home-based or center-based, whether or not the facility is licensed, registered, or regulated, that provides care to infants, toddlers, and children aged 5 and younger.

H. Indicia of licensure. No person who is not a law enforcement officer, may carry a badge, patch, card, or any other indication of authority to carry a concealed handgun in New Mexico other than the license issued by the department or a license issued by a state that has been accepted by transfer, recognition or reciprocity by New Mexico pursuant to the act.

I. Notice of change in circumstances. A licensee shall, within 10 calendar days, notify the department in writing of any of the following: (1) adjudication of mental incompetence; (2) commitment to a facility for the treatment of mental illness; (3) commitment to a facility for treatment of addiction to alcohol, controlled substances, or other drugs; (4) issuance of an order of protection by a court; (5) indictment for or charge with a felony or one of the misdemeanor offenses described in Subsection B of NMSA 1978 Section 29-19-4; (6) is no longer a full time salaried law enforcement officer; and (7) is required to turn in the license within 10 calendar days of the change.

NEW YORK

FIREARM FRIENDLY: D

Permit Holders

Permit: "May issue" state.

Open Carry: Permissible in some counties, but not in others; every county enacts its own carry laws.

Travel: Permissible but firearm should be concealed and in direct control and on the person of the carrier; laws for travel are different in New York City.

Disclose Presence of Handgun to Law Enforcement: Only required if requested by the officer.

Restaurants: Permissible to carry in restaurants and bars unless posted.

Recognizes Permits From: No states (but NY does recognize permits issued by New York City).

Non-Permit

Firearm Ownership: Firearms must be registered to be legally owned/possessed.

Loaded Carry: Residents of NY cannot even possess a handgun without a permit, so open carry is forbidden.

Travel: Carriers must comply with federal regulations (unloaded, locked, cased, out of carrier's reach, ammo stored separately).

General Info

State Parks: Forbidden.

Carry Law Uniformity: There is no state law preemption, and counties enact their own respective carry laws. Carriers should take special care when traveling within the state, as there is wide variation county-to-county.

Self-Defense Model: Duty to retreat outside the home; Stand Your Ground inside the home. Force must be authorized, reasonable, and necessary to be justifiable.

Notes: Postings forbidding firearms by private businesses do not carry the force of law; business owners may deny service or admittance, but a carrier is only punishable for a crime in the event a trespass occurs because of a refusal to leave an establishment. Carry permits are issued in New York City by the New York City Police Commissioner, but in all other counties of NY, carry permits are issued by respective county court judges. In NY, one must have a permit to even possess a handgun, and all handguns must be registered. The prohibition against possessing a handgun without a permit is so strictly enforced that stores that sell handguns remove the slides from them before handing them to customers who want to feel the grip of the gun in their hands. The only legal possession of a handgun by a person without a permit occurs when persons aged 14-21 possess handguns at a shooting range under the supervision of an NRA instructor; even at the range under the same instructor's supervision, an adult may not possess a handgun without a permit. New residents who move to NY and seek to register their firearms should be prepared to surrender them to law enforcement in the interim until registration is actually finalized and issued.

NEW YORK

New York Penal Code § 35.15 Justification; use of physical force in defense of a person.

1. A person may, subject to the provisions of subdivision two, use physical force upon another person when and to the extent he or she reasonably believes such to be necessary to defend himself, herself or a third person from what he or she reasonably believes to be the use or imminent use of unlawful physical force by such other person, unless:

(a) The latter's conduct was provoked by the actor with intent to cause physical injury to another person; or

(b) The actor was the initial aggressor; except that in such case the use of physical force is nevertheless justifiable if the actor has withdrawn from the encounter and effectively communicated such withdrawal to such other person but the latter persists in continuing the incident by the use or threatened imminent use of unlawful physical force; or

(c) The physical force involved is the product of a combat by agreement not specifically authorized by law.

2. A person may not use deadly physical force upon another person under circumstances specified in subdivision one unless:

(a) The actor reasonably believes that such other person is using or about to use deadly physical force. Even in such case, however, the actor may not use deadly physical force if he or she knows that with complete personal safety, to oneself and others he or she may avoid the necessity of so doing by retreating; except that the actor is under no duty to retreat if he or she is:

(i) in his or her dwelling and not the initial aggressor; or

(ii) a police officer or peace officer or a person assisting a police officer or a peace officer at the latter's direction, acting pursuant to section 35.30; or

(b) He or she reasonably believes that such other person is committing or attempting to commit a kidnapping, forcible rape, forcible criminal sexual act or robbery; or

(c) He or she reasonably believes that such other person is committing or attempting to commit a burglary, and ... deadly physical force is authorized by subdivision three of section 35.20.

§ 400.00 Licenses to carry, possess, repair, and dispose of firearms

...2. Types of licenses. A license for gunsmith or dealer in firearms shall be issued to engage in such business. A license for a pistol or revolver, other than an assault weapon or a disguised gun, shall be issued to

(a) have and possess in his dwelling by a householder;

(b) have and possess in his place of business by a merchant or storekeeper;

(c) have and carry concealed while so employed by a messenger employed by a banking institution or express company;

(d) have and carry concealed by a justice of the supreme court in the first or second judicial departments, or by a judge of the New York city civil court or the New York city criminal court;

(e) have and carry concealed while so employed by a regular employee of an institution of the state, or of any county, city, town or village, under control of a commissioner of correction of the city or any warden, superintendent or head keeper of any state prison, penitentiary, workhouse, county jail or other institution for the detention of persons convicted or accused of crime or held as witnesses in criminal cases, provided that application is made therefor by such commissioner, warden, superintendent or head keeper;

(f) have and carry concealed, without regard to employment or place of possession, by any person when proper cause exists for the issuance thereof; and

(g) have, possess, collect and carry antique pistols which are defined as follows:

(i) any single shot, muzzle loading pistol with a matchlock, flintlock, percussion cap, or similar type of ignition system manufactured in or before 1898, which is not designed for using rimfire or conventional centerfire fixed ammunition; and

(ii) any replica of any pistol described in clause (i) hereof if such replica--

(1) is not designed or redesigned for using rimfire or conventional centerfire fixed ammunition, or

(2) uses rimfire or conventional centerfire fixed ammunition which is no longer manufactured in the United States and which is not readily available in the ordinary channels of commercial trade.

3. Applications.

(a) Applications shall be made and renewed, in the case of a license to carry or possess a pistol or revolver, to the licensing officer in the city or county, as the case may be, where the applicant resides, is principally employed or has his or her principal place of business as merchant or storekeeper....

... 6. License: validity. Any license issued pursuant to this section shall be valid not withstanding the provisions of any local law or ordinance. No license shall be transferable to any other person or premises. A license to carry or possess a pistol or revolver, not otherwise limited as to place or time of possession, shall be effective throughout the state, except that the same shall not be valid within the city of New York unless a special permit granting validity is issued by the police commissioner of that city. Such license to carry or possess shall be valid within the city of New York in the absence of a permit issued by the police commissioner of that city, provided that

(a) the firearms covered by such license have been purchased from a licensed dealer within the city of New York and are being transported out of said city forthwith and immediately from said dealer by the licensee in a locked container during a continuous and uninterrupted trip; or provided that

(b) the firearms covered by such license are being transported by the licensee in a locked container and the trip through the city of NewYork is continuous and uninterrupted; or provided that

(c) the firearms covered by such license are carried by armored car security guards transporting money or other valuables, in, to, or from motor vehicles commonly known as armored cars, during the course of their employment; or provided that

(d) the licensee is a retired police officer as police officer is defined pursuant to subdivision thirty-four of section 1.20 of the criminal procedure law or a retired federal law enforcement officer, as defined in section 2.15 of the criminal procedure law, who has been issued a license by an authorized licensing officer as defined in subdivision ten of section 265.00 of this chapter; provided, further, however, that if such license was not issued in the city of New York it must be marked "Retired Police Officer" or "Retired Federal Law Enforcement Officer", as the case may be, and, in the case of a retired officer the license shall be deemed to permit only police or federal law enforcement regulations weapons; or provided that

(e) the licensee is a peace officer described in subdivision four of section 2.10 of the criminal procedure law and the license, if issued by other than the city of New York, is marked "New York State Tax Department Peace Officer" and in such case the exemption shall apply only to the firearm issued to such licensee by the department of taxation and finance. A license as gunsmith or dealer in firearms shall not be valid outside the city or county, as the case may be, where issued....

...15. Any violation by any person of any provision of this section is a class A misdemeanor....

Contact for Additional Information:

New York State Police
1220 Washington Avenue, Bldg. 22 • Albany, NY 12226
518-783-3211

NORTH CAROLINA  FIREARM FRIENDLY: 

Permit Holders

Permit: "Shall issue" state.

Open Carry: Permitted except at certain public functions and properties. Certain cities have restrictions.

Travel: Loaded handguns may be transported anywhere in a vehicle for self-defense purposes and may be concealed. Long arms should be transported unloaded in plain view or locked in a trunk, carrying case, or gun rack.

Disclose Presence of Handgun to Law Enforcement: Must immediately inform officer of presence of weapon.

Restaurants: May carry with permit unless posted as prohibited.

Recognizes Permits From: All states.

Non-Permit

Firearm Ownership: Permitted, but must obtain a pistol permit or NC concealed carry permit to purchase or receive a pistol.

Loaded Carry: Open carry permitted in certain areas, but certain cities have a display ban. Concealed carry requires a permit.

Travel: May open carry in a vehicle, but may not conceal. If not openly holstered, handguns must remain in plain view or locked in a case, not readily accessible. The law is somewhat ambiguous about storing a handgun in a glove box or console and is generally discouraged. Long arms must be unloaded and locked in a trunk, carrying case, or gun rack.

General Info

State Parks: Only permit holders.

Carry Law Uniformity: State law preempts that of local agencies/municipalities on most laws. Law is somewhat vague concerning a city's ability to regulate open carry.

Self-Defense Model: Castle Doctrine, No Duty to Retreat in home, workplace, or vehicle.

Notes: Firearms are not permitted in any school or school grounds. All citizens must acquire a pistol permit or possess a NC issued concealed carry permit in order to purchase or receive a pistol. Citizens without a permit should use extreme caution when transporting firearms in NC, as the law is vague on the definition of what is concealed and readily accessible. Concealed and readily accessible firearms are not permitted in a vehicle to non-permit carriers.

Contact for Additional Information:

North Carolina Department of Justice
9001 Mail Service Center • Raleigh, NC 27699
919-716-6400

North Carolina General Statutes § 14-415.11. Permit to carry concealed handgun; scope of permit.

(a) Any person who has a concealed handgun permit may carry a concealed handgun unless otherwise specifically prohibited by law. The person shall carry the permit together with valid identification whenever the person is carrying a concealed handgun, shall disclose to any law enforcement officer that the person holds a valid permit and is carrying a concealed handgun when approached or addressed by the officer, and shall display both the permit and the proper identification upon the request of a law enforcement officer. In addition to these requirements, a military permittee whose permit has expired during deployment may carry a concealed handgun during the 90 days following the end of deployment and before the permit is renewed provided the permittee also displays proof of deployment to any law enforcement officer.

(b) The sheriff shall issue a permit to carry a concealed handgun to a person who qualifies for a permit under G.S. 14-415.12. The permit shall be valid throughout the State for a period of five years from the date of issuance.

(c) Except as provided in G.S. 14-415.27, a permit does not authorize a person to carry a concealed handgun in any of the following:

(1) Areas prohibited by G.S. 14-269.2, 14-269.3, and 14-277.2.

(2) Areas prohibited by G.S. 14-269.4, except as allowed under G.S. 14-269.4(6).

(3) In an area prohibited by rule adopted under G.S. 120-32.1.

(4) In any area prohibited by 18 U.S.C. § 922 or any other federal law.

(5) In a law enforcement or correctional facility.

(6) In a building housing only State or federal offices.

(7) In an office of the State or federal government that is not located in a building exclusively occupied by the State or federal government.

(8) On any private premises where notice that carrying a concealed handgun is prohibited by the posting of a conspicuous notice or statement by the person in legal possession or control of the premises.

(c1) Any person who has a concealed handgun permit may carry a concealed handgun on the grounds or waters of a park within the State Parks System as defined in G.S. 113-44.9.

(c2) It shall be unlawful for a person, with or without a permit, to carry a concealed handgun while consuming alcohol or at any time while the person has remaining in the person's body any alcohol or in the person's blood a controlled substance previously consumed, but a person does not violate this condition if

a controlled substance in the person's blood was lawfully obtained and taken in therapeutically appropriate amounts or if the person is on the person's own property.

(c3) As provided in G.S. 14-269.4(5), it shall be lawful for a person to carry any firearm openly, or to carry a concealed handgun with a concealed carry permit, at any State-owned rest area, at any State-owned rest stop along the highways, and at any State-owned hunting and fishing reservation.

(d) A person who is issued a permit shall notify the sheriff who issued the permit of any change in the person's permanent address within 30 days after the change of address. If a permit is lost or destroyed, the person to whom the permit was issued shall notify the sheriff who issued the permit of the loss or destruction of the permit. A person may obtain a duplicate permit by submitting to the sheriff a notarized statement that the permit was lost or destroyed and paying the required duplicate permit fee.

G. S. § 14-415.21. Violations of this Article punishable as an infraction.

(a) A person who has been issued a valid permit who is found to be carrying a concealed handgun without the permit in the person's possession or who fails to disclose to any law enforcement officer that the person holds a valid permit and is carrying a concealed handgun, as required by G.S. 14-415.11, shall be guilty of an infraction and shall be punished in accordance with G.S. 14-3.1. In lieu of paying a fine the person may surrender the permit.

(a1) A person who has been issued a valid permit who is found to be carrying a concealed handgun in violation of subdivision (c)(8) or subsection (c2) of G.S. 14-415.11 shall be guilty of a Class 1 misdemeanor.

(b) A person who violates the provisions of this Article other than as set forth in subsection (a) or (a1) of this section is guilty of a Class 2 misdemeanor.

NORTH DAKOTA

Permit: "Shall issue" state.

Open Carry: Must conceal unless unloaded.

Travel: Loaded handguns may be transported in a vehicle for self-defense purposes, but they may not be in plain view.

Disclose Presence of Handgun to Law Enforcement: Required only if requested by officer.

Restaurants: May carry in any restaurant or area of a restaurant and bar where children are permitted; any area dedicated to the consumption of alcohol that restricts the entry of children is off limits for carry.

Recognizes Permits From: AL, AK, AZ, AR, CO, DE, FL, GA, ID, IN, IA, KS, KY, LA, ME, MI, MO, MT, NE, NH, NM, NC, OH, OK, PA, SC, SD, TN, TX, UT, VA, WA, WV, WI, WY

Permit Holders

Firearm Ownership: Permitted to all qualified citizens without license or permit.

Loaded Carry: Loaded carry is forbidden, but residents may carry firearms openly during the hours from sunrise to sunset, as long as the firearm is unloaded. Ammunition may also be carried on the carrier's person, but it may not be in the firearm.

Travel: Transport of unloaded firearms is permitted as long as the firearm is fully exposed during the hours from sunrise to sunset or secured in the non-passenger compartment, locked, or disassembled after sunset.

Non-Permit

State Parks: Only if hunting is permitted on the park property.

Carry Law Uniformity: State law preempts that of local agencies/municipalities.

Self-Defense Model: No Castle Doctrine, Duty to Retreat in public.

Notes: Postings forbidding firearms on private property have the force of law, and violations are punishable as misdemeanor criminal charges. The state does not explicitly codify requirements for postings as to size, location, font, etc. Carry is not permitted in bars or package stores, and alcohol consumption is forbidden while carrying. Carry is forbidden at public gatherings like sporting events or concerts and is not allowed in publicly owned or operated buildings.

General Info

Contact for Additional Information:

North Dakota Attorney General,
Bureau of Criminal Investigation
State Capitol, 600 East Boulevard Avenue,
Department 125 • Bismarck, ND 58505
701-328-5500

NORTH DAKOTA

North Dakota Century Code § 62.1-04-01. Definition of concealed. A firearm or dangerous weapon is concealed if it is carried in such a manner as to not be discernible by the ordinary observation of a passerby. There is no requirement that there be absolute invisibility of the firearm or dangerous weapon, merely that it not be ordinarily discernible. A firearm or dangerous weapon is considered concealed if it is not secured, and is worn under clothing or carried in a bundle that is held or carried by the individual, or transported in a vehicle under the individual's control or direction and available to the individual, including beneath the seat or in a glove compartment. A firearm or dangerous weapon is not considered concealed if it is:

1. Carried in a belt holster which is wholly or substantially visible or carried in a case designed for carrying a firearm or dangerous weapon and which is wholly or substantially visible;

2. Locked in a closed trunk or luggage compartment of a motor vehicle;

3. Carried in the field while lawfully engaged in hunting, trapping, or target shooting, whether visible or not; or

4. Carried by any person permitted by law to possess a handgun unloaded and in a secure wrapper from the place of purchase to that person's home or place of business, or to a place of repair, or back from those locations.

5. A bow and arrow, an unloaded rifle or shotgun, or an unloaded weapon that will expel, or is readily capable of expelling, a projectile by the action of a spring, compressed air, or compressed gas including any such weapon commonly referred to as a BB gun, air rifle, or CO2 gun, while carried in a motor vehicle.

§ 62.1-04-03. License to carry a firearm or dangerous weapon concealed - Class 1 firearm license and class 2 firearm and dangerous weapon license.

1. The director of the bureau of criminal investigation shall issue a license to carry a firearm or dangerous weapon concealed upon review of an application submitted to the director if the following criteria are met:

a. The applicant is at least twenty-one years of age for a class 1 firearm license or at least eighteen years of age for a class 2 firearm and dangerous weapon license;

b. The applicant can demonstrate that the applicant is a resident of this state by providing a copy of a valid driver's license or state-issued identification card from this state that establishes personal identification through photographic means and shows the applicant's name associated with a valid residential street address in this state or the applicant possesses a valid driver's license from the applicant's state of residence that establishes personal identification through photographic means and shows the applicant's name associated with a valid residential street address and a valid concealed weapons license from the applicant's state of residence, which state has reciprocity with this state under section 62.1-04-03.1;

c. The applicant is not an individual specified in section 62.1-02-01 and for a class 1 firearm license the applicant: (1) Has not been convicted of a felony; (2) Has not been convicted of a crime of violence; Page No. 1(3) Has not been convicted of an offense involving the use of alcohol within ten years prior to the date of application; (4) Has not been convicted of a misdemeanor offense involving the unlawful use of narcotics or other controlled substances within ten years prior to the date of application; (5) Has not been convicted of an offense involving moral turpitude; (6) Has not been convicted of an offense involving domestic violence; (7) Has not been adjudicated by a state or federal court as mentally incompetent, unless the adjudication has been withdrawn or reversed; and (8) Is qualified to purchase and possess a firearm under federal law;

d. The applicant has successfully completed the testing procedure conducted by a certified test administrator. The person conducting the testing may assess a charge of up to fifty dollars for conducting this testing. The attorney general may certify a test administrator based upon criteria and guidelines prescribed by the director of the bureau of criminal investigation;

e. The applicant satisfactorily completes the bureau of criminal investigation application form and has successfully passed the criminal history records check conducted by the bureau of criminal investigation and the federal bureau of investigation. The applicant shall provide all documentation relating to any court-ordered treatment or commitment for mental health or alcohol or substance abuse. The applicant shall provide the director of the bureau of criminal investigation written authorizations for disclosure of the applicant's mental health and alcohol or substance abuse evaluation and treatment records. The bureau may deny approval for a license if the bureau has reasonable cause to believe that the applicant or licenseholder has been or is a danger to self or others as demonstrated by evidence, including past pattern of behavior involving unlawful violence or threats of unlawful violence; past participation in incidents involving unlawful violence or threats of unlawful violence; or conviction of a weapons offense. In determining whether the applicant or licenseholder has been or is a danger to self or others, the bureau may inspect expunged records of arrests and convictions of adults and juvenile court records; and f. The applicant is not prohibited under federal law from owning, possessing, or having a firearm under that individual's control.

OHIO

FIREARM FRIENDLY: 

Permit Holders

Permit: "Shall issue" state.

Open Carry: Permitted.

Travel: Loaded handguns may be transported anywhere in a vehicle for self-defense purposes.

Disclose Presence of Handgun to Law Enforcement: Immediately upon contact with an officer.

Restaurants: May carry unless posted, but may not drink or be intoxicated.

Recognizes Permits From: AK, AZ, AR, DE, FL, ID, KS, KY, LA, MI, MO, NE, NM, NC, ND, OK, SC, TN, UT, VA, WA, WV, WY

Non-Permit

Firearm Ownership: Permitted to all citizens without license or permit.

Loaded Carry: Open carry is permissible.

Travel: Travel with firearms is permitted, as long as all ammunition is stored in a separate compartment of the car. A carrier must not be able to access both ammunition and the firearm from the same area of the vehicle.

General Info

State Parks: Only permit holders and only in parks (not while inside structures on park property).

Carry Law Uniformity: State law preempts that of local agencies/municipalities.

Self-Defense Model: Castle Doctrine, Duty to Retreat.

Notes: Postings forbidding firearms on private property do have the force of law, and violations are punishable as level 4 misdemeanors. Permit holders may not consume alcohol while carrying. Several changes to carry law will go into effect on March 23, 2015 through the passage of House Bill 234. One change will allow the Attorney General to enter into reciprocity agreements with other states without legislative involvement. Another change will allow residents of contiguous states to acquire OH carry permits upon proof of employment in OH. Another will lower the mandatory training for permit acquisition from 12 hours to 8 hours and would allow 6 of those hours to be acquired online. Still another will change the requirement that an NRA Basic Pistol training program be used and allow for programs originating from any national gun advocacy group.

Contact for Additional Information:

Attorney General of Ohio
30 East Broad Street, 14th Floor
Columbus, OH 43215
614-466-4986

Ohio Revised Code 2923.126 [Effective 3/23/2015]
Duties of licensed individual.

(A) A concealed handgun license that is issued under section 2923.125 of the Revised Code shall expire five years after the date of issuance. A licensee who has been issued a license under that section shall be granted a grace period of thirty days after the licensee's license expires during which the licensee's license remains valid. Except as provided in divisions (B) and (C) of this section, a licensee who has been issued a concealed handgun license under section 2923.125 or 2923.1213 of the Revised Code may carry a concealed handgun anywhere in this state if the licensee also carries a valid license and valid identification when the licensee is in actual possession of a concealed handgun. The licensee shall give notice of any change in the licensee's residence address to the sheriff who issued the license within forty-five days after that change.

If a licensee is the driver or an occupant of a motor vehicle that is stopped as the result of a traffic stop or a stop for another law enforcement purpose and if the licensee is transporting or has a loaded handgun in the motor vehicle at that time, the licensee shall promptly inform any law enforcement officer who approaches the vehicle while stopped that the licensee has been issued a concealed handgun license and that the licensee currently possesses or has a loaded handgun; the licensee shall not knowingly disregard or fail to comply with lawful orders of a law enforcement officer given while the motor vehicle is stopped, knowingly fail to remain in the motor vehicle while stopped, or knowingly fail to keep the licensee's hands in plain sight after any law enforcement officer begins approaching the licensee while stopped and before the officer leaves, unless directed otherwise by a law enforcement officer; and the licensee shall not knowingly have contact with the loaded handgun by touching it with the licensee's hands or fingers, in any manner in violation of division (E) of section 2923.16 of the Revised Code, after any law enforcement officer begins approaching the licensee while stopped and before the officer leaves. Additionally, if a licensee is the driver or an occupant of a commercial motor vehicle that is stopped by an employee of the motor carrier enforcement unit for the purposes defined in section 5503.04 of the Revised Code and if the licensee is transporting or has a loaded handgun in the commercial motor vehicle at that time, the licensee shall promptly inform the employee of the unit who approaches the vehicle while stopped that the licensee has been issued a concealed handgun license and that the licensee currently possesses or has a loaded handgun.

If a licensee is stopped for a law enforcement purpose and if the licensee is carrying a concealed handgun at the time the officer approaches, the licensee shall promptly inform any law enforcement officer who approaches the licensee while stopped that the licensee has been issued a concealed handgun license and that the licensee currently is carrying a concealed handgun; the licensee shall not knowingly disregard or fail to comply with lawful orders of a law enforcement officer given while the licensee is stopped or knowingly fail to keep the licensee's hands in plain sight after any law enforcement officer begins approaching the licensee while stopped and before the officer leaves, unless directed otherwise by a law enforcement officer; and the licensee shall not knowingly remove, attempt to remove, grasp, or hold the loaded handgun or knowingly have contact with the loaded handgun by touching it with the licensee's hands or fingers, in any manner in violation of division (B) of section 2923.12 of the Revised Code, after any law enforcement officer begins approaching the licensee while stopped and before the officer leaves.

(B) ... A valid license does not authorize the licensee to carry a concealed handgun into any of the following places:

(1) A police station, sheriff's office, or state highway patrol station, premises controlled by the bureau of criminal identification and investigation, a state correctional institution, jail, workhouse, or other detention facility, an airport passenger terminal, or an institution that is maintained, operated, managed, and governed pursuant to division (A) of section 5119.14 of the Revised Code or division (A)(1) of section5123.03 of the Revised Code;

(2) A school safety zone if the licensee's carrying the concealed handgun is in violation of section 2923.122of the Revised Code;

(3) A courthouse or another building or structure in which a courtroom is located, in violation of section2923.123 of the Revised Code;

(4) Any premises or open air arena for which a D permit has been issued under Chapter 4303. of the Revised Code if the licensee's carrying the concealed handgun is in violation of section 2923.121 of the Revised Code;

(5) Any premises owned or leased by any public or private college, university, or other institution of higher education, unless the handgun is in a locked motor vehicle or the licensee is in the immediate process of placing the handgun in a locked motor vehicle;

(6) Any church, synagogue, mosque, or other place of worship, unless the church, synagogue, mosque, or other place of worship posts or permits otherwise;

(7) A child day-care center, a type A family day-care home, or a type B family day-care home, except that this division does not prohibit a licensee who resides in a type A family day-care home or a type B family day-care home from carrying a concealed handgun at any time in any part of the home that is not dedicated or used for day-care purposes, or from carrying a concealed handgun in a part of the home that is dedicated or used for day-care purposes at any time during which no children, other than children of that licensee, are in the home;

(8) An aircraft that is in, or intended for operation in, foreign air transportation, interstate air transportation, intrastate air transportation, or the transportation of mail by aircraft;

(9) Any building that is a government facility of this state or a political subdivision of this state and that is not a building that is used primarily as a shelter, restroom, parking facility for motor vehicles, or rest facility and is not a courthouse or other building or structure in which a courtroom is located that is subject to division (B)(3) of this section;

(10) A place in which federal law prohibits the carrying of handguns.

FIREARM FRIENDLY:  OKLAHOMA

Permit: "Shall issue" state, limited to .45 caliber or smaller.

Open Carry: Permitted with permit, limited to .45 caliber or smaller.

Travel: Loaded firearms may be transported while visible or concealed in a vehicle with a permit.

Disclose Presence of Handgun to Law Enforcement: Must inform officer immediately upon contact.

Restaurants: May carry with permit if establishment earns less than 50% of its revenue from alcohol sales and permit carrier does not consume alcohol. May not carry in bar area of a restaurant.

Recognizes Permits From: All states.

Permit Holders

Firearm Ownership: Permitted to all qualified citizens without license or permit.

Loaded Carry: Generally forbidden in public without carry permit.

Travel: May transport unloaded firearms in a vehicle open, in plain view, or in a firearms case which is fully or partially visible, in a mounted gun rack, in an exterior locked compartment, or in the trunk of a vehicle.

Non-Permit

State Parks: Only permit holders and only in parks (not while inside buildings on park property).

Carry Law Uniformity: State law preempts that of local agencies/municipalities.

Self-Defense Model: Castle Doctrine, Stand Your Ground.

Notes: Any handgun carried concealed or unconcealed for self-defense purposes may not be larger than .45 caliber. The law allows citizens with a firearm to legally store the firearm in a locked vehicle while at prohibited locations. Posted "no gun" signs do not have the force of law, but an individual may be issued a citation if they refuse to leave the premises. OK allows residents of constitutional carry states (non-permitting carry states) to carry without a permit while traveling in OK.

General Info

Contact for Additional Information:

Oklahoma Bureau of Investigation
Self-Defense Act Licensing Unit
6600 North Harvey Place
Oklahoma City, Oklahoma 73116
405-879-2690

OKLAHOMA

Oklahoma Statutes § 21-1272. Unlawful carry.

A. It shall be unlawful for any person to carry upon or about his or her person, or in a purse or other container belonging to the person, any pistol, revolver, shotgun or rifle whether loaded or unloaded... whether such weapon be concealed or unconcealed...

B. Any person convicted of violating the foregoing provision shall be guilty of a misdemeanor....

§ 21-1272.1. Carrying firearms where liquor is consumed.

A. It shall be unlawful for any person to carry or possess any weapon designated in Section 1272 of this title in any establishment where low-point beer, as defined by Section 163.2 of Title 37 of the Oklahoma Statutes, or alcoholic beverages, as defined by Section 506 of Title 37 of the Oklahoma Statutes, are consumed. ... Provided however, a person possessing a valid handgun license pursuant to the provisions of the Oklahoma Self-Defense Act may carry the concealed or unconcealed handgun into any restaurant or other establishment licensed to dispense low-point beer or alcoholic beverages where the sale of low-point beer or alcoholic beverages does not constitute the primary purpose of the business....

§ 21-1272.2. Penalty for firearm in liquor establishment.

Any person who intentionally or knowingly carries on his or her person any weapon in violation of Section 1272.1 of this title, shall, upon conviction, be guilty of a felony punishable by a fine not to exceed One Thousand Dollars ($1,000.00), or imprisonment in the custody of the Department of Corrections for a period not to exceed two (2) years, or by both such fine and imprisonment.

§ 21-1277. Unlawful carry in certain places.

A. It shall be unlawful for any person in possession of a valid handgun license issued pursuant to the provisions of the Oklahoma Self-Defense Act to carry any concealed or unconcealed handgun into any of the following places:

1. Any structure, building, or office space which is owned or leased by a city, town, county, state, or federal governmental authority for the purpose of conducting business with the public;

2. Any prison, jail, detention facility or any facility used to process, hold, or house arrested persons, prisoners or persons alleged delinquent or adjudicated delinquent;

3. Any public or private elementary or public or private secondary school, except as provided in subsection C of this section;

4. Any sports arena during a professional sporting event;

5. Any place where pari-mutuel wagering is authorized by law; and

6. Any other place specifically prohibited by law.

B. For purposes of paragraphs 1, 2, 3, 4 and 5 of subsection A of this section, the prohibited place does not include and specifically excludes the following property:

1. Any property set aside for the use or parking of any vehicle, whether attended or unattended, by a city, town, county, state, or federal governmental authority;

2. Any property set aside for the use or parking of any vehicle, whether attended or unattended, by any entity offering any professional sporting event which is open to the public for admission, or by any entity engaged in pari-mutuel wagering authorized by law;

3. Any property adjacent to a structure, building, or office space in which concealed or unconcealed weapons are prohibited by the provisions of this section;

4. Any property designated by a city, town, county, or state governmental authority as a park, recreational area, or fairgrounds; provided, nothing in this paragraph shall be construed to authorize any entry by a person in possession of a concealed or unconcealed handgun into any structure, building, or office space which is specifically prohibited by the provisions of subsection A of this section; and

5. Any property set aside by a public or private elementary or secondary school for the use or parking of any vehicle, whether attended or unattended; provided, however, said handgun shall be stored and hidden from view in a locked motor vehicle when the motor vehicle is left unattended on school property.

Nothing contained in any provision of this subsection or subsection C of this section shall be construed to authorize or allow any person in control of any place described in paragraph 1, 2, 3, 4 or 5 of subsection A of this section to establish any policy or rule that has the effect of prohibiting any person in lawful possession of a handgun license from possession of a handgun allowable under such license in places described in paragraph 1, 2, 3, 4 or 5 of this subsection.

C. A concealed or unconcealed weapon may be carried onto private school property or in any school bus or vehicle used by any private school for transportation of students or teachers by a person who is licensed pursuant to the Oklahoma Self-Defense Act, provided a policy has been adopted by the governing entity of the private school that authorizes the carrying and possession of a weapon on private school property or in any school bus or vehicle used by a private school....

D. Any person violating the provisions of subsection A of this section shall, upon conviction, be guilty of a misdemeanor punishable by a fine not to exceed Two Hundred Fifty Dollars ($250.00).

E. No person in possession of a valid handgun license issued pursuant to the provisions of the Oklahoma Self-Defense Act shall be authorized to carry the handgun into or upon any college, university, or technology center school property, except as provided in this subsection. For purposes of this subsection, the following property shall not be construed as prohibited for persons having a valid handgun license:

1. Any property set aside for the use or parking of any vehicle, whether attended or unattended, provided the handgun is carried or stored as required by law and the handgun is not removed from the vehicle without the prior consent of the college or university president or technology center school administrator while the vehicle is on any college, university, or technology center school property;

2. Any property authorized for possession or use of handguns by college, university, or technology center school policy; and

3. Any property authorized by the written consent of the college or university president or technology center school administrator, provided the written consent is carried with the handgun and the valid handgun license while on college, university, or technology center school property.

...upon a determination that the licensee has violated any provision of this subsection, the licensee may be subject to an administrative fine of Two Hundred Fifty Dollars ($250.00) and may have the handgun license suspended for three (3) months....

F. The provisions of this section shall not apply to any peace officer or to any person authorized by law to carry a pistol in the course of employment....

FIREARM FRIENDLY: C

OREGON

Permit: "Shall issue" state.

Open Carry: Generally permitted.

Travel: Loaded handguns may be transported concealed or openly in a vehicle, with a permit.

Disclose Presence of Handgun to Law Enforcement: Required only if requested by officer.

Restaurants: Permitted unless posted as prohibited.

Recognizes Permits From: No states.

Firearm Ownership: Permitted to all citizens without license or permit.

Loaded Carry: Open carry generally permitted in rural areas, but many metropolitan localities forbid carry for non-permit holders. May not carry concealed without a permit. Carry in any public building is prohibited without a permit.

Travel: Handguns may not be concealed or readily accessible to the person in a vehicle without a permit. According to OR law, a handgun is readily accessible if the handgun is within the passenger compartment of a vehicle. If a vehicle has no storage outside the passenger compartment, a handgun may be stored in a locked glove box, center console, or other locked container, as long as the key is not kept inserted in the lock. Non-permit holders may openly carry in belt holsters in a vehicle, except in areas where a local municipality has prohibited open carry.

State Parks: Open carry permitted for all law-abiding citizens. Concealed carry only permitted for permit holders.

Carry Law Uniformity: State law preempts that of local agencies/ municipalities on most laws, but cities, counties, or municipalities may enact ordnances regulating the possession of loaded firearms in public places. City or county regulations regulating possession of loaded firearms in public places do not apply to permit holders.

Self-Defense Model: Castle Doctrine, Stand Your Ground.

Notes: Oregon shall issue permits to residents and "may issue" to non-residents in bordering states only. Each county sheriff's office issues carry permits. Localities prohibiting non-permit holders from loaded, open carry include (but not limited to): Astoria, Beaverton, Gladstone, Independence, Multnomah County, Newport, Oregon City, Portland, Salem, and Tigard.

Contact for Additional Information:

Oregon Legislative Administration
900 Court Street Northeast,
Room 140A • Salem, OR 97301
503-986-1848

OREGON

Oregon Revised Statutes § 166.170 State Preemption. (1) Except as expressly authorized by state statute, the authority to regulate in any matter whatsoever the sale, acquisition, transfer, ownership, possession, storage, transportation or use of firearms or any element relating to firearms and components thereof, including ammunition, is vested solely in theLegislative Assembly. (2) Except as expressly authorized by state statute, no county, city or other municipal corporation or district may enact civil or criminal ordinances, including but not limited to zoning ordinances, to regulate, restrict or prohibit the sale, acquisition, transfer, ownership, possession, storage, transportation or use of firearms or any element relating to firearms and components thereof, including ammunition. Ordinances that are contrary to this subsection are void.

§ 166.250 Unlawful Possession of Firearms. (1) Except as otherwise provided in this section or ORS 166.260, 166.270, 166.274, 166.291, 166.292 or 166.410 to 166.470, a person commits the crime of unlawful possession of a firearm if the person knowingly: (a) Carries any firearm concealed upon the person; (b) Possesses a handgun that is concealed and readily accessible to the person within any vehicle; or (c) Possesses a firearm and: (A) Is under 18 years of age; (B)(i) While a minor, was found to be within the jurisdiction of the juvenile court for having committed an act which, if committed by an adult, would constitute a felony or a misdemeanor involving violence, as defined in ORS 166.470; and (ii) Was discharged from the jurisdiction of the juvenile court within four years prior to being charged under this section; (C) Has been convicted of a felony or found guilty, except for insanity under ORS 161.295, of a felony; (D) Was committed to the Department of Human Services under ORS 426.130; or (E) Was found to be mentally ill and subject to an order under ORS 426.130 that the person be prohibited from purchasing or possessing a firearm as a result of that mental illness. (2) This section does not prohibit: (a) A minor, who is not otherwise prohibited under subsection (1)(c) of this section, from possessing a firearm: (A) Other than a handgun, if the firearm was transferred to the minor by the minor's parent or guardian or by another person with the consent of the minor's parent or guardian; or (B) Temporarily for hunting, target practice or any other lawful purpose; or (b) Any citizen of the United States over the age of 18 years who resides in or is temporarily sojourning within this state, and who is not within the excepted classes prescribed by ORS 166.270 and subsection (1) of this section, from owning, possessing or keeping within the person's place of residence or place of business any handgun, and no permit or license to purchase, own, possess or keep any such firearm at the person's place of residence or place of business is required of any such citizen. As used in this subsection, "residence" includes a recreational vessel or recreational vehicle while used, for whatever period of time, as residential quarters. (3) Firearms carried openly in belt holsters are not concealed within the meaning of this section. (4) Unlawful possession of a firearm is a Class A misdemeanor.

§ 166.370 Possession of Firearm or Dangerous Weapon in Public Building or Court Facility; Exceptions; Discharging Firearm at School. (1) Any person who intentionally possesses a loaded or unloaded firearm or any other instrument used as a dangerous weapon, while in or on a public building, shall upon conviction be guilty of a Class C felony.

(2)(a) Except as otherwise provided in paragraph (b) of this subsection, a person who intentionally possesses: (A) A firearm in a court facility is guilty, upon conviction, of a Class C felony. A person who intentionally possesses a firearm in a court facility shall surrender the firearm to a law enforcement officer. (B) A weapon, other than a firearm, in a court facility may be required to surrender the weapon to a law enforcement officer or to immediately remove it from the court facility. A person who fails to comply with this subparagraph is guilty, upon conviction, of a Class C felony. (b) The presiding judge of a judicial district may enter an order permitting the possession of specified weapons in a court facility.

(3) Subsection (1) of this section does not apply to: (a) A sheriff, police officer, other duly appointed peace officers or a corrections officer while acting within the scope of employment. (b) A person summoned by a peace officer to assist in making an arrest or preserving the peace, while the summoned person is engaged in assisting the officer. (c) An active or reserve member of the military forces of this state or the United States, when engaged in the performance of duty. (d) A person who is licensed under ORS 166.291 and 166.292 to carry a concealed handgun. (e) A person who is authorized by the officer or agency that controls the public building to possess a firearm or dangerous weapon in that public building. (f) An employee of the United States Department of Agriculture, acting within the scope of employment, who possesses a firearm in the course of the lawful taking of wildlife. (g) Possession of a firearm on school property if the firearm: (A) Is possessed by a person who is not otherwise prohibited from possessing the firearm; and (B) Is unloaded and locked in a motor vehicle.

(4) The exceptions listed in subsection (3)(b) to (g) of this section constitute affirmative defenses to a charge of violating subsection (1) of this section....

PENNSYLVANIA FIREARM FRIENDLY: A

Permit Holders

Permit: "Shall issue" to residents, shall issue to non-residents if non-resident has a carry permit in his/her home state.

Open Carry: Permitted with or without permit, except the city of Philadelphia, which requires a permit to carry.

Travel: May carry a firearm in a vehicle with a permit, openly or concealed.

Disclose Presence of Handgun to Law Enforcement: Required only if requested by officer.

Restaurants: Permitted unless posted as prohibited.

Recognizes Permits From: AK, AZ, AR, CO, FL, GA, IN, IA, KS, KY, LA, MI, MS, MO, MT, NC, ND, NH, OH, OK, PA, SD, TN, TX, UT, VA, WV, WI, WY

Non-Permit

Firearm Ownership: Permitted to all citizens without license or permit.

Loaded Carry: All law abiding citizens over 18 years of age may carry openly a loaded firearm in public, except in Philadelphia, where a permit is required for any type of carry. A permit is required to carry (open or concealed) on one's person in a vehicle.

Travel: Firearms must be unloaded in a vehicle. Firearms may not be carried openly or concealed on a person without a permit, while in a vehicle. To transport a handgun in a vehicle, a carrier must fit an exemption in 18 Pa.C.S. § 6106 (b); the list includes law enforcement personnel; military personnel; traveling to/from target shooting; U.S governmental employees authorized to carry; dealers, manufacturers, or repairers of firearms; (and hunters or fisherman); and others.

General Info

State Parks: Must have a valid carry permit to carry openly or concealed in state parks.

Carry Law Uniformity: State law preempts that of local agencies/municipalities, with the exception of open carry restrictions in a "city of the 1st class" which is Philadelphia.

Self-Defense Model: Castle Doctrine, Stand Your Ground.

Notes: Carry laws for non-permit holders in vehicles is somewhat convoluted—See PA laws 18 Pa.C.S. § 6106 for detailed info. The city of Philadelphia has additional restrictions on open carry.

Pennsylvania Consolidated Statutes

§ 6106. Firearms not to be carried without a license.

(a) Offense defined.-- (1) Except as provided in paragraph (2), any person who carries a firearm in any vehicle or any person who carries firearm concealed on or about his person, except in his place of abode or fixed place of business, without a valid and lawfully issued license under this chapter commits a felony of the third degree. (2) A person who is otherwise eligible to possess a valid license under this chapter but carries a firearm in any vehicle or any person who carries a firearm concealed on or about his person, except in his place of abode or fixed place of business, without a valid and lawfully issued license and has not committed any other criminal violation commits a misdemeanor of the first degree....

§ 6106.1. Carrying loaded weapons other than firearms.

(a) General rule.--Except as provided in Title 34 (relating to game), no person shall carry a loaded pistol, revolver, shotgun or rifle, other than a firearm as defined in section 6102 (relating to definitions), in any vehicle. The provisions of this section shall not apply to persons excepted from the requirement of a license to carry firearms under section 6106(b)(1), (2), (5) or (6) (relating to firearms not to be carried without a license) nor shall the provisions of this section be construed to permit persons to carry firearms in a vehicle where such conduct is prohibited by section 6106. (b) Penalty.-- A person who violates the provisions of this section commits a summary offense.

§ 6108. Carrying firearms on public streets or public property in Philadelphia.

No person shall carry a firearm, rifle or shotgun at any time upon the public streets or upon any public property in a city of the first class unless: (1) such person is licensed to carry a firearm; or (2) such person is exempt from licensing under section 6106(b) of this title relating to firearms not to be carried without a license.

§ 6120. Limitation on the regulation of firearms and ammunition.

(a) General rule.-- No county, municipality or township may in any manner regulate the lawful ownership, possession, transfer or transportation of firearms, ammunition or ammunition components when carried or transported for purposes not prohibited by the laws of this Commonwealth....

§ 11-47-52 Carrying of weapon while under the influence of liquor or drugs. – It is unlawful to carry or transport any firearm in this state when intoxicated or under the influence of intoxicating liquor or narcotic drugs.

Contact for Additional Information:

Pennsylvania Office of Attorney General
16th Floor / Strawberry Square • Harrisburg, PA 17120
717-787-3391

RHODE ISLAND FIREARM FRIENDLY: D

Permit Holders

Permit: "May issue" from state Attorney General, "shall issue" from local authority. Permits limited and issued with discretion.

Open Carry: Permitted with a permit in certain areas, but generally forbidden in most of the state.

Travel: Firearms may be transported in a vehicle with a permit. Non-residents, with a permit in another state, may transport a firearm only while passing through RI for travel requirements and without stopping for an extended time. Proceed with caution when traveling through this state with a firearm.

Disclose Presence of Handgun to Law Enforcement: Required only if requested by officer.

Restaurants: Permitted unless posted as prohibited and may not consume alcohol.

Recognizes Permits From: No states.

Non-Permit

Firearm Ownership: Permitted, but must complete an application to purchase a rifle or shotgun. Purchasing a handgun requires a DEM Pistol/ Revolver Certification (Blue Card) or a RI Hunter Safety Course Card and completion of an application to purchase and a waiting period of seven days.

Loaded Carry: Prohibited without a permit.

Travel: Transporting a handgun in a vehicle is only permitted if the handgun is unloaded and "securely wrapped from the place of purchase" to his/her residence or place of business, or while moving to another residence. A non-permit holder may also transport a handgun to a "bona fide target practice range" if the handgun is unloaded, broken-down to a non-functional state, and secured in a separate compartment or case away from any passengers. Use extreme caution when traveling with a firearm in this state and check any and all local laws and regulations.

General Info

State Parks: Prohibited outside of a vehicle. Permitted if firearm is left in vehicle, unloaded and cased while abiding by state laws.

Carry Law Uniformity: State law preempts that of local agencies/municipalities.

Self-Defense Model: Castle Doctrine, Stand Your Ground inside a home.

Notes: Proceed with caution when traveling through this state with a firearm. It is recommended for individuals to disassemble and secure any firearm as much as possible and separate ammunition. Rhode Island does not recognize carry permits from any other state, so concealed carry for non-residents is strictly prohibited, without a RI-issued non-resident permit. Permits are issued with discretion in RI by either the local sheriff's office or the Attorney General and either may deny a request for a permit. Long arms may not be transported in a vehicle on any public road with any ammunition in them at all, unless the carrier is a member of law enforcement or the military. Carriers may not consume alcohol or be intoxicated while carrying or transporting firearms.

State of Rhode Island General Laws § 11-47-8 License or permit required for carrying pistol – Possession of machine gun. –

(a) No person shall, without a license or permit issued as provided in §§ 11-47-11, 11-47-12 and 11-47-18, carry a pistol or revolver in any vehicle or conveyance or on or about his or her person whether visible or concealed, except in his or her dwelling house or place of business or on land possessed by him or her or as provided in §§ 11-47-9 and 11-47-10. The provisions of these sections shall not apply to any person who is the holder of a valid license or permit issued by the licensing authority of another state, or territory of the United States, or political subdivision of the state or territory, allowing him or her to carry a pistol or revolver in any vehicle or conveyance or on or about his or her person whether visible or concealed, provided the person is merely transporting the firearm through the state in a vehicle or other conveyance without any intent on the part of the person to detain him or herself or remain within the state of Rhode Island. No person shall manufacture, sell, purchase, or possess a machine gun except as otherwise provided in this chapter. Every person violating the provision of this section shall, upon conviction, be punished by imprisonment for not less than one nor more than ten (10) years, or by a fine up to ten thousand dollars ($10,000), or both, and except for a first conviction under this section shall not be afforded the provisions of suspension or deferment of sentence, nor a probation....

§ 11-47-10 License or permit not required to carry to target range. –

No license or permit shall be required for the purpose of carrying or transporting any pistol or revolver from one's home or place of business to a bona fide target practice range, nor from a bona fide target practice range to one's home or place of business, to engage in any shoot meet, or practice, provided that the pistol or revolver is broken down, unloaded and carried as openly as circumstances will permit, or provided that the pistols or revolvers are unloaded and secured in a separate container suitable for the purpose.

§ 11-47-52 Carrying of weapon while under the influence of liquor or drugs. – It is unlawful to carry or transport any firearm in this state when intoxicated or under the influence of intoxicating liquor or narcotic drugs.

Contact for Additional Information:

RI Office of the Attorney General
150 South Main Street • Providence, RI 02903
401-274-4400

SOUTH CAROLINA FIREARM FRIENDLY: A

Permit Holders

Permit: "Shall issue" state.

Open Carry: Prohibited.

Travel: Loaded handguns may be transported openly or concealed within a vehicle.

Disclose Presence of Handgun to Law Enforcement: Must inform immediately upon contact with a police officer.

Restaurants: Permissible, unless otherwise posted. Alcohol may not be consumed.

Recognizes Permits From: The following states, as long as the permit holder is a resident there: AK, AZ, AR, FL, GA, KS, KY, LA, MI, MO, MS (enhanced permit only), NM, NC, OH, OK, TN, TX, VA, WV, WY

Non-Permit

Firearm Ownership: Permitted to all citizens without license or permit.

Loaded Carry: Non-permitted citizens may not carry a loaded firearm on their person.

Travel: A loaded handgun may be transported concealed within the glove box or console of a vehicle. It may also be carried in the trunk, or if there is no trunk, it may be carried in the luggage area of a vehicle so long as it is securely held in place.

General Info

State Parks: Permissible, some restrictions may apply.

Carry Law Uniformity: State law preempts that of local agencies/municipalities.

Self-Defense Model: Castle Doctrine, Stand Your Ground.

Notes: Carriers may not consume alcohol. Any carrier who enters the dwelling of another without express permission to bring a firearm is punishable for a crime.

South Carolina Code of Laws § 23-31-215. Issuance of permits.

... (M) A permit issued pursuant to this section does not authorize a permit holder to carry a concealable weapon into a:

(1) law enforcement, correctional, or detention facility;

(2) courthouse or courtroom;

(3) polling place on election days;

(4) office of or the business meeting of the governing body of a county, public school district, municipality, or special purpose district;

(5) school or college athletic event not related to firearms;

(6) daycare facility or preschool facility;

(7) place where the carrying of firearms is prohibited by federal law;

(8) church or other established religious sanctuary unless express permission is given by the appropriate church official or governing body;

(9) hospital, medical clinic, doctor's office, or any other facility where medical services or procedures are performed unless expressly authorized by the employer; or

(10) place clearly marked with a sign prohibiting the carrying of a concealable weapon on the premises pursuant to Sections 23-31-220 and 23-31-235. Except that a property owner or an agent acting on his behalf, by express written consent, may allow individuals of his choosing to enter onto property regardless of any posted sign to the contrary. A person who violates a provision of this item, whether the violation is wilful or not, only may be charged with a violation of Section 16-11-620 and must not be charged with or penalized for a violation of this subsection.

Except as provided for in item (10), a person who wilfully violates a provision of this subsection is guilty of a misdemeanor and, upon conviction, must be fined not less than one thousand dollars or imprisoned not more than one year, or both, at the discretion of the court and have his permit revoked for five years....

... (N) Valid out-of-state permits to carry concealable weapons held by a resident of a reciprocal state must be honored by this State, provided, that the reciprocal state requires an applicant to successfully pass a criminal background check and a course in firearm training and safety. A resident of a reciprocal state carrying a concealable weapon in South Carolina is subject to and must abide by the laws of South Carolina regarding concealable weapons. SLED shall maintain and publish a list of those states as the states with which South Carolina has reciprocity....

§ 23-31-220. Right to allow or permit concealed weapons upon premises; signs.

Nothing contained in this article shall in any way be construed to limit, diminish, or otherwise infringe upon:

(1) the right of a public or private employer to prohibit a person who is licensed under this article from carrying a concealable weapon upon the premises of the business or work place or while using any machinery, vehicle, or equipment owned or operated by the business;

(2) the right of a private property owner or person in legal possession or control to allow or prohibit the carrying of a concealable weapon upon his premises. The posting by the employer, owner, or person in legal possession or control of a sign stating "No Concealable Weapons Allowed" shall constitute notice to a person holding a permit issued pursuant to this article that the employer, owner, or person in legal possession or control requests that concealable weapons not be brought upon the premises or into the work place. A person who brings a concealable weapon onto the premises or work place in violation of the provisions of this paragraph may be charged with a violation of Section 16-11-620. In addition to the penalties provided in Section 16-11-620, a person convicted of a second or subsequent violation of the provisions of this paragraph must have his permit revoked for a period of one year....

§ 23-31-225. Carrying concealed weapons into residences or dwellings.

No person who holds a permit issued pursuant to Article 4, Chapter 31, Title 23 may carry a concealable weapon into the residence or dwelling place of another person without the express permission of the owner or person in legal control or possession, as appropriate. A person who violates this provision is guilty of a misdemeanor and, upon conviction, must be fined not less than one thousand dollars or imprisoned for not more than one year, or both, at the discretion of the court and have his permit revoked for five years.

§ 23-31-230. Carrying concealed weapons between automobile and accommodation.

Notwithstanding any provision of law, any person may carry a concealable weapon from an automobile or other motorized conveyance to a room or other accommodation he has rented and upon which an accommodations tax has been paid.

§ 23-31-235. Sign requirements.

(A) Notwithstanding any other provision of this article, any requirement of or allowance for the posting of signs prohibiting the carrying of a concealable weapon upon any premises shall only be satisfied by a sign expressing the prohibition in both written language interdict and universal sign language.

(B) All signs must be posted at each entrance into a building where a concealable weapon permit holder is prohibited from carrying a concealable weapon and must be:

(1) clearly visible from outside the building;

(2) eight inches wide by twelve inches tall in size;

(3) contain the words "NO CONCEALABLE WEAPONS ALLOWED" in black one-inch tall uppercase type at the bottom of the sign and centered between the lateral edges of the sign;

(4) contain a black silhouette of a handgun inside a circle seven inches in diameter with a diagonal line that runs from the lower left to the upper right at a forty-five degree angle from the horizontal;

(5) a diameter of a circle; and

(6) placed not less than forty inches and not more than sixty inches from the bottom of the building's entrance door.

(C) If the premises where concealable weapons are prohibited does not have doors, then the signs contained in subsection (A) must be:

(1) thirty-six inches wide by forty-eight inches tall in size;

(2) contain the words "NO CONCEALABLE WEAPONS ALLOWED" in black three- inch tall uppercase type at the bottom of the sign and centered between the lateral edges of the sign;

(3) contain a black silhouette of a handgun inside a circle thirty-four inches in diameter with a diagonal line that is two inches wide and runs from the lower left to the upper right at a forty-five degree angle from the horizontal and must be a diameter of a circle whose circumference is two inches wide;

(4) placed not less than forty inches and not more than ninety-six inches above the ground;

(5) posted in sufficient quantities to be clearly visible from any point of entry onto the premises.

§ 23-31-400. Definitions; unlawful use of firearm; violations.

... (B) It is unlawful for a person who is under the influence of alcohol or a controlled substance to use a firearm in this State.

(C) A person who violates the provisions of subsection (B) is guilty of a misdemeanor and, upon conviction, must be fined not less than two thousand dollars or imprisoned not more than two years.

(D) This article does not apply to persons lawfully defending themselves or their property.

Contact for Additional Information:

South Carolina Law Enforcement Division
P.O. Box 21398 • Columbia, SC 29221
803-896-7015

SOUTH DAKOTA FIREARM FRIENDLY: A+

Permit Holders

Permit: "Shall issue" state.

Open Carry: Permitted.

Travel: Loaded handguns may be transported openly or concealed anywhere in a vehicle for self-defense purposes.

Disclose Presence of Handgun to Law Enforcement: Required only if requested by officer.

Restaurants: May carry if establishment earns less than 50% of its revenue from alcohol sales and unless establishment posts forbidding carry.

Recognizes Permits From: All states except VT.

Non-Permit

Firearms Ownership: Permitted to all citizens without license or permit.

Loaded Carry: All citizens over 21 years of age may openly carry a loaded firearm in public.

Travel: Loaded firearms are permissible as long as they are in plain view. They may be concealed if unloaded and secured in a case that is placed in the trunk or is too large to be concealed on someone's person.

General Info

State Parks: Permissible for anyone to carry, but non-permit holders must carry openly.

Carry Law Uniformity: State law preempts that of local agencies/municipalities.

Self-Defense Model: Castle Doctrine, Stand Your Ground.

Notes: South Dakota is atypical in that the state doesn't require a training component at all for acquisition of a carry permit. Carry is not permissible in bars, but alcohol may be consumed while carrying up to a blood alcohol content of 0.08%. Postings forbidding firearms on private property do not have the force of law; establishments may deny service or admittance if a carrier comes on the property, but no criminal penalty will result from the carrier's possession of a firearm on the property. Carriers may carry on school grounds if they have pre-approval from the school.

Contact for Additional Information:

South Dakota Security of State, Capitol Building
500 East Capitol Avenue • Pierre, SD 57501
605-773-3537

South Dakota Codified Laws § 23-7-7.1. Requirements for issuance of temporary permit--Time requirement--Appeal of denial. A temporary permit to carry a concealed pistol shall be issued within five days of application to a person if the applicant:

(1) Is eighteen years of age or older;

(2) Has never pled guilty to, nolo contendere to, or been convicted of a felony or a crime of violence;

(3) Is not habitually in an intoxicated or drugged condition;

(4) Has no history of violence;

(5) Has not been found in the previous ten years to be a "danger to others" or a "danger to self" as defined in § 27A-1-1 or is not currently adjudged mentally incompetent;

(6) Has physically resided in and is a resident of the county where the application is being made for at least thirty days immediately preceding the date of the application;

(7) Has had no violations of chapter 23-7, 22-14, or 22-42 constituting a felony or misdemeanor in the five years preceding the date of application or is not currently charged under indictment or information for such an offense;

(8) Is a citizen or legal resident of the United States; and

(9) Is not a fugitive from justice.

A person denied a permit may appeal to the circuit court pursuant to chapter 1-26.

§ 23-7-7.4. Nonresident permit to carry concealed pistol--Validity in South Dakota--Application. Any valid permit to carry a concealed pistol, issued to a nonresident of South Dakota, is valid in South Dakota according to the terms of its issuance in the state of its issue, but only to the extent that the terms of issuance comply with any appropriate South Dakota statute or promulgated rule. However, if the holder of such a nonresident permit to carry a concealed pistol becomes, at any time, a legal resident of South Dakota, the provisions of this section no longer apply.

§ 23-7-44. Possession of pistols by minors prohibited--Misdemeanor. No person under the age of eighteen years may knowingly possess a pistol. A violation of this section is a Class 1 misdemeanor.

TENNESSEE FIREARM FRIENDLY: A

Permit Holders

Permit: "Shall issue" state.

Open Carry: Permissible.

Travel: Firearms may be transported in vehicles but must be "kept from ordinary observation" and locked in a compartment of the vehicle when the carrier is not present.

Disclose Presence of Handgun to Law Enforcement: Required only if requested by officer.

Restaurants: Permissible unless posted.

Recognizes Permits From: All states.

Non-Permit

Firearms Ownership: Permissible without license or permit.

Loaded Carry: Forbidden, unless incidental to hunting or sport shooting.

Travel: Unloaded firearms may be transported in vehicles but may not be on the driver's person and ammunition must not be present in the driver's immediate vicinity.

General Info

State Parks: Only permit holders.

Carry Law Uniformity: State law preempts that of localities and municipalities.

Self-Defense Model: Castle Doctrine, Stand Your Ground.

Notes: Several changes to carry law, specifically T.C.A. § 39-17-1351, went into effect on January 1, 2016. Carriers may not consume alcohol while carrying and violations are punishable as class A misdemeanors. If a resident and permit holder of a state that has no reciprocity with TN works in TN for at least six months, that carrier may apply for and be issued a TN permit, as long as a couple of requirements are met. Possessing a firearm on posted property carries the force of law and is punishable as a class B misdemeanor. Firearms are forbidden in judicial proceedings, on any school property (unless it is kept in a vehicle and not handled), on playgrounds, and in government buildings.

Contact for Additional Information:

Department of Public Safety

1150 Foster Avenue • Nashville, TN 37243

615-251-8590

Tennessee Code Annotated § 39-17-1306. Carrying weapons during judicial proceedings.

(a) No person shall intentionally, knowingly, or recklessly carry on or about the person while inside any room in which judicial proceedings are in progress any weapon prohibited by § 39-17-1302(a), for the purpose of going armed; provided, that if the weapon carried is a firearm, the person is in violation of this section regardless of whether the weapon is carried for the purpose of going armed....

(b) Any person violating subsection (a) commits a Class E felony....

§ 39-17-1311. Carrying weapons on public parks, playgrounds, civic centers and other public recreational buildings and grounds.

(a) It is an offense for any person to possess or carry, whether openly or concealed, with the intent to go armed, any weapon prohibited by § 39-17-1302(a), not used solely for instructional, display or sanctioned ceremonial purposes, in or on the grounds of any public park, playground, civic center or other building facility, area or property owned, used or operated by any municipal, county or state government, or instrumentality thereof, for recreational purposes....

...(c) (1) Each chief administrator of public recreational property shall display in prominent locations about the public recreational property a sign, at least six inches (6") high and fourteen inches (14") wide, stating:

MISDEMEANOR. STATE LAW PRESCRIBES A MAXIMUM PENALTY OF ELEVEN (11) MONTHS AND TWENTY-NINE (29) DAYS AND A FINE NOT TO EXCEED TWO THOUSAND FIVE HUNDRED DOLLARS ($2,500) FOR CARRYING WEAPONS ON OR IN PUBLIC RECREATIONAL PROPERTY....

§ 39-17-1313. Transporting and storing a firearm or firearm ammunition in permit holder's motor vehicle.

(a) Notwithstanding any provision of law or any ordinance or resolution adopted by the governing body of a city, county or metropolitan government, including any ordinance or resolution enacted before April 8, 1986, that prohibits or regulates the possession, transportation or storage of a firearm or firearm ammunition by a handgun carry permit holder, the holder of a valid handgun carry permit recognized in Tennessee may, unless expressly prohibited by federal law, transport and store a firearm or firearm ammunition in the permit holder's motor vehicle, as defined in § 55-1-103, while on or utilizing any public or private parking area if:

(1) The permit holder's motor vehicle is parked in a location where it is permitted to be; and

(2) The firearm or ammunition being transported or stored in the motor vehicle:

(A) Is kept from ordinary observation if the permit holder is in the motor vehicle; or

(B) Is kept from ordinary observation and locked within the trunk, glove box, or interior of the person's motor vehicle or a container securely affixed to such motor vehicle if the permit holder is not in the motor vehicle....

§ 39-17-1321. Possession of handgun while under influence -- Penalty.

(a) Notwithstanding whether a person has a permit issued pursuant to § 39-17-1315 or § 39-17-1351, it is an offense for a person to possess a handgun while under the influence of alcohol or any controlled substance or controlled substance analogue.

(b) It is an offense for a person to possess a firearm if the person is both:

(1) Within the confines of an establishment open to the public where liquor, wine or other alcoholic beverages, as defined in § 57-3-101(a)(1)(A), or beer, as defined in § 57-6-102, are served for consumption on the premises; and

(2) Consuming any alcoholic beverage listed in subdivision (b)(1).

(c) (1) A violation of this section is a Class A misdemeanor.

(2) In addition to the punishment authorized by subdivision (c)(1), if the violation is of subsection (a), occurs in an establishment described in subdivision (b)(1), and the person has a handgun permit issued pursuant to § 39-17-1351, such permit shall be suspended in accordance with § 39-17-1352 for a period of three (3) years.

§ 39-17-1351. Handgun carry permits. [Updated January 1, 2016.]

... (r) (1) A facially valid handgun permit, firearms permit, weapons permit or license issued by another state shall be valid in this state according to its terms and shall be treated as if it is a handgun permit issued by this state; provided, however, this subsection (r) shall not be construed to authorize the holder of any out-of-state permit or license to carry, in this state, any firearm or weapon other than a handgun.

(2) For a person to lawfully carry a handgun in this state based upon a permit or license issued in another state, the person must be in possession of the permit or license at all times the person carries a handgun in this state.

(3) (A) The commissioner of safety shall enter into written reciprocity agreements with other states that require the execution of the agreements. The commissioner of safety shall prepare and publicly publish a current list of states honoring permits issued by the state of Tennessee and shall make the list available to anyone upon request. The commissioner of safety shall also prepare and publicly publish a

current list of states who, after inquiry by the commissioner, refuse to enter into a reciprocity agreement with this state or honor handgun carry permits issued by this state. To the extent that any state may impose conditions in the reciprocity agreements, the commissioner of safety shall publish those conditions as part of the list. If another state imposes conditions on Tennessee permit holders in a reciprocity agreement, the conditions shall also become a part of the agreement and apply to the other state's permit holders when they carry a handgun in this state....

....(C) (i) If a person who is a resident of and handgun permit holder in another state is employed in this state on a regular basis and desires to carry a handgun in this state, the person shall have six (6) months from the last day of the sixth month of regular employment in this state to obtain a Tennessee handgun carry permit. The permit may be issued based on the person having a permit from another state provided the other state has substantially similar permit eligibility requirements as this state. However, if during the six-month period the person applies for a handgun permit in this state and the application is denied, the person shall not be allowed to carry a handgun in this state based upon the other state's permit.

(ii) This subdivision (r)(3)(C) shall not apply if the state of residence of the person employed in Tennessee has entered into a handgun permit reciprocity agreement with this state pursuant to this subsection (r).

(iii) As used in this subdivision (r)(3)(C), "employed in this state on a regular basis" means a person has been gainfully employed in this state for at least thirty (30) hours a week for six (6) consecutive months not counting any absence from employment caused by the employee's use of sick leave, annual leave, administrative leave or compensatory time.

§ 39-17-1359. Prohibition at certain meetings -- Posting notice.

(a) (1) Except as provided in § 39-17-1313, an individual, corporation, business entity or local, state or federal government entity or agent thereof is authorized to prohibit the possession of weapons by any person who is at a meeting conducted by, or on property owned, operated, or managed or under the control of the individual, corporation, business entity or government entity.

(2) The prohibition in subdivision (a)(1) shall apply to any person who is authorized to carry a firearm by authority of § 39-17-1351.

(b) (1) Notice of the prohibition permitted by subsection (a) shall be accomplished by displaying one (1) or both of the notices described in subdivision (b)(3) in prominent locations, including all entrances primarily used by persons entering the property, building, or portion of the property or building where weapon possession is prohibited. Either form of notice used shall be of a size that is plainly visible to the average person entering the building, property, or portion of the building or property, posted.

(2) The notice required by this section shall be in English, but a duplicate notice may also be posted in any language used by patrons, customers or persons who frequent the place where weapon possession is prohibited.

(3) (A) If a sign is used as the method of posting, it shall contain language substantially similar to the following:

AS AUTHORIZED BY T.C.A. § 39-17-1359, POSSESSION OF A WEAPON ON POSTED PROPERTY OR IN

A POSTED BUILDING IS PROHIBITED AND IS A CRIMINAL OFFENSE....

... (C) A building, property or a portion of a building or property, shall be considered properly posted in accordance with this section if one (1) or both of the following is displayed in prominent locations, including all entrances primarily used by persons entering the property, building, or portion of the property or building where weapon possession is prohibited:

(i) The international circle and slash symbolizing the prohibition of the item within the circle; or

(ii) The posting sign described in this subdivision (b)(3)

(c) (1) It is an offense to possess a weapon in a building or on property that is properly posted in accordance with this section.

(2) Possession of a weapon on posted property in violation of this section is a Class B misdemeanor punishable by fine only of five hundred dollars ($500)....

TEXAS

Permit: "Shall issue" state.

Open Carry: Permitted with state license.

Travel: Loaded handguns may be transported anywhere in a vehicle for self-defense purposes but they may not be in plain view.

Disclose Presence of Handgun to Law Enforcement: Immediately upon contact with an officer.

Restaurants: May carry if establishment earns less than 50% of its revenue from alcohol sales, and the onus is on the establishment to post if that is true. Posts must comply with § 30.06 of the Texas Penal Code, which mandates that posts be present at every entrance open to the public. Violation by a carrier has force of law and is punishable as a Class A misdemeanor.

Recognizes Permits From: AL, AK, AZ, AR, CA, CO, CT, DE, FL, GA, HI, ID, IL, IN, IA, KS, KY, LA, MD, MA, MI, MS, MO, MT, NE, NV, NJ, NM, NY, NC, ND, OH, OK, PA, RI, SC, SD, TN, UT, VA, WA, WV, WY

Firearm Ownership: Permitted to all citizens without license or permit.

Loaded Carry: Forbidden.

Travel: Since the Castle Doctrine extends to motor vehicles in the state, even non-permitted residents may transport loaded firearms anywhere in a vehicle for self-defense purposes as long as they are not in plain view.

State Parks: Permitted unless posted.

Carry Law Uniformity: State law preempts that of local agencies/municipalities.

Self-Defense Model: Castle Doctrine, Stand Your Ground.

Notes: Permit holders may not consume alcohol while carrying. Carry is not permissible in courthouses or state buildings. Residents involved in hunting and shooting events may carry a loaded handgun without permit while in transit to and from events. Permit holders may not carry in amusement parks that meet the following requirements: more than 75 acres, open for a minimum of 120 days a year, security staff on site, located in a city with at least 1 million in population. Suppressors are permissible for hunting.

Contact for Additional Information:

Texas Department of Public Safety
P.O. Box 4087 • Austin, TX 78773
512-424-7293

Texas Government Code § 411.194. REDUCTION OF FEES DUE TO INDIGENCY.

(a) Notwithstanding any other provision of this subchapter, the department shall reduce by 50 percent any fee required for the issuance of an original, duplicate, modified, or renewed license under this subchapter if the department determines that the applicant is indigent.

(b) The department shall require an applicant requesting a reduction of a fee to submit proof of indigency with the application materials. (c) For purposes of this section, an applicant is indigent if the applicant's income is not more than 100 percent of the applicable income level established by the federal poverty guidelines.

Texas Government Code § 411.195. REDUCTION OF FEES FOR SENIOR CITIZENS.

Notwithstanding any other provision of this subchapter, the department shall reduce by 50 percent any fee required for the issuance of an original, duplicate, modified, or renewed license under this subchapter if the applicant for the license is 60 years of age or older.

Texas Government Code § 411.2032. TRANSPORTATION AND STORAGE OF FIREARMS AND AMMUNITION BY LICENSE HOLDERS IN PRIVATE VEHICLES ON CERTAIN CAMPUSES.

... (b) An institution of higher education or private or independent institution of higher education in this state may not adopt or enforce any rule, regulation, or other provision or take any other action, including posting notice under Section 30.06, Penal Code, prohibiting or placing restrictions on the storage or transportation of a firearm or ammunition in a locked, privately owned or leased motor vehicle by a person, including a student enrolled at that institution, who holds a license to carry a concealed handgun under this subchapter and lawfully possesses the firearm or ammunition: (1) on a street or driveway located on the campus of the institution; or (2) in a parking lot, parking garage, or other parking area located on the campus of the institution.

Texas Penal Code §9.42. DEADLY FORCE TO PROTECT PROPERTY.

A person is justified in using deadly force against another to protect land or tangible, movable property: TEXAS CONCEALED HANDGUN LAWS 36TEXAS CONCEALED HANDGUN LAWS 37 (1) if he would be justified in using force against the other under Section 9.41; and (2) when and to the degree he reasonably believes the deadly force is immediately necessary: (A) to prevent the other's imminent commission of arson, burglary, robbery, aggravated robbery, theft during the nighttime, or criminal mischief during the nighttime; or (B) to prevent the other who is fleeing immediately after committing burglary, robbery, aggravated robbery, or theft during the night-time from escaping with the property; and (3) he reasonably believes that: (A) the land or property cannot be protected or recovered by any other means; or (B) the use of force other than deadly force to protect or recover the land or property would expose the actor or another to a substantial risk of death or serious bodily injury.

FIREARM FRIENDLY:  UTAH

Permit: "Shall issue" state.

Open Carry: Permitted.

Travel: Loaded handguns may be transported anywhere in a vehicle for self-defense purposes. Long arms in vehicles may not have a round chambered.

Disclose Presence of Handgun to Law Enforcement: Only required if requested.

Restaurants: May carry unless posted.

Recognizes Permits from: All states.

Firearm Ownership: Permitted to all citizens without license or permit.

Loaded Carry: Residents may carry a firearm with a loaded magazine openly as long as the chamber is empty on a semi-auto and the next chamber in rotation is empty on a revolver.

Travel: Residents may transport loaded firearms as long as the chamber is empty on a semi-auto and the next chamber in rotation is empty on a revolver.

State Parks: Only permit holders and only in parks (not while inside structures on park property).

Carry Law Uniformity: State law preempts that of local agencies/municipalities.

Self-Defense Model: Castle Doctrine, Stand Your Ground.

Notes: Castle Doctrine extends to any place a resident lays his head, be it a hotel room, an RV, or a tent; it even extends to motor vehicles, but the carrier must own or have permission to possess the vehicle. Firearms may be carried in bars that do not post forbidding them. Employees whose places of employment post forbidding firearms may still carry as long as firearms are left in the car while on the property. Carry is permissible on public trains but not in courthouses. Posts forbidding firearms in restaurants, etc. do not carry the force of law; carriers will be denied admittance or service, but will not be subject to criminal penalties for violation. Carry is permissible in state buildings and churches unless posted. Carry is even permissible on property of "secured" areas like jails and psychological institutions. Secured areas are required by law to provide storage for weapons of permit holders when permit holders enter the area that is actually "secured"; while carriers' weapons are stored by these secured institutions, the institutions are responsible for them. Both concealed and open carry are permissible in schools for grades K-12.

Contact for Additional Information:
Utah Department of Public Safety
5500 West Amelia Earhart Drive • Salt Lake City, UT 84116
801-532-2168

Utah Code § 53-5-704. Bureau duties -- Permit to carry concealed firearm -- Certification for concealed firearms instructor -- Requirements for issuance -- Violation -- Denial, suspension, or revocation -- Appeal procedure.

(1) (a) The bureau shall issue a permit to carry a concealed firearm for lawful self defense to an applicant who is 21 years of age or older within 60 days after receiving an application, unless the bureau finds proof that the applicant does not meet the qualifications set forth in Subsection (2).

(b) The permit is valid throughout the state for five years, without restriction, except as otherwise provided by Section 53-5-710.

(c) The provisions of Subsections 76-10-504(1) and (2), and Section 76-10-505 do not apply to a person issued a permit under Subsection (1)(a).

(d) Subsection (4)(a) does not apply to a nonresident:

(i) active duty service member, who present to the bureau orders requiring the active duty service member to report for duty in this state; or

(ii) an active duty service member's spouse, stationed with the active duty service member, who presents to the bureau the active duty service member's orders requiring the service member to report for duty in this state.

(2) (a) The bureau may deny, suspend, or revoke a concealed firearm permit if the applicant or permit holder:

(i) has been or is convicted of a felony;

(ii) has been or is convicted of a crime of violence;

(iii) has been or is convicted of an offense involving the use of alcohol;

(iv) has been or is convicted of an offense involving the unlawful use of narcotics or other controlled substances;

(v) has been or is convicted of an offense involving moral turpitude;

(vi) has been or is convicted of an offense involving domestic violence;

(vii) has been or is adjudicated by a state or federal court as mentally incompetent, unless the adjudication has been withdrawn or reversed; and

(viii) is not qualified to purchase and possess a firearm pursuant to Section 76-10-503 and federal law.

(b) In determining whether an applicant or permit holder meets the qualifications set forth in Subsection (2)(a), the bureau shall consider mitigating circumstances.

(3) (a) The bureau may deny, suspend, or revoke a concealed firearm permit if it has reasonable cause to believe that the applicant or permit holder has been or is a danger to self or others as demonstrated by evidence, including:

(i) past pattern of behavior involving unlawful violence or threats of unlawful violence;

(ii) past participation in incidents involving unlawful violence or threats of unlawful violence; or

(iii) conviction of an offense in violation of Title 76, Chapter 10, Part 5, Weapons.

(b) The bureau may not deny, suspend, or revoke a concealed firearm permit solely for a single conviction of an infraction violation of Title 76, Chapter 10, Part 5, Weapons....

Permit: None issued, Vermont is a "Constitutional Carry" state.

Open Carry: Permitted.

Travel: Loaded handguns may be transported openly or concealed within a vehicle.

Disclose Presence of Handgun to Law Enforcement: Required only if requested by a law enforcement officer.

Restaurants: Permissible, unless otherwise posted.

Recognizes Permits From: AL, AK, AZ, AR, CA, CO, CT, DE, FL, GA, HI, ID, IL, IN, IA, KS, KY, LA, ME, MD, MA, MI, MN, MS, MO, MT, NE, NV, NH, NJ, NM, NY, NC, ND, OH, OK, OR, PA, RI, SC, SD, TN, TX, UT, VA, WA, WV, WI, WY

Firearm Ownership: Permitted to all qualified citizens without license or permit.

Loaded Carry: All citizens of age (18+) may openly carry a loaded firearm in public.

Travel: A loaded handgun may be transported openly or concealed in a vehicle.

State Parks: Permissible, some restrictions may apply.

Carry Law Uniformity: State law preempts that of local agencies/municipalities.

Self-Defense Model: No Castle Doctrine, no Stand Your Ground laws.

Notes: As a "Constitutional Carry" state, Vermont equates the U.S. Constitution with a citizen's carry permit. Thus, there are no strict state laws or regulations on firearms. However, federal laws must still be followed. Vermont law does not distinguish between residents and non-residents of the state, so both groups of people have the same rights within the state's borders.

Contact for Additional Information:

Attorney General of Vermont
109 State Street • Montpelier, VT 05609
802-828-3171

Vermont Statutes Title 13 Chapter 85 § 4003. Carrying dangerous weapons

A person who carries a dangerous or deadly weapon, openly or concealed, with the intent or avowed purpose of injuring a fellow man, or who carries a dangerous or deadly weapon within any state institution or upon the grounds or lands owned or leased for the use of such institution, without the approval of the warden or superintendent of the institution, shall be imprisoned not more than two years or fined not more than $200.00, or both.

§ 4004. Possession of dangerous or deadly weapon in a school bus or school building or on school property

(a) No person shall knowingly possess a firearm or a dangerous or deadly weapon while within a school building or on a school bus. A person who violates this section shall, for the first offense, be imprisoned not more than one year or fined not more than $1,000.00, or both, and for a second or subsequent offense shall be imprisoned not more than three years or fined not more than $5,000.00, or both.

(b) No person shall knowingly possess a firearm or a dangerous or deadly weapon on any school property with the intent to injure another person. A person who violates this section shall, for the first offense, be imprisoned not more than two years or fined not more than $1,000.00, or both, and for a second or subsequent offense shall be imprisoned not more than three years or fined not more than $5,000.00, or both.

(c) This section shall not apply to: (1) A law enforcement officer while engaged in law enforcement duties. (2) Possession and use of firearms or dangerous or deadly weapons if the board of school directors, or the superintendent or principal if delegated authority to do so by the board, authorizes possession or use for specific occasions or for instructional or other specific purposes.

(d) As used in this section: (1) "School property" means any property owned by a school, including motor vehicles. (2) "Owned by the school" means owned, leased, controlled or subcontracted by the school. (3) "Dangerous or deadly weapon" has the meaning defined in section 4016 of this title. (4) "Firearm" has the meaning defined in section 4016 of this title. (5) "Law enforcement officer" has the meaning defined in section 4016 of this title.

(e) The provisions of this section shall not limit or restrict any prosecution for any other offense, including simple assault or aggravated assault.

§ 4008. Possession of firearms by children

A child under the age of 16 years shall not, without the consent of his or her parents or guardian, have in his or her possession or control a pistol or revolver constructed or designed for the use of gunpowder or other explosive substance with leaden ball or shot. A child who violates a provision of this section shall be deemed a delinquent child under the provisions of chapter 52 of Title 33.

Permit: "Shall issue" state.

Open Carry: Generally permitted, statutes prohibit open carry in some areas.

Travel: A handgun may be transported openly or concealed by a permit holder.

Disclose Presence of Handgun to Law Enforcement: Required only if requested by a law enforcement officer.

Restaurants: Permissible, must not consume alcohol.

Recognizes Permits From: All states.

Permit Holders

Firearm Ownership: All qualified citizens may own firearms, no license or permit needed for purchase.

Loaded Carry: Open carry for adults 18+ is permissible without a permit, with the exception of some cities and counties that have outlawed open carry.

Travel: Handgun must be secured within a container or compartment of the vehicle; container or case does not have to be locked. The handgun may be loaded and within reach of the driver or any passengers.

Non-Permit

State Parks: Permissible, some restrictions may apply.

Carry Law Uniformity: State law preempts most local municipality/agency implemented laws regarding firearms.

Self-Defense Model: Castle Doctrine (broad application), Stand Your Ground.

Notes: Virginia state law states that individuals who are innocent in an altercation, meaning they did not provoke the situations, have a legal right to stand their ground and defend themselves with whatever force is necessary to neutralize the situation. Deadly force is only permissible if you are under an immediate threat and in fear for your life.

General Info

Contact for Additional Information:

Virginia State Police

P.O. Box 27472 • Richmond, VA 23261

804-674-2000

§ 18.2-308. Carrying concealed weapons; exceptions; penalty.

A. If any person carries about his person, hidden from common observation,

(i) any pistol, revolver, or other weapon designed or intended to propel a missile of any kind by action of an explosion of any combustible material;

(ii) any dirk, bowie knife, switchblade knife, ballistic knife, machete, razor, slingshot, spring stick, metal knucks, or blackjack;

(iii) any flailing instrument consisting of two or more rigid parts connected in such a manner as to allow them to swing freely, which may be known as a nun chahka, nun chuck, nunchaku, shuriken, or fighting chain;

(iv) any disc, of whatever configuration, having at least two points or pointed blades which is designed to be thrown or propelled and which may be known as a throwing star or oriental dart; or

(v) any weapon of like kind as those enumerated in this subsection, he is guilty of a Class 1 misdemeanor. A second violation of this section or a conviction under this section subsequent to any conviction under any substantially similar ordinance of any county, city, or town shall be punishable as a Class 6 felony, and a third or subsequent such violation shall be punishable as a Class 5 felony. For the purpose of this section, a weapon shall be deemed to be hidden from common observation when it is observable but is of such deceptive appearance as to disguise the weapon's true nature. It shall be an affirmative defense to a violation of clause (i) regarding a handgun, that a person had been issued, at the time of the offense, a valid concealed handgun permit....

...C. Except as provided in subsection A of § 18.2-308.012, this section shall not apply to:

...10. Any person who may lawfully possess a firearm and is carrying a handgun while in a personal, private motor vehicle or vessel and such handgun is secured in a container or compartment in the vehicle or vessel...

§ 18.2-308.01. Carrying a concealed handgun with a permit.

A. The prohibition against carrying a concealed handgun in clause (i) of subsection A of § 18.2-308 shall not apply to a person who has a valid concealed handgun permit issued pursuant to this article....

B. Failure to display the permit and a photo identification upon demand by a law-enforcement officer shall be punishable by a $25 civil penalty....

C. The granting of a concealed handgun permit pursuant to this article shall not thereby authorize the possession of any handgun or other weapon on property or in places where such possession is otherwise prohibited by law or is prohibited by the owner of private property.

§ 18.2-308.012. Prohibited conduct.

A. Any person permitted to carry a concealed handgun who is under the influence of alcohol or illegal drugs while carrying such handgun in a public place is guilty of a Class 1 misdemeanor....

B. No person who carries a concealed handgun onto the premises of any restaurant or club as defined in § 4.1-100 for which a license to sell and serve alcoholic beverages for on-premises consumption has been granted by the Virginia Alcoholic Beverage Control Board under Title 4.1 may consume an alcoholic beverage while on the premises. A person who carries a concealed handgun onto the premises of such a restaurant or club and consumes alcoholic beverages is guilty of a Class 2 misdemeanor....

WASHINGTON

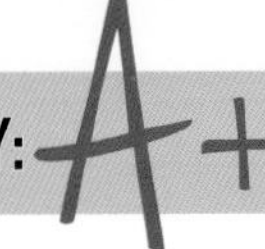

Permit Holders

Permit: "Shall issue" state.

Open Carry: Permitted.

Travel: Loaded handguns may be transported openly or concealed within a vehicle. Loaded long guns may not be transported.

Disclose Presence of Handgun to Law Enforcement: Not mandatory unless asked by a law enforcement officer.

Restaurants: May carry if permit holder does not consume alcohol, must not enter areas of restaurants that are restricted to patrons aged 21+.

Recognizes Permits From: KS, LA, MI, NC, ND, OH, OK, UT

Non-Permit

Firearm Ownership: Permitted to all qualified citizens without license or permit.

Loaded Carry: All citizens of age (18+) may openly carry a loaded firearm in public.

Travel: It is illegal to openly carry a loaded handgun in a vehicle without a permit. Unloaded handguns may be carried but not concealed, chamber must be empty and loaded magazine removed. Loaded long guns are prohibited.

General Info

State Parks: Permissible, some restrictions may apply.

Carry Law Uniformity: State law preempts that of local agencies/municipalities.

Self-Defense Model: No Castle Doctrine, no Duty to Retreat.

Notes: Firearms are forbidden in judicial proceedings but not in general common areas of courthouses, and statute requires courthouses to provide lock boxes for the purpose of storing the firearms of permit holders while they visit restricted areas of the building. Interestingly, the legislative authority is responsible for the firearms while they are held and is accountable for any damage or loss due to negligence during that time.

Revised Code of Washington § 9.41.073
Concealed pistol license—Reciprocity.

(1)(a) A person licensed to carry a pistol in a state the laws of which recognize and give effect in that state to a concealed pistol license issued under the laws of the state of Washington is authorized to carry a concealed pistol in this state if: (i) The licensing state does not issue concealed pistol licenses to persons under twenty-one years of age; and background checks of criminal and mental health history for all persons who apply for a concealed pistol license. (ii) The licensing state requires mandatory fingerprint-based (b) This section applies to a license holder from another state only while the license holder is not a resident of this state. A license holder from another state must carry the handgun in compliance with the laws of this state.

(2) The attorney general shall periodically publish a list of states the laws of which recognize and give effect in that state to a concealed pistol license issued under the laws of the state of Washington and which meet the requirements of subsection (1)(a)(i) and (ii) of this section.

§ 9.41.240 Possession of pistol by person from eighteen to twenty-one.

Unless an exception under RCW 9.41.042, 9.41.050, or 9.41.060 applies, a person at least eighteen years of age, but less than twenty-one years of age, may possess a pistol only: (1) In the person's place of abode; (2) At the person's fixed place of business; or (3) On real property under his or her control.

§ 9.41.290 State preemption.

The state of Washington hereby fully occupies and preempts the entire field of firearms regulation within the boundaries of the state, including the registration, licensing, possession, purchase, sale, acquisition, transfer, discharge, and transportation of firearms, or any other element relating to firearms or parts thereof, including ammunition and reloader components. Cities, towns, and counties or other municipalities may enact only those laws and ordinances relating to firearms that are specifically authorized by state law, as in RCW 9.41.300, and are consistent with this chapter. Such local ordinances shall have the same penalty as provided for by state law. Local laws and ordinances that are inconsistent with, more restrictive than, or exceed the requirements of state law shall not be enacted and are preempted and repealed, regardless of the nature of the code, charter, or home rule status of such city, town, county, or municipality.

§ 9.41.300 Weapons prohibited in certain places—Local laws and ordinances—Exceptions—Penalty.

(1) It is unlawful for any person to enter the following places when he or she knowingly possesses or knowingly has under his or her control a weapon:

(a) The restricted access areas of a jail, or of a law enforcement facility, or any place used for the confinement of a person (i) arrested for, charged with, or convicted of an offense, (ii) held for extradition or as a material witness, or (iii) otherwise confined pursuant to an order of a court, except an order under chapter 13.32A or 13.34 RCW. Restricted access areas do not include common areas of egress or ingress open to the general public;

(b) Those areas in any building which are used in connection with court proceedings, including courtrooms, jury rooms, judge's chambers, offices and areas used to conduct court business, waiting areas, and corridors adjacent to areas used in connection with court proceedings. The restricted areas do not include common areas of ingress and egress to the building that is used in connection with court proceedings, when it is possible to protect court areas without restricting ingress and egress to the building. The restricted areas shall be the minimum necessary to fulfill the objective of this subsection (1)(b)....In addition, the local legislative authority shall provide either a stationary locked box sufficient in size for pistols and key to a weapon owner for weapon storage, or shall designate an official to receive weapons for safekeeping, during the owner's visit to restricted areas of the building. The locked box or designated official shall be located within the same building used in connection with court proceedings. The local legislative authority shall be liable for any negligence causing damage to or loss of a weapon either placed in a locked box or left with an official during the owner's visit to restricted areas of the building.

The local judicial authority shall designate and clearly mark those areas where weapons are prohibited, and shall post notices at each entrance to the building of the prohibition against weapons in the restricted areas;

(c) The restricted access areas of a public mental health facility certified by the department of social and health services for inpatient hospital care and state institutions for the care of the mentally ill, excluding those facilities solely for evaluation and treatment. Restricted access areas do not include common areas of egress and ingress open to the general public;

(d) That portion of an establishment classified by the state liquor control board as off-limits to persons under twenty-one years of age; or

(e) The restricted access areas of a commercial service airport designated in the airport security plan approved by the federal transportation security administration, including passenger screening checkpoints at or beyond the point at which a passenger initiates the screening process. These areas do not include airport drives, general parking areas and walkways, and shops and areas of the terminal that are outside the screening checkpoints and that are normally open to unscreened passengers or visitors to the airport. Any restricted access area shall be clearly indicated by prominent signs indicating that firearms and other weapons are prohibited in the area.

(2) Cities, towns, counties, and other municipalities may enact laws and ordinances: (a) Restricting the discharge of firearms in any portion of their respective jurisdictions where there is a reasonable likelihood that humans, domestic animals, or property will be jeopardized. Such laws and ordinances shall not abridge the right of the individual guaranteed by Article I, section 24 of the state Constitution to bear arms in defense of self or others; and (b) Restricting the possession of firearms in any stadium or convention center, operated by a city, town, county, or other municipality, except that such restrictions shall not apply to: (i) Any pistol in the possession of a person licensed under RCW 9.41.070 or exempt from the licensing requirement by RCW 9.41.060; or (ii) Any showing, demonstration, or lecture involving the exhibition of firearms.

(3)(a) Cities, towns, and counties may enact ordinances restricting the areas in their respective jurisdictions in which firearms may be sold, but, except as provided in (b) of this subsection, a business selling firearms may not be treated more restrictively than other businesses located within the same zone....

(b) Cities, towns, and counties may restrict the location of a business selling firearms to not less than five hundred feet from primary or secondary school grounds, if the business has a storefront, has hours during which it is open for business, and posts advertisements or signs observable to passersby that firearms are available for sale. A business selling firearms that exists as of the date a restriction is enacted under this subsection (3)(b) shall be grandfathered according to existing law.

(4) Violations of local ordinances adopted under subsection (2) of this section must have the same penalty as provided for by state law.

(5) The perimeter of the premises of any specific location covered by subsection (1) of this section shall be posted at reasonable intervals to alert the public as to the existence of any law restricting the possession of firearms on the premises.

(6) Subsection (1) of this section does not apply to: (a) A person engaged in military activities ... while engaged in official duties; (b) Law enforcement personnel, except that subsection (1)(b) of this section does apply to a law enforcement officer who is present at a courthouse building as a party to an action under chapter 10.14, 10.99, or 26.50 RCW, or an action under Title 26 RCW where any party has alleged the existence of domestic violence as defined in RCW 26.50.010; or (c) Security personnel while engaged in official duties.

(7) Subsection (1)(a), (b), (c), and (e) of this section does not apply to correctional personnel or community corrections officers, as long as they are employed as such, who have completed government-sponsored law enforcement firearms training, except that subsection (1)(b) of this section does apply to a correctional employee or community corrections officer who is present at a courthouse building as a party to an action under chapter 10.14, 10.99, or 26.50 RCW, or an action under Title 26 RCW where any party has alleged the existence of domestic violence as defined in RCW 26.50.010.

(8) Subsection (1)(a) of this section does not apply to a person licensed pursuant to RCW 9.41.070 who, upon entering the place or facility, directly and promptly proceeds to the administrator of the facility or the administrator's designee and obtains written permission to possess the firearm while on the premises or checks his or her firearm. The person may reclaim the firearms upon leaving but must immediately and directly depart from the place or facility.

(9) Subsection (1)(c) of this section does not apply to any administrator or employee of the facility or to any person who, upon entering the place or facility, directly and promptly proceeds to the administrator of the facility or the administrator's designee and obtains written permission to possess the firearm while on the premises.

(10) Subsection (1)(d) of this section does not apply to the proprietor of the premises or his or her employees while engaged in their employment.

(11) Government-sponsored law enforcement firearms training must be training that correctional personnel and community corrections officers receive as part of their job requirement and reference to such training does not constitute a mandate that it be provided by the correctional facility.

(12) Any person violating subsection (1) of this section is guilty of a gross misdemeanor....

Contact for Additional Information:

Washington State Department of Licensing
P.O. Box 9649 • Olympia, WA 98507
360-664-6616

WEST VIRGINIA  FIREARM FRIENDLY: A

Permit Holders

Permit: "Shall issue" state.

Open Carry: Generally permitted, some restrictions apply.

Travel: A handgun may be transported openly or concealed by a permit holder.

Disclose Presence of Handgun to Law Enforcement: Required only if requested by a law enforcement officer.

Restaurants: Permissible, must not consume alcohol.

Recognizes Permits From: AL, AK, AZ, AR, CO, DE, FL, GA, IA, IN, KS, KY, LA, MI, MS, MO, NH, NM, NV, NC, ND, OH, OK, PA, SC, SD, TN, TX, UT, VA, WY

Non-Permit

Firearm Ownership: All qualified citizens may own firearms, no license or permit needed for purchase.

Loaded Carry: Open carry for adults 18+ is permissible without a permit.

Travel: If you plan to travel in West Virginia with a handgun and do not have a permit, then unload and case your gun, putting it in a place where it is not easily accessible by the driver or passengers. Ammunition should be stored separately from the firearm.

General Info

State Parks: Permissible, some restrictions may apply.

Carry Law Uniformity: State Law preempts that of local municipalities/agencies. However, there are some local laws that predate the state preemption law that remain valid.

Self-Defense Model: Castle Doctrine, Stand Your Ground.

Notes: If a person is found to be unlawfully in possession of a concealed firearm, it is punishable as a misdemeanor with a minimum fine of $200 for the first offense.

West Virginia Code § 61-7-3. Carrying deadly weapon without license or other authorization; penalties.

(a) Any person who carries a concealed deadly weapon, without a state license or other lawful authorization established under the provisions of this code, shall be guilty of a misdemeanor, and, upon conviction thereof, shall be fined not less than one hundred dollars nor more than one thousand dollars and may be imprisoned in the county jail for not more than twelve months for the first offense; but upon conviction of a second or subsequent offense, he or she shall be guilty of a felony, and, upon conviction thereof, shall be imprisoned in the penitentiary not less than one nor more than five years and fined not less than one thousand dollars nor more than five thousand dollars....

§ 61-7-6a. Reciprocity and recognition; out-of-state concealed handgun permits.

(a) A valid out-of-state permit or license to possess or carry a handgun is valid in this state for the carrying of a concealed handgun, if the following conditions are met:

(1) The permit or license holder is twenty-one years of age or older;

(2) The permit or license is in his or her immediate possession;

(3) The permit or license holder is not a resident of the State of West Virginia; and

(4) The Attorney General has been notified by the Governor of the other state that the other state allows residents of West Virginia who are licensed in West Virginia to carry a concealed handgun to carry a concealed handgun in that state or the Attorney General has entered into a written reciprocity agreement with the appropriate official of the other state....

(b) A holder of a valid permit or license from another state who is authorized to carry a concealed handgun in this state pursuant to provisions of this section is subject to the same laws and restrictions with respect to carrying a concealed handgun as a resident of West Virginia who is so permitted and must carry the concealed handgun in compliance with the laws of this state.

(c) A license or permit from another state is not valid in this state if the holder is or becomes prohibited by law from possessing a firearm....

§ 61-7-11a. Possessing deadly weapons on premises of educational facilities; reports by school principals; suspension of driver's license; possessing deadly weapons on premises housing courts of law and in offices of family law master.

... (b) (1) It is unlawful for a person to possess a firearm or other deadly weapon on a school bus as defined in section one, article one, chapter seventeen-a of this code, or in or on a public or private primary or secondary education building, structure, facility or grounds including a vocational education building, structure, facility or grounds where secondary vocational education programs are conducted or at a school-sponsored function.

... (b) (3) A person violating this subsection is guilty of a felony and, upon conviction thereof, shall be imprisoned in a state correctional facility for a definite term of years of not less than two years nor more than ten years, or fined not more than $5,000, or both.

... (g) (1) It is unlawful for a person to possess a firearm or other deadly weapon on the premises of a court of law, including family courts.

(2) This subsection does not apply to:

(A) A law-enforcement officer acting in his or her official capacity; and

(B) A person exempted from the provisions of this subsection by order of record entered by a court with jurisdiction over the premises or offices.

(3) A person violating this subsection is guilty of a misdemeanor and, upon conviction thereof, shall be fined not more than $1,000, or shall be confined in jail not more than one year, or both....

§ 61-7-14. Right of certain persons to limit possession of firearms on premises.

Notwithstanding the provisions of this article, any owner, lessee or other person charged with the care, custody and control of real property may prohibit the carrying openly or concealed of any firearm or deadly weapon on property under his or her domain: Provided, That for purposes of this section "person" means an individual or any entity which may acquire title to real property.

Any person carrying or possessing a firearm or other deadly weapon on the property of another who refuses to temporarily relinquish possession of such firearm or other deadly weapon, upon being requested to do so, or to leave such premises, while in possession of such firearm or other deadly weapon, shall be guilty of a misdemeanor, and, upon conviction thereof, shall be fined not more than one thousand dollars or confined in the county jail not more than six months, or both: Provided, That the provisions of this section shall not apply to those persons set forth in subsections (3) through (6) of section six of this code while such persons are acting in an official capacity: Provided, however, That under no circumstances may any person possess or carry or cause the possession or carrying of any firearm or other deadly weapon on the premises of any primary or secondary educational facility in this state unless such person is a law-enforcement officer or he or she has the express written permission of the county school superintendent.

Contact for Additional Information:

West Virginia State Police Headquarters
725 Jefferson Road • South Charleston, WV 25309
304-746-2100

FIREARM FRIENDLY: 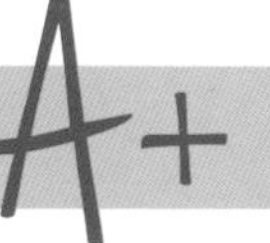  WISCONSIN

Permit: "Shall issue" state.

Open Carry: Permitted.

Travel: Loaded handguns may be transported openly or concealed in a vehicle. Long arms must remain unloaded, but can be uncased. Confusion persists as to whether or not a cased long gun is considered concealed. If cased, keep a long gun out of reach.

Disclose Presence of Handgun to Law Enforcement: Required only if requested by a law enforcement officer.

Restaurants: May carry if permit holder does not consume alcohol, not permitted to carry inside establishment that has a "no guns" sign posted.

Recognizes Permits From: AL, AZ, AR, CA, CO, CT, GA, HI, ID, IL, IN, IA, KS, KY, LA, MA (Class A permits only), MD, MI, MN, MO, MS, MT, NE, NV, NM, NY, NC, ND, PA, SC, SD (Enhanced and Gold licenses only), SC, TN, TX, UT, VA, WA, WV, WY

Permit Holders

Firearm Ownership: Permitted to all qualified citizens without license or permit.

Loaded Carry: All citizens of age (18+) may openly carry a loaded firearm in public.

Travel: A loaded handgun, cased or uncased, may be transported openly in a vehicle, but it may not be concealed.

Non-Permit

State Parks: Permissible, unless otherwise posted.

Carry Law Uniformity: State law preempts that of local agencies/municipalities.

Self-Defense Model: Castle Doctrine, Stand Your Ground.

Notes: Castle Doctrine applies to a citizen's personal dwelling, business, or automobile. Non-permitted citizens may not carry a concealed firearm; it must be visibly holstered on the carrier's person while in public.

Wisconsin Statutes § 175.60 License to carry a concealed weapon.

... (15m) Employer restrictions.

(a) Except as provided in par. (b), an employer may prohibit a licensee or an out-of-state licensee that it employs from carrying a concealed weapon or a particular type of concealed weapon in the course of the licensee's or out-of-state licensee's employment or during any part of the licensee's or out-of-state licensee's course of employment.

(b) An employer may not prohibit a licensee or an out-of-state licensee, as a condition of employment, from carrying a concealed weapon, a particular type of concealed weapon, or ammunition or from storing a weapon, a particular type of weapon, or ammunition in the licensee's or out-of-state licensee's own motor vehicle, regardless of whether the motor vehicle is used in the course of employment or whether the motor vehicle is driven or parked on property used by the employer.

(16) Prohibited activity.

(a) Except as provided in par. (b), neither a licensee nor an out-of-state licensee may knowingly carry a concealed weapon, a weapon that is not concealed, or a firearm that is not a weapon in any of the following places:

General Info

1. Any portion of a building that is a police station, sheriff's office, state patrol station, or the office of a division of criminal investigation special agent of the department.

2. Any portion of a building that is a prison, jail, house of correction, or secured correctional facility.

3. The facility established under s. 46.055.

4. The center established under s. 46.056.

5. Any secured unit or secured portion of a mental health institute under s. 51.05, including a facility designated as the Maximum Security Facility at Mendota Mental Health Institute.

6. Any portion of a building that is a county, state, or federal courthouse.

7. Any portion of a building that is a municipal courtroom if court is in session.

8. A place beyond a security checkpoint in an airport.

(b) The prohibitions under par. (a) do not apply to any of the following:

1. A weapon in a vehicle driven or parked in a parking facility located in a building that is used as, or any portion of which is used as, a location under par. (a).

2. A weapon in a courthouse or courtroom if a judge who is a licensee is carrying the weapon or if another licensee or out-of-state licensee, whom a judge has permitted in writing to carry a weapon, is carrying the weapon.

3. A weapon in a courthouse or courtroom if a district attorney, or an assistant district attorney, who is a licensee is carrying the weapon.

(17) Penalties.

(a) Any person who violates sub. (2g) (b) or (c) may be required to forfeit not more than $25, except that the person shall be exempted from the forfeiture if the person presents, within 48 hours, his or her license document or out-of-state license and photographic identification to the law enforcement agency that employs the requesting law enforcement officer.

(ac) Except as provided in sub. (11) (b) 2., any person who violates sub. (11) (b) 1. may be required to forfeit $50.

(ag) Any person who violates sub. (2m) (e), (12), or (12g) may be fined not more than $500 or sentenced to a term of imprisonment of not more than 30 days or both....

(b) Any person who violates sub. (16) may be fined not more than $500 or imprisoned for not more than 30 days or both.

(c) An instructor of a training course under sub. (4) (a) who intentionally submits false documentation indicating that an individual has met the training requirements under sub. (4) (a) may be prosecuted for a violation of s. 946.32.

(e) Any person required under sub. (14) (b) 3. to relinquish or deliver a license document to the department who intentionally violates the requirements of that subdivision shall be fined not more than $500 and may be imprisoned for not more than 30 days or both.

Contact for Additional Information:

Wisconsin Department of Justice
P.O. Box 7857 • Madison, WI 53707
608-266-1221

FIREARM FRIENDLY:  WYOMING

Permit: "Shall issue" to residents only; a permit isn't necessary to carry concealed, but some residents acquire one to gain reciprocity rights in states that honor WY permits.

Open Carry: Generally permitted in all areas not specifically prohibiting firearms.

Travel: Loaded handguns may be transported on a person or anywhere in a vehicle. Long guns may be loaded, but must remain in plain view.

Disclose Presence of Handgun to Law Enforcement: Only required if requested by officer.

Restaurants: May carry unless establishment has posted signs noting otherwise. May not carry in portion of restaurant primarily devoted to dispensing alcohol.

Recognizes Permits From: AL, AK, AZ, AR, CO, FL, GA, ID, IN, IA, KS, KY, LA, ME, MI, MS, MO, MT, NE, NH, NM, NC, ND, NV, OH, OK, PA, SC, SD, TN, TX, UT, VA, WV, WI

Permit Holders

Firearm Ownership: Permitted to all qualified citizens without license or permit.

Loaded Carry: All law-abiding citizens 21 years of age or older may carry a loaded firearm in public, openly without a permit. Residents of WY may carry concealed without a permit. Non-residents must have a permit for concealed carry.

Travel: Loaded firearms may be transported in plain view or anywhere in a vehicle if the gun is cased. Those 21 years of age or older may carry a concealed handgun anywhere in a vehicle. Long arms should be cased or kept in plain view.

Non-Permit

State Parks: Only permit holders and only in parks (not while inside structures on park property).

Carry Law Uniformity: State law preempts that of local agencies/municipalities.

Self-Defense Model: Castle Doctrine, Stand Your Ground (only in your home).

Notes: As of 2011, the state no longer requires a permit for a citizen to carry. Permits in this state only apply to concealed carry of a handgun and no other types of weapons. Postings forbidding firearms on private property have the force of law. Permit law in WY requires an applicant to be at least 21 years of age, but residents as young as 18 can acquire a carry permit with written permission of a sheriff.

General Info

Contact for Additional Information:

Attorney General of Wyoming

208 South College Drive • Cheyenne, WY 82002

307-777-7181

Wyoming Statutes §6-8-104. Wearing or carrying concealed weapons; penalties; exceptions; permits.

(a) A person who wears or carries a concealed deadly weapon is guilty of a misdemeanor punishable by a fine of not more than seven hundred fifty dollars ($750.00), imprisonment in the county jail for not more than six (6) months, or both for a first offense, or a felony punishable by a fine of not more than two thousand dollars ($2,000.00), imprisonment for not more than two (2) years, or both, for a second or subsequent offense, unless:

(i) The person is a peace officer;

(ii) The person possesses a permit under this section;

(iii) The person holds a valid permit authorizing him to carry a concealed firearm authorized and issued by a governmental agency or entity in another state that recognizes Wyoming permits and is a valid statewide permit; or

(iv) The person does not possess a permit issued under this section, but otherwise meets the requirements specified in paragraphs (b)(i) through (vi), (viii) and (ix) of this section and possession of the firearm by the person is not otherwise unlawful....

... (j) The sheriff of the applicant's county of residence may, at his discretion, submit a written report to the division recommending the issuance of a concealed firearm permit to an applicant between eighteen (18) and twenty-one (21) years of age who meets the requirements specified in this section. The written recommendation shall specifically state that the sheriff has personal knowledge of the applicant's situation or circumstances which warrant the issuance of a concealed firearm permit. The division may issue a permit to carry a concealed firearm to those individuals between eighteen (18) and twenty-one (21) years of age under circumstances that a reasonable, prudent person would believe warrant the issuance of a permit to carry a concealed firearm. The decision to issue a concealed firearm permit shall be based on the satisfactory completion of the requirements of this section and any voluntary written report offered by the sheriff of the county of the applicant's residence which shall clearly state the reasons the applicant should be issued a permit. The applicant may submit a written report containing relevant facts for consideration by the division.

...(t) No person authorized to carry a concealed weapon pursuant to paragraphs (a)(ii) through (iv) of this section shall carry a concealed firearm into:

(i) Any facility used primarily for law enforcement operations or administration without the written consent of the chief administrator;

(ii) Any detention facility, prison or jail;

(iii) Any courtroom, except that nothing in this section shall preclude a judge from carrying a concealed weapon or determining who will carry a concealed weapon in the courtroom;

(iv) Any meeting of a governmental entity;

(v) Any meeting of the legislature or a committee thereof;

(vi) Any school, college or professional athletic event not related to firearms;

(vii) Any portion of an establishment licensed to dispense alcoholic liquor and malt beverages for consumption on the premises, which portion of the establishment is primarily devoted to that purpose;

(viii) Any place where persons are assembled for public worship, without the written consent of the chief administrator of that place;

(ix) Any elementary or secondary school facility;

(x) Any college or university facility without the written consent of the security service of the college or university; or

(xi) Any place where the carrying of firearms is prohibited by federal law or regulation or state law.

DISTRICT OF COLUMBIA FIREARM FRIENDLY:

Permit Holders

Permit: "May issue."

Open Carry: Forbidden.

Travel: May travel with loaded firearm in vehicle, but must be concealed and on carrier's person if loaded.

Disclose Presence of Handgun to Law Enforcement: Must immediately disclose to law enforcement upon making investigative contact; applies to all carriers in the vehicle.

Restaurants: Permissible in restaurants unless posted, even if establishment serves alcohol (as long as establishment is primarily a restaurant and not a bar where carry is forbidden).

Recognizes Permits from: No states.

Non-Permit

Firearms Ownership: Handgun ownership is only permissible with a permit. Handguns must be registered within 48 hours of new resident's arrival into the state. Established residents may only register one firearm per month.

Loaded Carry: Forbidden.

Travel: Non-permit holders must comply with federal requirements when traveling with a firearm (unloaded, locked, out of reach, ammunition stored separately, cased).

General Info

State Parks: Not applicable.

Carry Law Uniformity: Not applicable.

Self-Defense Model: Castle Doctrine provides that there's no duty to retreat in the home; Stand Your Ground in public.

Notes: Any firearm possessed and not properly registered/permitted is an "unregistered firearm" under DC law, and possession of one is punishable as a felony offense. DC has extensive training requirements associated with permit acquisition. Private property or businesses forbidding firearms must post conspicuously, and postings carry force of law. DC has a ban on high capacity magazines, but this jurisdiction takes ammunition restrictions a step further by mandating that a carrier not only be prohibited from possessing a magazine that holds in excess of ten rounds, but also that a carrier be prohibited from carrying additional loaded magazines that, together with the one in the firearm, yield a total number of rounds in excess of 20. Firearms are forbidden in bars, in nightclubs, in taverns, on federal property, at schools, at colleges, in churches, in entertainment stadiums/complexes, in government buildings, at the National Mall, on the Metro Rail Subway System, within 1000 feet from Congress and the White House properties, and within 1000 feet of any principal who is being protected by a detail associated with law enforcement or the Secret Service (but the public must have proper notice for violations to be enforceable). Concealed carry is extremely new in the state, so there are few test cases interpreting DC carry law. Due to the newness of its creation, the only existing law to govern concealed carry in DC is in the form of an emergency ruling making amending Chapter 23 (Guns and Other Weapons) of Title 24 (Public Space and Safety) of the District of Columbia Municipal Regulations; that rulemaking went into effect on February 13, 2015, and should yield a final, formal promulgation within the District of Columbia Official Code by June 13, 2015. The rulemaking allows for permit issuance only upon a showing of "good reason to fear injury," "other proper reason for carrying a pistol," and "suitability to obtain" on the part of the applicant. Selected excerpts of that rulemaking follow in italics:

2343 AMMUNITION CARRIED BY LICENSEE

2343.1 A person issued a concealed carry license by the Chief, while carrying the pistol, shall not carry more ammunition than is required to fully load the pistol twice, and in no event shall that amount be greater than twenty (20) rounds of ammunition.

2343.2 A person issued a concealed carry license by the Chief may not carry any restricted pistol bullet as that term is defined in the Act.

2344 PISTOL CARRY METHODS

2344.1 A licensee shall carry any pistol in a manner that it is entirely hidden from view of the public when carried on or about a person, or when in a vehicle in such a way as it is entirely hidden from view of the public.

2344.2 A licensee shall carry any pistol in a holster on their person in a firmly secure manner that is reasonably designed to prevent loss, theft, or accidental discharge of the pistol.

2345 NON-RESIDENT APPLICATIONS FOR CONCEALED CARRY LICENSE

2345.1 A non-resident of the District, as defined by the Act, may apply to the Firearms Registration Section for a concealed carry license upon a showing that the applicant meets all of the eligibility requirements of § 2332.

2345.2 A non-resident may satisfy some or all of the firearms training requirements in § 2336 by providing proof of completion of a firearms training course in another state or subdivision of the United States.

2345.3 A non-resident shall obtain a certification from a firearms trainer that the applicant has received and completed training in District firearms law and the District law of self-defense.

2345.4 A non-resident must demonstrate to the Chief that he or she has a good reason to fear injury to his or her person or property, as defined by the Act and these regulations, by showing that the fear is from a cause that will likely be present in the District and is not a cause that is likely to be present only in another jurisdiction.

2345.5 A non-resident must demonstrate to the Chief that he or she has any other proper reason for carrying a pistol, as defined by the Act and these regulations, by showing that the other proper reason exists in the District.

2346 SIGNAGE TO PREVENT ENTRANCE BY CONCEALED CARRY LICENSEE ONTO NON-RESDIENTIAL PRIVATE PROPERTY

2346.1 Signs stating that the carrying of firearms is prohibited on any private property shall be clearly and conspicuously posted at any entrance, open to the public, of a building, premises, or real property.

2346.2 A sign shall be considered conspicuous if it is at least eight (8) inches by ten (10) inches in size and contains writing in contrasting ink using not less than thirty-six (36) point type.

District of Columbia Official Code § 7-2502.01. Registration requirements. (a) Except as otherwise provided in this unit, no person or organization in the District of Columbia ("District") shall receive, possess, control, transfer, offer for sale, sell, give, or deliver any destructive device, and no person or organization in the District shall possess or control any firearm, unless the person or organization holds a valid registration certificate for the firearm. A registration certificate may be issued:

(1) To an organization if:

(A) The organization employs at least 1 commissioned special police officer or employee licensed to carry a firearm whom the organization arms during the employee's duty hours; and

(B) The registration is issued in the name of the organization and in the name of the president or chief executive officer of the organization;

(2) In the discretion of the Chief of Police, to a police officer who has retired from the Metropolitan Police Department;

(3) In the discretion of the Chief of Police, to the Fire Marshal and any member of the Fire and Arson Investigation Unit of the Fire Prevention Bureau of the Fire Department of the District of Columbia, who is designated in writing by the Fire Chief, for the purpose of enforcing the arson and fire safety laws of the District of Columbia;

(4) To a firearms instructor, or to an organization that employs a firearms instructor, for the purpose of conducting firearms training; or

(5) To a person who complies with, and meets the requirements of, this unit.

(b) Subsection (a) of this section shall not apply to:

(1) Any law enforcement officer or agent of the District or the United States, or any law enforcement officer or agent of the government of any state or subdivision thereof, or any member of the armed forces of the United States, the National Guard or organized reserves, when such officer, agent, or member is authorized to possess such a firearm or device while on duty in the performance of official authorized functions;

(2) Any person holding a dealer's license; provided, that the firearm or destructive device is:

(A) Acquired by such person in the normal conduct of business;

(B) Kept at the place described in the dealer's license; and

(C) Not kept for such person's private use or protection, or for the protection of his business;

(3) With respect to firearms, any nonresident of the District participating in any lawful recreational firearm-related activity in the District, or on his way to or from such activity in another jurisdiction; provided, that such person, whenever in possession of a firearm, shall upon demand of any member of the Metropolitan Police Department, or other bona fide law enforcement officer, exhibit proof that he is on his way to or from such activity, and that his possession or control of such firearm is lawful in the jurisdiction in which he resides; provided further, that such weapon shall be transported in accordance with § 22-4504.02;

(4) Any person who temporarily possesses a firearm registered to another person while in the home of the registrant; provided, that the person is not otherwise prohibited from possessing firearms and the person reasonably believes that possession of the firearm is necessary to prevent imminent death or great bodily harm to himself or herself; or

(5) Any person who temporarily possesses a firearm while participating in a firearms training and safety class conducted by a firearms instructor.

(c) For the purposes of subsection (b)(3) of this section, the term "recreational firearm-related activity" includes a firearms training and safety class.

§ 7-2502.06. Time for filing registration applications.

(a) An application for a registration certificate shall be filed (and a registration certificate issued) prior to taking possession of a firearm from a licensed dealer or from any person or organization holding a registration certificate therefor. In all other cases, an application for registration shall be filed immediately after a firearm is brought into the District. It shall be deemed compliance with the preceding sentence if such person personally communicates with the Metropolitan Police Department (as determined by the Chief to be sufficient) and provides such information as may be demanded; provided, that such person files an application for a registration certificate within 48 hours after such communication....

§ 7-2506.01. Persons permitted to possess ammunition.

(a) No person shall possess ammunition in the District of Columbia unless:

(1) He is a licensed dealer pursuant to subchapter IV of this unit;

(2) He is an officer, agent, or employee of the District of Columbia or the United States of America, on duty and acting within the scope of his duties when possessing such ammunition;

(3) He is the holder of a valid registration certificate for a firearm pursuant to subchapter II of this chapter; except, that no such person shall possess one or more restricted pistol bullets;

(4) He holds an ammunition collector's certificate on September 24, 1976; or

(5) He temporarily possesses ammunition while participating in a firearms training and safety class conducted by a firearms instructor.

(b) No person in the District shall possess, sell, or transfer any large capacity ammunition feeding device regardless of whether the device is attached to a firearm. For the purposes of this subsection, the term "large capacity ammunition feeding device" means a magazine, belt, drum, feed strip, or similar device that has a capacity of, or that can be readily restored or converted to accept, more than 10 rounds of ammunition. The term "large capacity ammunition feeding device" shall not include an attached tubular device designed to accept, and capable of operating only with, .22 caliber rimfire ammunition.

§ 22-4504.01. Authority to carry firearm in certain places and for certain purposes.

Notwithstanding any other law, a person holding a valid registration for a firearm may carry the firearm:

(1) Within the registrant's home;

(2) While it is being used for lawful recreational purposes;

(3) While it is kept at the registrant's place of business; or

(4) While it is being transported for a lawful purpose as expressly authorized by District or federal statute and in accordance with the requirements of that statute.

Contact for Additional Information:
Metropolitan Police Department,
Firearms Registration Section
300 Indiana Avenue Northwest • Washington D.C. 20001
202-727-4225

Handgun Instructors by State

The following handgun instructors, listed by jurisdiction, are recommended and endorsed by the editors of *Legally Armed*. Some of them were gracious enough to review the manuscript of the first edition, and we appreciate their help as we strive for clarity and accuracy.

Alabama: Southern Belle Firearms Training, Kristi Collins, *www.southernbellefirearmstraining.com*, 256-479-6738. Classes held at multiple gun ranges.

Gun Logic Firearms Training, *www.gunlogic.com*, 205-333-3258, gunlogic@charter.net, 14695 Bel Aire East, Coker, AL 35452

Alaska: RRR Alaska Firearms Instruction, Mike Rawalt, *www.rrrfi.com*, 907-344-1946, mbrawalt@gmail.com, P.O. Box 110572, Anchorage, AK 99511

Alaska Tactical and Security Inc., Steve McDaniel, 907-338-5434, *www.alaskatactical.com*, akshooter@gci.net, 210 Muldoon Road, Anchorage, AK 99504

Arizona: Shots Ranch, Jeffery Jolly, *www.shotsranch.com*, 928-554-6002, 4628 N Diamond M Ranch Road, Kingman, AZ 86401

C2 Tactical, *www.c2tactical.com*, vincent.vasquez@c2tactical.com, 480-588-8802, 8475 S. Emerald Drive, Suite 106, Tempe, AZ 85284

Arkansas: Nighthawk Custom Training Academy, Thomas See, *www.nighthawkcustomtraining.com*, 479-366-8256, thomas_see@ymail.com. Classes held at Rogers Police Department.

THOR Global Defense Group, Max Rodriguez, 479-474-3434, *www.thortraining.com*, info@thortraining.com, 1206 Knesek Lane, Van Buren, AR 72956

California: Best Handgun Training, John Taylor, *www.besthandguntraining.com*, 916-295-8489, 2270 Nicolaus Road #109, Lincoln, CA 95648

Firearms Training Associates, *www.ftatv.com*, 714-701-9918, P.O. Box 554, Yorba Linda, CA 92885

Colorado: Colorado CCW and Firearm Training, Jacob Paulsen, *www.coloradofirearmtraining.com*, 303-719-1209. Classes held at multiple gun ranges.

Have Gun Will Train Colorado, Rick Sindeband, 719-821-3958, *www.havegunwilltraincolorado.com*, 700 W. 6th Street, Pueblo, CO 81003

Connecticut: A Call to Arms, *www.acall2arms.net*, 860-265-7620, 90 Enfield Street, #3, Enfield, CT 06082

HF LearnSafety, LLC, Herb Furhman, 203-947-4327, *www.hflearnsafety.com*, learnsafety@gmail.com, 280 Kent Road, New Milford, CT 06776

Delaware: Trinity Tactical USA, Carl Pace, 302-355-1772 *www.trintacusa.com*, training@trintacusa.net, 4435 Summitt Bridge Road, Middletown, DE 19709

JD Defense, *www.jddefense.com*, 302-856-6910, 18140 County Seat Highway (US Route 9), Georgetown, DE 19947

Florida: Florida Firearms Training, Paul Molloy, 561-450-9586, *www.floridafirearmstraining.com*. Classes held at multiple gun ranges.

Shooters World, 116 East Fletcher Ave., Tampa, FL 33612, 813-381-1111 *www.shootersworld.com/training-classes/concealed-permit.aspx*

Georgia: Atlanta Firearms Training, Tom Mulheron, 404-451-6061, *www.atlantafirearmstraining.com*, P.O. Box 942203, Atlanta, GA 31141, tommulheron@atlantafirearmstraining.com

4G Tactical Firearms Training, Paul Forgey, 678-283-5104, *www.4gtactical.com*, pwforgey@msn.com, Jodeco Road, McDonough, GA 30253

Hawaii: Sean Choo, cfpinstructor808@gmail.com, 808-754-0130, P. O. Box 941221, Unit 108-132, Waipahu, HI 96797

Wayne Holu, 808-292-7321, 66-250 Kamehameha Hwy, Ste. C-201, Haleiwa, HI

Idaho: Ultimate Firearms Training, Keith Owen, 2420 East Kuna Mora Road, Kuna, ID 83634, *www.boisefirearmstraining.com*, 208-846-9119

Northwest Concealed Carry Outfitters, Bert Moore, 208-949-3763, *www.ncco.biz*, ncco@centurylink.net. Classes held at multiple gun ranges.

Illinois: Fidelity Investigative Training Academy, Andre Queen, *www.illinois-concealed-carry-permit-classes.com*, 224-678-0311, 4224 W. Belmont Avenue, Chicago, IL 60641

Condition Yellow Academy, Steve Watson, 847-341-5711, *www.conditionyellowacademy.com*, info@conditionyellowacademy.com, 3 W. College Drive, Arlington Heights, IL 60004

Indiana: Indy Gun Safety, Randall DeWitt, 317-345-3263, *www.indygunsafety.com*, info@indygunsafety.com, 55 S. State Ave., Indianapolis, IN 46202

Hard Target Firearms Training, 812-774-0235, P.O. Box 1495, Newburgh, IN 47629, *www.hardtargetfirearms.com*

Iowa: Cedar Valley Outfitters, 319-447-6140, *www.cedarvalleyoutfitters.org*, julie@cedarvalleyoutfitters.org, 1177 Grand Ave., Marion, IA 52302

Hawkeye Firearms Instruction, Steve Hensyel, 641-660-0070, *www.hawkeyefirearmsinstruction.com*, 1006 Penn Boulevard, Oskaloosa, Iowa 52577, steve@hawkeyefirearmsinstruction.com

Kansas: KC Concealed Carry LLC, *www.kcconcealedcarry.com*, 816-215-1002, 1358 NE Windsor Dr., Lees Summit, MO 64086

Bullseye Shooting Range, Mike Relihan, *www.bullseyewichita.com*, 316-686-7264, mrelihan@bullseye.com, 1455 North Terrace, Wichita, KS 67208

Kentucky: Firearm Safety and Security Training, LLC, Joshua McFadden, *www.kygunclass.com*, 859-576-3083, 694 East New Circle Road, Suite 210, Lexington, KY 40505a

Kentucky CCDW Classes, Matt Preston, *www.kentuckyccdwclasses.com*, 606-636-6464, 1220 Highway 235, Nancy, KY 42544

Louisiana: Acadiana Tactical Firearms, Damian Leger, 855-999-4867, *www.acadianatactical.com*, info@acadianatactical.com, P.O. Box 507, Carencro, LA 70520

Elite Arms Training, LLC, Jack Ragsdale, *www.elitearmstraining.com*, 601-528-2410, jack@elitearmstraining.com, 34A O.T. Davis Road, Lumberton, MS 39455

Maine: Maine Defensive Firearms Academy, Bob Henckel, 207-310-8603, *www.mainefirearmsacademy.com*, P.O. Box 943, Gorham, ME 04038

Weaponcraft Firearms Training and Professional Development, *www.weaponcrafttraining.com*, 207-553-2266, 27 Industrial Park Road, Saco, ME 04072

Maryland: WORTH-A-SHOT INC., Curtis Worthy, 443-688-6521, *www.worth-a-shot.com*, 8424 Veterans Hwy #5, Millersville, MD 21108, customerservice@worth-a-shot.com

Defensive & Protective Solutions, LLC, 240-383-4763, *www.defensiveprotectivesolutions.com*, info@dpsmd.com, P.O. Box 1032, La Plata, MD 20646

Massachusetts: Complete Firearm Instruction, Alan Klammer, *www.completefirearminstruction.com*, 508-465-0501, 240 Meadow Street, Carver, MA 02330

2nd Amendment Firearms Training, 413-888-4519, 28 Smith Ave., West Springfield, MA 01089

Michigan: 906 Concealed Carry, *www.906concealedcarry.com*, 906-249-9250, 279 Kawbawgam Road, Marquette, MI 49855

Tulip City Rod and Gun Club, 616-786-0223, 4381 136th Avenue, Holland, MI 49424, *www.tcrgc.org,* Phil@TCRCG.org

Minnesota: Brian Duer Firearms Training Academy, LLC, Brian Duerr, 507-993-0778, 5233 Belmoral Lane NW, Rochester, MN 55901 *www.brianduerrfirearmstrainingacademy.com*, brianduerrfirearmstraining@gmail.com

Burnsville Rifle and Pistol Range, *www.bvpistol.com*, 952-890-6228, 14300 Ewing Avenue South, Burnsville, MN 55306

Mississippi: Focused Fire Training, *www.focusedfiretraining.com*, 228-313-6034, admin@focusedfiretraining.com, 2429 Sunkist Country Club Road, Biloxi, MS 39532

MidSouth Safety Training, *www.midsouthsafetytraining.com*, 901-568-7420, 2682 Lamar Place North, Hernando, MS 38632

Missouri: Advantage Training Center, 636-334-5300, *www.advantagetrainingcenter.com*, 2757 English Road, Pacific, MO 63069, training@advantagetrainingcenter.com

Constitutional Sports, Dr. Rodney Harrison, 816-286-7786, *www.sites.google.com/site/constitutionalprotection*, rod@constitutionalsports.com, 3801 NW 52nd, Kansas City, MO 64155

Montana: Fortress Personal Defense Solutions, 406-599-6766, *www.firearmsbozeman.com*, 1008 N 7th Ave., Suite C, Bozeman, MT 59715

Fish Creek Ventures, Dan Busarow, *www.fishcreekventures.com*, 406-287-2182, dan@fishcreekventures.com, 5913 State Hwy. 41, Whitehall, MT 59759

Nebraska: Great Plains Firearms Training, 402-676-0676, *www.gpftomaha.com*, info@gpftomaha.com, 3606 North 156th Street, Suite 101-198, Omaha, NE 68116

Midwest Concealed Carry, LLC, Tim Kostrunek, 308-325-4631, *www.midwestconcealedcarry.com*, midwestccw@yahoo.com

Nevada: CCW Las Vegas, *www.ccw-lasvegas.com*, 702-475-4078, 113v7 N Decatur Blvd, Las Vegas, NV 89131

Nevada Concealed Weapon Instruction, Anthony B. Wojcicki, *www.renoconcealedweapons.com*, 775-772-4508, tonycordevista@yahoo.com, P.O. Box 1720, Sparks, NV 89432

New Hampshire: Defensive Strategies, LLC, 603-566-1727, *www.defensivestrategies.org*, 680 Brent Street, Manchester, NH 03103

Response Ability Firearms Training, LLC, Ernest Castle, 603-703-3995, *www.response-ability.org*, info@response-ability.org, 855 Hanover Street # 425, Manchester, NH 03104

New Jersey: Lady Liberty Gunsmithing, LLC, Andrea & Guy Petinga, *www.ladylibertyllc.com*, 609-348-1900, ladylibertyllc@aol.com, 121 North LaClede Place, Atlantic City, NJ 08401

Shoot NJ, LLC, *www.shootnj.com*, 732-791-4880, 200 Yardville Allentown Rd., Hamilton Township, NJ 08620

New Mexico: New Mexico CHL Instruction, Steve Aikens, *www.nm-ccw.com*, 575-762-0365, 601 South Norris Street, Clovis, NM 88101

Deliberate Defense, Rick Davis, *www.deliberatedefense.com*, 505-369-6992, 2270-D Wyoming NE, #353, Albuquerque, NM 87112

New York: Aim Small Firearms Instruction, Paul J Conforti, *www.aimsmallinstruction.com*, paul@aimsmallinstruction.com, 914-447-7281, 1231 Audra Court, Mohegan Lake, NY 10547

New York CCW & Firearm Training, Lance Dashefsky, 917-688-2656, *www.newyorkfirearmtraining.com*. Classes held at multiple gun ranges.

North Carolina: North Carolina Concealed Carry, Lorne Kime, *www.northcarolina-concealed-carry.com*, 704-991-5467, 488 Anson High School Road, Wadesboro, NC 28170

Concealed Carry Pistol Classes for North Carolina, Thomas Cash, *www.concealedcarrypermitnc.com,* 919-902-0976, 4753 Swift Creek Road, Smithfield, NC 27577

North Dakota: Dakota Carry, Bruce Potts, 701-320-1547, dakotacarry@yahoo.com, 956 18th Avenue SW, Valley City, ND 58072

North Dakota Permit to Carry, *www.ndpermittocarry.com*, 612-240-2246, admin@ndpermittcarry.com. Classes held at multiple gun ranges.

Ohio: Tactical Defense Institute, John Benner, *www.tdiohio.com*, 937-544-7228, 2174 Bethany Ridge, West Union, OH 45693

Iron Element, Justin Miesse, *www.ironelement.net*, 567-279-1547, justin@ironelement.net, 1957 Celina-Mendon Road, Celina, OH 45822

Oklahoma: Tulsa Red Castle Gun Club, *www.tulsaredcastlegunclub.com/concealed-carry*, 918-582-3922, concealedcarry@trcgc.org, 1115 S. Zunis Avenue, Tulsa, OK 74104

Dale Spradlin 580-656-6225, 214 South Main Street, Waurika, OK 73573, *www.okconcealcarry.com*, okconcealcarry@yahoo.com

Oregon: MK Tactical, Michael and Susie Knoetig, *www.mktactical.com*, 503-577-6824, 128 West Main Street Ext., Hillsboro, OR 97123

Blackstone Gun Safety, Dan Blackstone, 971-238-2478, *www.blackstonegunsafety.com*, dan@blackstonegunsafety.com, 12360 SW Poppy Drive, Gaston, OR 97119

Pennsylvania: Philly Firearms Academy, José Morales, *www.phillyguntraining.com*, info@phillyguntraining.com, 215-765-7233, 935 Spring Garden Street, Philadelphia, PA 19123

Targetmaster, *www.targetmaster.com*, 610-459-5400, 255 Wilmington W Chester Pike, Suite 3, Chadds Ford, PA 19317

Rhode Island: Lock, Stock, and Daria, Daria Bruno, *www.lockstockanddaria.com*, 401-441-0111, 309 Sanford Road, Westport, MA 02790

South Carolina: Carolina Concealed Carry & Tactical Firearms Training, Jonathan Painter, *www.carolinaconcealedcarry.net*, 843-318-1743. Classes held at multiple gun ranges.

SouthCarolinaConcealedCarry.com, Jeff Barton, *www.southcarolinaconcealedcarry.com*, 803-359-4050, 1610 South Lake Drive, Lexington, SC 29073

South Dakota: Professional Firearms Training LLC, Jayson Gilbertson, 507-407-0004, *www.mngunclass.com*, 3942 O'Brien Court, SW, Pryor Lake, MN 55372

Smoking Gun Range & Training Center, *smokinggunsd.com*, 605-791-3656, info@smokinggunsd.com, 4711 S Interstate 90 Svc Road #B, Rapid City, SD 57703

Tennessee: The Armory, Curtis Dodson, *www.thearmorytn.com*, 615-257-0606, 628 S Cumberland Street, Lebanon, TN 37087

Guns and Leather, Chris Smith, *www.gandlacademy.com*, 615-824-7846, 600 West Main St., Hendersonville, TN 37075

Texas: Jeff's Gunslingers, Jeff Srygley, 806-433-0435, jeffs.gunslingers@sbcglobal.net, 7148 Bell Street, Amarillo, TX 79109

Texas Handgun Academy, *www.texashandgunacademy.com*, 214-340-3101, tha.messages@gmail.com, 10201 Plano Road, Suite 107, Dallas, TX 75238

Utah: Utah CCW Carry, Aaron Turner, *utahccwcarry.com*, 801-554-4833, aaron@utahccwcarry.com, 4641 Cherry Street, Murry, UT 84123

Pistol Pete's Self Protection Training, *www.pistolpetesspt.com*, 801-706-7363, info@pistolpetesspt.com, 63 East 11400 South #211, Sandy, UT 84070

Vermont: Vermont Tactical International LLC, Gary LeRoux, 802-734-6387

VT Firearms Training, John Jacob, 802-355-7554,
www.vtfirearmstraining.com, vtfirearmstraining@gmail.com,
854 Maquam Shore Road, St. Albans Bay, VT 05488

Virginia: Proactive Shooters, 804-307-8315,
www.proactiveshooters.com, training@proactiveshooters.com,
9702 Gayton Road, Suite 185, Henrico, VA 23238

Virginia Pistol LLC, "Buz" Grover, 540-636-9476,
www.virginiapistol.com, jim@virginiapistol.com,
5223 John Marshall Hwy, Linden, VA 22642

Washington: InSights Training Center, LLC, 888-958-0884,
www.insightstraining.com, Info@InSightsTraining.com,
P.O. Box 3585, Bellevue, WA 98009

Defensive Solutions, LLC, 509-540-1701, Harvey Shaw Road, Prescott, WA 99348

Washington, DC: dcConcealed Carry.com, Leon Spears,
www.dcconcealedcarry.com, contactus@dcconcealedcarry.com,
202-317-1964, 1425 K Street NW, Washington, D.C. 20005

VOU Gunsmith Firearm Safety and Training, B. Powers,
www.vougunsmith.com, training@vougunsmith.com,
202-415-8520, 5257 Buckeystown Pike, #215, Frederick, MD 21704

West Virginia: Tri-County-Training, 340-680-6230, 257
Linton Road, Independence, WV 26374

Second Amendment Sports & Defense LLC, 304-381-2674, 1212
Van Voorhis Road, Suite 5, Morgantown, WV 26505

Wisconsin: Wisconsin Firearms Training LLC, Jake Trussoni,
www.wi-firearmstraining.com, P.O. Box 210873, Milwaukee, WI 53221
jake@wi-firearmstraining.com, 414-405-1089,

BDJ-Ltd., Bill Schmitz, 920-295-9435, ccwtrainer@BDJ-LTD.com,
www.bdj-ltd.com, Classes held at multiple gun ranges.

Wyoming: Code Red Tactical, Steve Allred, 307-548-7154,
www.coderedtacticalwy.com, info@coderedtacticalwy.com,
459 Nevada Avenue, Lovell, WY 82431

Jackson Hole Shooting Experience, *www.shootinjh.com*,
307-690-7921, info@shootinjh.com, P.O. Box 7927, Jackson, WY 83002